# True Canadian UFO Stories

John Robert Colombo

PROSPERO
B·O·O·K·S

**Library and Archives Canada Cataloguing in Publication**

Colombo, John Robert, 1936-
    True Canadian UFO stories / John Robert Colombo.

ISBN 1-55267-874-1 (bound).—ISBN 978-1-55267-874-9 (pbk.)

1. Unidentified flying objects—Sightings and encounters—Canada. I. Title.

| TL789.6.C3C65 2004 | 001.9420971 | C2004-901239-8 |

This collection produced for Prospero Books.

Key Porter Books Limited
Six Adelaide Street East, Tenth Floor
Toronto, Ontario
Canada M5C 1H6

www.keyporter.com

Electronic formatting: Jean Lightfoot Peters

Printed and bound in Canada

07 08 09 10 11 6 5 4 3 2

To Dwight Whalen and W. Ritchie Benedict

*Fellow researchers of the unknown*

# Contents

*Our formulations of the regularities of nature are surely dependent on how the brain is built, but also, and to a significant degree, on how the universe is built.*

*For myself, I like a universe that includes much that is unknown and, at the same time, much that is knowable. A universe in which everything is known would be static and dull, as boring as the heaven of some weak-minded theologians. A universe that is unknowable is no fit place for a thinking being. The ideal universe for us is one very much like the universe we inhabit. And I would guess that this is not really much of a coincidence.*

Carl Sagan,
astronomer and author,
"Can We Know the Universe?
Reflections on a Grain of Salt,"
*Broca's Brain* (1979)

# Introduction

*When you think about it, the really astonishing thing would
be if they did not exist.*
—Jean Cocteau (on flying saucers)

If you have ever wondered about life on planets other than our own, or
life in dimensions beyond the ones we know, *True Canadian UFO
Stories* is the book for you. If you find that you are less interested in life
in its extraterrestrial or extra-dimensional forms than you are in the
human drama that takes place right here on the surface of the planet
Earth, this book is also for you. It is for you because the book is
designed to broaden and deepen your "sense of wonder," to encourage
you to think of life and the human conditions in extra-human terms.

There are more than eighty stories here, all of them Canadian in origin. They come from the past and from the recent present. Some of
these stories first appeared in the columns of early newspapers, maga-
zines, and books. Others originated in correspondence I conducted with
people who have had extraordinary true stories to tell. They are "stories" in the sense that they are narratives, not in the sense that they are
works of fiction or of the imagination. They are "true" in the sense that
they are "told as true." There is no way to confirm that these events
occurred or to prove that these experiences are faithfully and accurately
recorded. We have to take the word of the witnesses on these matters.
Folklorists have a name for accounts like these. They call them "memorates," which are told-as-true personal accounts of experiences, often
outlandish episodes, that are meant to be shared with sympathetic listeners or readers, not with everyone in the world at large.

These memorates are generally arranged in chronological order.
Part I is of historical interest and includes reports of "mystery lights"
from the past to the end of the nineteenth century. Part II focuses on

some "waves" or "flaps" that involve man-made and possibly alien-made vehicles of the early twentieth century. The first two sections also include accounts of meteor and comet sightings. Ancient and modern societies have looked up to the skies for centuries and continue to be baffled by what they see. Astrology, astronomy, and UFOlogy are attempts to explain what are mainly natural phenomena. It is important to note how humans have always been intrigued with gifts from outer space. Which begs the question: If celestial objects are often mistaken for UFOs, are UFOs often mistaken for celestial objects?

Part III is concerned with sightings of the modern era, and hence it takes as its starting point Kenneth Arnold's epochal sighting on 26 June 1947 of nine "saucer-shaped" craft streaming in a southwesterly direction across the state of Washington. (The direction of their flight suggests that the craft originated their journey in the province of British Columbia.) Part IV concentrates on contactees, that is, people who claim to be in communication with alien beings or extraterrestrial or extra-dimensional intelligences. Part V ponders the lot of UFO abductees, that is, people who maintain that they have been in some manner abducted by alien beings, and who sometimes argue that in some sense they have become alienated—perhaps "alienized" is a word that should exist—in the process. Part VI examines a few conspiracy theories, some crop circles, and a few probable hoaxes. The chapters make fascinating reading!

The arrangement of the sections reflects the work of the late J. Allen Hynek, the investigator who created the "close encounter" classification system. (He appears as himself in Stephen Spielberg's often ridiculous but nevertheless influential movie *Close Encounters of the Third Kind*.) Dr. Hynek began his professional life as an astronomer and a sceptic. In 1966 he dismissed a widely reported sighting of "mystery lights" as the result of "swamp gas." But he was intrigued and continued to examine sightings. By 1976 he was a professional investigator of the phenomenon and the world's first full-time UFOlogist. He devoted the second half of his professional life to the search for proof of the UFO phenomenon. He found much interesting evidence for the existence of UFOs, but no proof that our planet was ever visited in "flaps" or "waves" by "buzzing" or "hovering" alien-piloted or drone craft. Such evidence as does exist (as distinct from proof) is to be found in statistical studies (which are amenable to various interpretations). It is also to be found in interesting narratives like the ones included in this collection. These are haunting, not always readily explained. Dr. Hynek would have agreed.

The earliest Canadian sighting (dated 1796) is offered here; it is occasionally described as the earliest in North America. Over the years Canadians have made interesting contributions to UFOlogy (though these are seldom well or widely reported). We had our Project Magnet in 1950 and our Second Storey Committee in 1953. There was the test flight of the saucer-like *Avro Aerocar* built and flown by the A.V. Roe Company at Malton, Ontario. A very early report of UFO-related "crop circles" came in 1966 from a farmer's field outside Camrose, Alberta. The National Research Council's Search for Extra-Terrestrial Intelligence (or SETI) program utilized the Radio Telescope in Algonquin Provincial Park in 1974–76 and 1982–83. Throughout the 1980s there was the private SETI work of the dedicated amateur astronomer Robert W. Stephens, initially from his own Radio Observatory at Hay River, Northwest Territories. There are the nationally reported surveys of sightings prepared by Chris Rutkowski of Winnipeg. The research of psychologist Michael A. Persinger into the "entity experience" is relevant and of considerable value. Of great interest is Douglas Curran's book of photographs titled *In Advance of the Landing: Folk Concepts of Outer Space* (1985) and the television documentary based on it. Stanton T. Friedman, the ubiquitous "flying saucer physicist" (or "flying saucer publicist") promotes a cover-up theory which he calls "a cosmic Watergate." He lives in Fredericton, New Brunswick. (Does the T. in his name stand for Tiberius?) Canadians have reported a number of "classic cases," including the Falcon Lake Encounter, that deserve serious examination. These and other Canadian episodes cause one "to pause and wonder."

It is not clear from these accounts whether the aliens who pilot these craft (who might or might not exist) are Space Brothers or Space Invaders. The ETH (the Extra-Terrestrial Hypothesis) is of course only one way to account for the spectacle. Carl Jung's suggestion that UFOs are the "mandalas in the sky" onto which we project our hopes and our fears is another possibility. Then there is Dr. Hynek's "swamp gas," reflections of light, solar flares, the bright planet Venus, wishful thinking, fearful thinking, hoaxing, and so on. Whatever their causes, the phenomena of "things seen in the sky" will always be with us and may well be a defining characteristic of the human species.

# PART I
# MYSTERY LIGHTS

*All visitors from Earth or otherwise are welcome to this territory and to the town of St. Paul.*
—Official notice at the foot of the stairway leading up to the world's first UFO Landing Pad, which was erected as a Centennial project in 1967 by the city council of St. Paul, Alberta

Canadians were describing the appearance of "mystery lights" in the sky well before there were what we today call "airships," "space ships," "flying saucers," or "unidentified flying objects." Witnesses were reporting the sight of strange sources of illumination in the sky, usually in the night sky, and observers were surprised enough by what they saw to record the experiences in their diaries or to report them to the editors of their local newspapers. Such sights, whether "daylight discs" or "nocturnal lights," seemed to resist ready explanations by astronomers and physicists or interpretations by the meteorologists of the day. All this changed in 1947, when the words "flying saucers" came into vogue.

The modern period of flying-saucer sightings commenced with the epochal report of the sighting of Kenneth Arnold. While flying in the vicinity of the Cascade Mountains in the state of Washington on 24 June 1947, the civilian pilot was astonished to see a formation of nine disc-shaped objects in flight. It was not a fleet of flying saucers at all; the objects Arnold described were flat and crescent-shaped, not domed and disc-shaped. Yet a newspaperman's catchy epithet "flying saucer" caught on; soon the public was reporting skies full of flat and circular flying saucers. Before long there were hundreds and thousands and tens of thousands of reports of objects and non-objects being sighted in the skies; they were described as disc-shaped, sphere-shaped, cigar-shaped, sombrero-shaped, Saturn-shaped, and so on.

The term "flying saucers" remained a sentimental favourite—and it still is—until 1956 when Edward Ruppelt, the American investigator of the phenomenon with Project Blue Book, introduced a more sophisticated term, "unidentified flying object," which was soon shortened to UFO. Thereafter, theorist and astronomer J. Allen Hynek contributed such useful descriptions as "daylight disc" and "nocturnal light." He went on to create now-familiar categories for UFOs events, based on degrees of proximity and intimacy: Close Encounters of the First Kind (sightings), Close Encounters of the Second Kind (landings), and Close Encounters of the Third Kind (interactions). Some years later reports of UFO abductions necessitated an extension: Close Encounters of the Fourth Kind (abductions, kidnappings, examinations, inseminations, impregnations, etc.).

In this section appear some accounts of early sightings of seemingly anomalous lights and shapes and movements in the skies from the past, or at least from the pre-1947 period. Two points are of particular interest. There is the sense of wonder that these evanescent sightings evoked at the time. There is also the present-day temptation to interpret these sightings as flying saucers or unidentified flying objects, that is, to see them and account for them in terms of the Extraterrestrial Hypothesis (ETH) that their sources lie in outer space or perhaps inner space.

Yet again, perhaps they are evidence of "early sightings" of alien craft...

# Fleet of Ships

Fear was certainly felt by the observers of this curious sight in the sky above New Minas, a community on the Minas Basin on the northwest shore of the Bay of Fundy, Nova Scotia. The aerial feature, based on reported accounts, was described by the colonial judge Simeon Perkins (1735–1812), a prosperous resident of Liverpool, Nova Scotia. This account appears in his diary for 12 October 1796. It is reprinted from the third volume of *The Diary of Simeon Perkins* (1849–1961). It is often said that these "15 Ships" constitute the first recorded sighting of UFOs over the skies of North America.

◆ ◆ ◆

 A Strange Story is going that Fleet of Ships have been Seen in the Air in Some part of the Bay of Fundy. Mr. Darrow is lately from there by Land. I enquired of him. He Says they were Said to be Seen in New Minas, at one Mr. Ratchford's, by a Girl, about Sunrise, & that the Girl, being frightened, Called out, & two men that were in the House went out & Saw the Same Sight, being 15 Ships and a Man forward of them with his hand Stretched out. The Ships made to the Eastward. They were So Near that the people Saw their Sides & ports. The Story did not obtain universal Credit, but Some people believed it. My Own Opinion is that it was only an Imagination, as the Cloud at Sunrise might Make Some Such appearance, which being Improved by Imagination, might be all they Saw. Exceeding pleasant day & Evening.

# Stranger from the Sky

John Meares (1756–1809) was a lieutenant in the Royal Navy who resigned in 1771 to establish a fur-trading enterprise on the northwest coast of the United States. He served as sea captain on three voyages which took him from China to Nootka Sound. Meares was a fine observer of the beliefs and practices of the Nootka Indians in the late eighteenth century. The account of his travels, *Voyages Made in the Years 1788 and 1789, from China to the North West Coast of America...* (1790), preserves a number of the traditions of the Nootka people. Today, there is a Meares Island in Clayoquot Sound to recall the industrious and impressionistic merchant seaman.

Among these traditions recorded by Meares is the archetype or memory of "the extraordinary stranger... from the sky" who one day arrived among the native people and gave them instruction (moral advice) and instructions (practical tips). The man of old and his mission are recalled in "the images in their houses," which might be a round-about reference to totemic images, even poles, which recall the semblances of this man who "came from the sky," possibly an ancient astronaut. Meares' informant was "the son of Hanapa, a boy of very uncommon sagacity for a native Nootka...."

◆ ◆ ◆

*The Man from the Sky*

This discovery arose from our enquiries of a subject of a very different nature.—On expressing our wish to be informed of by what means they became acquainted with copper, and why it was such a peculiar object of their admiration,—this intelligent young man told us all he knew, and, as we believe, all that is known by this nation on the subject.

Where words were wanting, or not intelligible, which frequently happened in the course of his narration, he supplied the deficiency by those expressive actions which nature or necessity seems to have communicated to people whose language is confined; and the young Nootkan discovered so much skill in conveying his ideas by signs and symbols as to render his discourse perfectly intelligible whenever he found it necessary to have recourse to them. He related his story in the following manner:—

He first placed a certain number of sticks on the ground, at small distances from each other, to which he gave separate names. Thus he called the first his father and the next his grandfather: he then took what remained, and threw them all into confusion together; as much as to say that they were the general heap of his ancestors, whom he could not individually reckon. He then, pointing to this bundle, said that when they lived, an old man entered the Sound in a copper canoe, with copper paddles, and every thing else in his possession of the same metal:—That he paddled along the shore, on which all the people were assembled, to contemplate so strange a sight; and that, having thrown one of his copper paddles on shore, he himself landed. The extraordinary stranger then told the natives that he came from the sky,—to which the boy pointed with his hand,—that their country would one day be destroyed, when they would all be killed and rise again to live in the place from whence he came. Our young interpreter explained this circumstance of his narrative by lying down as if he were dead; and then, rising up suddenly, he imitated the action of soaring through the air.

He continued to inform us that the people killed the old man, and took his canoe, and that from this event they derived their fondness for copper. He also gave us to understand that the images in their houses were intended to represent the form and perpetuate the mission of the old man who came from the sky.

Such was the imperfect tradition which we received of what may be called the sacred history of this country, and on which the inhabitants rested the common hope of the human mind in every state and form of our nature,—that there will be an existence hereafter, beyond the reach of sublunary sorrow.

Thus have we given such an account of this people, country, and the customs of it, as occurred to our observations. We had not time, even if we had possessed the ability, to have pursued the track of the philosopher and the naturalist. We had other objects before us; and all the knowledge we had obtained was, as it were, accidentally acquired in the pursuit of them. Of the country we had no reason to complain, and we left Nootka Sound with no small share of esteem for the inhabitants of it.

# Thunder Power

Here is a traditional tale of belief (and disbelief) in the awesome spirit of the Thunderbird. The tale was told by an Ojibwa woman, Marjorie St. Germain, a resident of the Rama Reserve, near Orillia, Ontario. In 1921 she recounted it to Colonel G.E. Laidlaw, a local collector, who published the text in the *Ontario Sessional Papers* issued by the Provincial Government.

◆ ◆ ◆

A long time ago, the Indians lived on their own settlement. They all believed in Thunderbirds, except for one man who did not quite believe in them. He listened to the white-man preacher who said, "Quit worshipping idols!" The preacher just imagined that they were idols, but the Indians said to the preacher that they were not worshipping idols. If the Thunderbirds were just idols, they would not have the power to kill serpents. Every time it thunders, the serpents go underground. The Thunderbirds go after them like fish, the way Indians like to go fishing. Of course, the preacher would not believe it. (Lots of people nowadays say there are no such things as Thunderbirds.)

One day this Indian, as above-mentioned, thought he would go hunting. After climbing over the high rocks, he saw a pretty scene in the distance. It was a circle of a nice greenish colour. He went closer to investigate. The pretty scene seemed to vanish away before his eyes. It began to spread out longer. To his surprise, it turned into a serpent and a big white bird about the size of an eagle.

The serpent spoke to the man, saying, "Shoot the enemy, it's going to kill me."

The bird said, "No, don't shoot me with your bow and arrow, shoot the serpent."

The man got so bewildered that he did not know which to shoot at.

The serpent said, "If you shoot the enemy, I will give you power to kill any wild game you wish."

The bird again spoke. "I perhaps have a better power than the serpent. Anything you wish will happen and will aid you all along."

So the Indian shot the serpent.

The scene vanished, gradually, and then a big thunderstorm and lightning came on. The man noticed a big white feather, about so long. He picked it up and wished for the storm to cease, and it did. He went home, glad to tell of his fortune.

So again the white-man preacher came along to preach a sermon to the Indians. This Indian went and had a chat with the preacher about his "feather fortune." The preacher told the man, "Wish a big storm, just to see if it will come one." He did it, and the most awful storm that anyone had seen came on, and it ceased in a little while.

Everything went well in the village. The minister never thought of idols any more. That is the end of the story.

# The Man from the Sky

The appearance of "the Skyman" is a traditional tale told by Jonas George, a Chippewa who lived on the Rama Reserve, Lake Couchiching. In 1917 he related the tale to the collector Colonel G.E. Laidlaw, who printed the text in the *Ontario Sessional Papers* issued by the provincial government.

At first glance this radiant tale may seem to be a description of the tradition of an encounter with an "ancient astronaut," à la Erich von Däniken, the Swiss theorist. Yet it should be borne in mind that when this tale was collected by Colonel G.E. Laidlaw in the mid-1910s, the skies were full of airships. There were balloons and dirigibles aplenty. Pilots barnstormed from cleared farmers' fields. There was exhibition flying in August 1909 at Scarborough Beach in the east end of Toronto, where, in 1915, the Curtiss School was established to train pilots for the war effort. Eyes were focused on the skies as never before.

At the same time, not all aerial phenomena are so easily explained. Awe and wonder was elicited by the procession of meteors that streaked across the skies of North America on the evening of 9 February 1913. Today the display is known as Chant's Meteors, named after C.A. Chant, Professor of Astronomy at the University of Toronto, who published the two definitive scientific papers on the subject.

Between November 1896 and April 1897 there were sightings across North America of "mystery airships," as noted by Daniel Cohen in *The Great Airship Mystery* (1981).

Perhaps the Chippewa informant Jonas George, whose myths and legends are "vague and mysterious, and have a local colouring to suit the expressions of the times," according to Colonel Laidlaw, had in mind "ancient astronauts" and what would later be called UFOs; then again, perhaps not.

◆ ◆ ◆

About four hundred years ago there were five or six hundred Indians living together somewhere south of Barrie on what is now called Pine Plains. These Indians had a big time at that place.

Two Indians walked up and looked around those plains. They went a little ways and saw somebody sitting on the grass. This was a man, so they went to see. The man put up his hand to keep them back, so they stopped and looked. After a while the man spoke and said, "I don't belong to this land, I dropped down from above, yesterday, so I am here now."

Those two men wanted him to go with them down home. "Yes," he said, "you go home and clean the place where I will stay, and come back again, then I will go with you for a few days."

The two men went home and told the people about it. They began to clean the place where they were to keep the Skyman for two days. Then they went to get him.

Skyman was a nice-looking man, clean and shining bright. Just at sundown, he looked up, just like he was watching. He spoke sometimes in a clear voice. Just after dark he spoke. He said, "Stay for two days. I'll go up, something will come down and get me to go up."

This wise man said that he was running from where he came. There was an open place and he could not stop running, so he got in and dropped. The next day he said, "It's a nice country where we live, everything good. Tomorrow noon, I am going up, I will leave you, and you people all be good. Every Indian must be home tomorrow to see me go up."

Just after noon the next day, he looked up and said, "It's coming." Everybody looked up but could see nothing for a long time. The man that kept Skyman at his home could see good and saw something like a bright star shining away up. The other people did not see anything till it came near the ground. This thing was the nicest thing ever seen in this world. Two men got hold of it and pulled down heavy, then Skyman got in and said, "All right," and away he went up happy.

I guess he is living there yet.

# A Streak of Light

Here is a brief account of a sighting recorded by pioneers. John Langton and his sister Anne emigrated from England to Canada in 1837 and settled near Sturgeon Lake in the Township of Verulam in present-day Ontario. Langton, a graduate of Oxford, wrote about his impressions of life in the new land in a series of letters that he addressed to members of his family in the Old Country. His sister did the same. John's letters were collected and published in book form in 1926.

Anne's journals and letters were also published, appearing under the title *A Gentlewoman in Upper Canada: The Journals of Anne Langton* (1950). Edited by her nephew H.H. Langton, they give a good account of how a refined woman related to the rough conditions of farm life in the backwoods of the New World. The extract below comes from a letter written by Anne Langton and dated 14 April 1843. In it she refers to "a streak of light" that has appeared "at many different times" in the daytime sky in the vicinity of their farm not far from Cobourg.

Today that "streak" might be described in terms of an unidentified flying object.

◆ ◆ ◆

The roads have been good for sleighing, and I made my *début* in driving the other day. John had more grist for the mill than he could take at once, so I volunteered to drive one load whilst he drove the other. Our journey was performed very prosperously. A strange, luminous appearance in the heavens has been seen by many at different times lately. John saw it twice while on his travels—a streak of light following the sun, neither resembling a comet nor zodiacal light. We have no wise men here to interpret it.

# The Men in the Air

Charles Cooper, a farmer, observed something strange crossing the sky in the middle of the afternoon on Tuesday, 3 October 1843. At the time of the sighting he was working in his field outside Warwick, a small farming community located between Strathroy and Sarnia, Canada West, today's Ontario. Cooper claimed that he saw "a cloud of very remarkable appearance" but also "the appearance of three men, perfectly white, sailing through the air." Two labourers in an adjoining field said they observed the cloud but not the men. Other witnesses in the community admitted that they saw "the cloud and persons."

These testimonies are included in the millennialist tract that is titled *Wonderful Phenomena: Wonders of the Age...Carefully Compiled by Eli Curtis, Proprietor and Publisher, New York, 1850.*

◆ ◆ ◆

Warwick, C.W., Nov. 1, 1843

On the 3rd day of October, as I was labouring in the field, I saw a remarkable rainbow, after a slight shower of rain. Soon after, the bow passed away and the sky became clear, and I heard a distant rumbling sound resembling thunder. I laid by my work, and looked towards the west from whence the sound proceeded, but seeing nothing returned to my labour. The sound continued to increase until it became very heavy, and seemed to approach nearer. I again laid by my work, and looking towards the west once more, to ascertain its cause, I beheld a cloud of very remarkable appearance approaching, and underneath it, the appearance of three men, perfectly white, sailing through the air, one following the other, the foremost one appearing a little the latest. My surprise was great, and concluding that I was deceived, I watched them carefully. They still approached me underneath the cloud, and came directly over my head, little higher up than the tops of the trees, so that I could view every feature as perfectly as one standing directly before me. I could see nothing but a milk-white body, with extended arms, destitute of motion, while they continued to utter doleful moans, which, I found as they approached, to be the distant roar that first attracted my attention. These moans sounded much like Wo—Wo—Wo! I watched them until they passed out of sight. The effect can be better imagined than described. Two men were labouring at a distance, to whom I called to see the men in the air; but they say they did not see them. I never believed in such an appearance until that time.

# The Spirits of the Dead

The aurora borealis or northern lights that play over the northern skies are sights never to be forgotten—and not to be disregarded or dismissed when discussing "nocturnal lights." The auroral displays figure in the belief systems of the aboriginal inhabitants of the land.

Here is how they were traditionally regarded by the Cree. The description is a passage from the journal kept by Paul Kane (1810–1871), the artist and traveller who crossed the continent to sketch and paint the traditional Native Indian way of life.

In late December 1847, Kane was resting at Fort Edmonton, in present-day Alberta; in his journal he described the Christmas and New Year's festivities. One evening, upon his return from a buffalo hunt, he was overcome by the sight of the aurora borealis. He described the spectacular display of the northern lights and its effect on him in his classic tome *Wanderings of an Artist among the Indians of North America* (1859). It is true that on that occasion he did not see spirits, or UFOs, but he was so moved that he felt that he had.

◆ ◆ ◆

Tired as I was at night after my day's hunt, I was kept long from my bed, fascinated by the appearance of the heavens, which presented to the view one of the most splendid meteoric phenomena I had ever witnessed. Soon after dark a zone of light began to appear, increasing rapidly in brilliancy until nine or ten o'clock, when it attained its greatest intensity. It was about four degrees in breadth, and extended from the east to the west across the zenith. In its centre, immediately overhead, appeared a blood-red ball of fire, of greater diameter than the full moon rising in a misty horizon; from the ball emanated rays of crimson light, merging into a brilliant yellow at the northern edges. The belt also on the northern side presented the same dazzling brightness; while the snow and every object surrounding us was tinted by the same hues. I continued lost in admiration of this splendid phenomenon until past one in the morning, when it still shone with undiminished, if not increasing, brilliancy. Tired out at last, I was compelled to retire to bed, but those who still sat up told me that it faded away about three o'clock in the morning, without varying its position or form. The Indians have a poetical superstition in regard to the aurora borealis, which is in this high latitude remarkably brilliant, shooting up coruscations of surprising splendour. These, they think, are "the spirits of the dead dancing before the Manitou, or Great Spirit."

# Remarkable Phenomenon

"Remarkable Phenomenon" appeared in *The Nor'Wester* (Winnipeg, Red River Settlement), 28 August 1860.

◆ ◆ ◆

The attention of numerous persons in the vicinity of Fort Garry was on Monday night arrested by a singular appearance in the Heavens. They described it as a bright body of fire, spheroidal in form, two feet in diameter, and having a luminous tail from ten to fifteen feet in length, moving towards the north, "as fast as a trotting horse," and at an altitude of about 300 feet from the earth. It was visible for several minutes, and when it disappeared, the aurora borealis shone forth in the northern sky in the greatest splendour and magnificence. This was no doubt one of numerous small bodies, moving through the celestial spaces, composed of iron, a peculiar mineral known as olivine, nickel, and other ingredients. When they descend so low as to meet the earth's atmosphere they rush onwards with such prodigious velocity (probably travelling fifty or sixty times swifter than a cannon-ball), that the compression of the air before them produces intense light and heat, rendering their paths clearly visible. Sometimes, as in this case, they go by without coming in contact with the earth—they then disappear and are no more seen; but they frequently strike the earth, and are then known as meteoric stones. There are numerous instances of these "stones," as they are improperly called—being almost entirely composed of metal—falling to the earth, and they are not unusually found far away from the spot in which they were supposed to descend, being known by their peculiar composition. A similar body was seen three or four years ago travelling from Lake Manitoba towards Fort Garry.

# Mirage

This odd item, which originally appeared in the *Montreal Witness* on 13 February 1862, describes first-hand, the appearance of a mirage that formed above the far shore of a lake near the village of Barnston in Quebec's Eastern Townships. The airborne mirage began with "a train of cars," presumably carriages of a train; continued with "an army of men"; and ended with "a ship." In turn, each of the images collapsed into itself and turned perpendicular to the horizon.

Meteorologists are familiar with atmospheric inversions that turn the sky into something of an upside-down mirror. But where were to be found the cars, army, and ship that were being reflected and refracted?

◆ ◆ ◆

Singular Phenomenon.—Mr. G.W. Kinney, of Barnston, communicates to the Stanstead *Journal* the following statement of an extraordinary appearance on the west side of a small lake in that Township. It was evidently what is termed a *mirage*, but the question is, where was the army thus reflected? Were they British troops on their way from Halifax to Canada?—"Two weeks ago today in the morning, I discovered that the mountains on the west side of the lake looked very different from what they usually do. It came to my mind what I had heard had been seen a few days before this in the same place. I stopped and saw, apparently, a train of cars, four in number; presently they changed their position and came together, forming into one body, one side of which was perpendicular to a great height; and then another similar form made its appearance at a short distance, I then saw, as it looked to me, an army of men advance towards each other and then disappear; it then passed away into some different position. I then saw a ship come in sight, turn broadside to the apparent army of men, and thus they appeared and disappeared for six hours, passing before my eyes like a splendid panorama. There were no clouds to be seen in the sky that day in that direction, or any fog. This is no idle dream or fancy, and I can substantiate it with the testimony of a very good number of people who were with me in the morning and saw the same sight.

# The Lachine Aërolite

An "aërolite" is defined by *The Shorter Oxford English Dictionary* as "a mass which has fallen to the earth through the atmosphere; a meteorite." The word, first recorded in 1815, has the same meaning as "aërolith." In later usage it means "a mass of stone, not of meteoritic iron."

Falls of aërolites, or meteorites, dazzle the senses and are wonders to behold. They were regarded as "stones from the gods" in the past; in some quarters their divine origin is still asserted.

"The Lachine Aërolite" is reprinted from the columns of *Nature*, 2 August 1883. There is no record that the informant, E.W. Claypole, found "further details" to report.

◆ ◆ ◆

The most remarkable fall of an aërolite that has yet been recorded took place at Lachine, about eight miles from Montreal, on Saturday, July 7, 1883. I give the following account from the Montreal *Daily Star* of July 11:—

"The fall of the aërolite transpired during a rain shower on the forenoon of Saturday, and there were no premonitory indications to show that the air was more than usually charged with electricity. The person who witnessed the fall of the aërolite more clearly than anyone else was Mrs. Popham, wife of Mr. John Popham, insurance agent. Mrs. Popham was seated in her house upstairs sewing, when all of a sudden the apartment became illuminated with a blinding flash of light. The lady instantly glanced out of the window, when to her astonishment she beheld a huge mass of fire descending towards the earth in a diagonal direction. This brilliant body had a solid nucleus that appeared to the eye about four feet square, and a strange, indescribable noise was caused by its flight through the air. Simultaneously, as it seemed to Mrs. Popham, she received a paralysing shock that affected her from head to foot, as if the entire contents of a highly-charged battery had been discharged into her body at once. The astonishing brilliancy of the meteor caused a temporary loss of sight, and it was fully half an hour before the lady could distinguish surrounding objects. When Mrs. Popham first beheld the falling mass she fancied that it was about to strike the house, and is still of the opinion that it must have passed alarmingly close. The lady took several hours to recover from the shock, and when Mr. Popham returned home several hours after, he found her partially prostrated from its effects.

"Mr. McNaughton, a brother of Mrs. Popham, was sitting downstairs reading when the flash came. He jumped up, and, looking out of the window under the trees towards the river, he plainly saw the fiery ball strike the water at a little distance from the shore, causing a mountainous upheaval and sending splashes in every direction.

"Mr. Horace Baby also saw the glare caused by the flight of the meteor, although he did not actually see the body itself. He said that he felt a tremendous shock, and that he could feel the electricity oozing out of his finger-ends for some time after.

"Mr. C.P. Davidson, Q.C., was sitting down to lunch at the time, and describes the crash as being tremendous. The Rawlings family also felt the shock severely, as indeed did half the village. Mr. Popham's cottage stands about seventy feet from the water's edge at Stony Point, and it is thought that the aërolite fell into the stream about twenty or thirty yards from the shore, in about twenty feet of water. Owing to the high winds since the occurrence, the water has been so muddy that it has been impossible to locate the whereabouts of the meteor. An attempt, however, will shortly be made to bring it to the surface."

I will send further details when they come to hand.

E.W. Claypole
New Bloomfield, Perry Co., Pennsylvania, July 15

# Singular Phenomena

Today we are inclined to lump sightings of strange lights or shapes seen in the sky into categories, categories to which we attach such labels as "mystery lights," "flying saucers," and "unidentified flying objects."

When the following newspaper account appeared, accounts of strange sights in the skies were regarded as exceptional and were described as "singular phenomena." This news story appeared as an untitled item in the *Nova Scotia Herald* (Yarmouth, N.S.), 22 November 1833. Apparently, the article is reprinted from the columns of the *Novascotian* (Halifax).

◆ ◆ ◆

Singular Phenomenon.—The following account of a singular phenomenon has been handed to us by a gentleman who resides on the eastern side of Halifax harbour:—

On looking out of the west window of my cottage in Dartmouth this morning, I was surprised to observe a number of stars shooting rapidly from the zenith towards the horizon, leaving very brilliant trains of light after them. I immediately went to the southern, also to the eastern windows, and observed the same appearance, twenty or thirty stars were in motion; in consequence of this extraordinary occurrence, I immediately called my family, who also observed the same thing, and sat at the windows for the space of half an hour, admiring.

While we were looking out of the window, the town and harbour became suddenly illuminated, as I thought, by lightning, but on running to the south windows, we perceived a brilliant meteor had burst to the east of Fort Clarence, leaving a brilliant train of light in the sky which lasted, I suppose, 20 seconds after we reached the window; at the time we saw the greatest light, we heard an explosion distinctly—the shooting of the stars continued until daylight had so far advanced as to obscure them; a strong breeze to the west was blowing at the same time. Being determined to see as much as possible of this singular phenomena, I went out and observed a bright cloud in the N.E. and this surprising shower of stars falling in every direction.

# Wonderful Mirages in the Sky

From travellers in northern latitudes come remarkable accounts of strange sights including "cities in the sky." Actual cities are seen from an aerial perspective to be floating or shimmering in the atmosphere. These are optical illusions, to be sure, but they are fascinating to behold. In a handful of instances, the cities, which come complete with "moving parts," have been identified. Quite often they are cities located in the north of England. How is that possible? For a variety of optical, visual, and meteorological reasons, such effects do occur. Images are transported in the upper atmosphere halfway around the world, to the astonishment of homesick travellers.

William Parker was an officer with the North-West Mounted Police. He enlisted as a sub-constable in 1874 and retired as an inspector in 1912. He kept a record of his experiences and observations. One of these experiences was the sight of a remarkable mirage. He saw it in 1876, while on a march approaching the South Saskatchewan River on his way to Fort Carleton. The passage is reprinted from *William Parker: Mounted Policeman* (Calgary: Glenbow-Alberta, 1973), edited by Hugh A. Dempsey.

◆ ◆ ◆

The next day, September 27th, the prairie was black with herds of buffalo and numerous bands of antelope. In the evening we camped at Egg Lake, which was covered with ducks and geese; we shot over fifty of them. When travelling across this vast plain we would see a ridge ahead of us and wondered what we would see on the other side of it. On arrival, there was nothing but another similar ridge ahead, and this went on day after day.

We did see some wonderful mirages in the sky. One especially was like a large city upside down, showing houses, large buildings and churches, even to the spires. Another showed beautiful trees. Then there was a ground mirage showing lovely lakes of water in the distance; these have fooled many a traveller who, in driving to the place, discovered there was no lake or water to be seen.

# Is the Earth Flat?

Flat Earthers are less in evidence than they used to be. Today almost all of us are Round Earthers.

Today, with telecommunication satellites and the space platform *Freedom*, with manned landings on the Moon and unmanned landings on Mars, with the twin *Voyager* spacecraft travelling through interstellar space, it has become is increasingly difficult to argue that the earth has the shape of a pancake, outlined by a fast-flowing river, or by nothing at all, a flat island in the sea of space, with the heavens being a vast darkness illuminated with tiny suns.

Yet the notion that the Earth is flat appeals to the senses (it looks flat, after all) and to the temperaments given to good argument rather than to common sense. "Is the Earth Flat?" appeared in the *London Daily Advertiser*, 29 October 1880.

◆ ◆ ◆

*IS THE EARTH FLAT?*
*A Goderich Man Makes It Plane*
*And Wants a Chance to Prove It*

To the Editor of the *Advertiser*.

Sir,—I see your perambulating editor, or reporter, has taken the liberty of bringing my name very prominently before your readers in connection with the question of the rotundity of the earth. Now, it is well known that it is more convenient for indolence and ignorance to ridicule the opinions of others who happen to differ with them than to examine the grounds of their belief. I have arrived at the conclusion that the earth is a plane from careful observation, and also from reading books and discussions lately published in England on the subject.

Now, science is knowledge based upon facts, not specious conjectures or mathematical devices. The assumption that because navigators, by sailing due east, have circumnavigated the earth is no proof that the earth is a globe. The same result would happen on a plane surrounded by water, if we suppose the North Pole to be in the centre, as the compass would continue to turn to the north, causing the navigator to keep his ship at right angles to the North Pole till he returned to the place of departure. Therefore, according to the dictionary, "any fact bearing upon and being inconsistent with a certain theory is sufficient to overthrow that theory." Now, according to this proposition, the globular theory is very awkwardly situated, for we have not only one fact, but scores, yes, hundreds of facts, which are grossly inconsistent with it. If the foundation of the globular theory is false, the whole superstructure must be wrong, and must in a short time vanish and disappear,

"Like the baseless fabric of a vision,
Which leaves no wreck behind."

But if Mr. Sparks is satisfied with the globular theory, let him enjoy his opinions and allow me to do the same, unless he would like at some future time to discuss the subject with me again before a Goderich audience. By publishing the above you will much oblige.

Yours & c.,
W.G. Smith,
Goderich, Oct. 27, 1880

# An Extraordinary Sky

The appearance of rare and spectacular effects in the sky has the effect of evoking fear and awe in the human race. Meteorologists may offer the last word on atmospheric phenomena, but the first word is that of members of the general public, as represented in accounts written by newspaper reporters who have their fingers on the public's pulse.

Here are articles about the "midday darkness" that covered the city of Toronto. They appeared in adjoining columns in *The Globe* (Toronto) on 6 September 1881. They describe the appearance of the sky and the city the previous day, Monday, 5 September. Descriptions of "midday darkness" are rare, but when they occur, they are described in terms that stress how awe-inspiring and fearsome they are.

There is a reference to Mother Shipton, a seventeenth-century English prophetess, a figure somewhat like doom-and-gloom Cassandra. The reference to "Grimmer's terrible predictions" is lost in the mists of time, though it may be assumed to refer to the prognostications of an American almanac-maker.

◆ ◆ ◆

*An Orange Dome of Rare Splendour Covers the City*
*The Phenomenon Lasts for Hours*
*The Whole Population in the Streets*
*Fears of Many that the End of the World Was Come.*

The one topic of conversation all over the city yesterday afternoon and evening was the wonderful appearance of the sky. Early in the forenoon the mercury had risen above 90° in the shade, and although the sky became clouded the heat was maintained long after darkness had commenced, the mercury in the city at midnight still being as high as 80°.

At half-past three in the afternoon the whole northern Heavens assumed a rich orange hue, and the rest of the sky a yellow. The orange deepened and extended as the day advanced, till at five o'clock the heavens presented the appearance of an orange dome of extraordinary beauty. The streets and buildings wore an orange tint: in fact, nearly everything looked as though viewed through an orange glass. The gas was not lit, and instead of its usual yellow, burned a brilliant white—almost as white as the electric light. As sunset approached the orange hue deepened on city and sky alike, and the streets were filled with an interested population gazing at the strange, weird glory of the scene, and indulging in all sorts of speculations—some of them terrifying—as to the cause of the unwonted spectacle. Bush fires were held responsible by some. Others said it was a solar eclipse. Orangemen jocularly claimed it as an Orange display a little late in the season, and thousands took a more serious view, and predictions of Mother Shipton's prophecy that

> "The world to an end shall come
> In eighteen hundred and eighty-one"

mingled strangely with Grimmer's terrible predictions, and produced a dread in the breasts of thousands that the end of the world has come.

Of course many knew that the phenomenon was simply due to the interception of the orange rays of old Sol, but between the anxious fears that the spread of bush fires throughout the Province was about to culminate in a whirlwind of flame which might destroy the city, and dread that the last trump was about to sound, a feeling of tremulousness prevailed, and the like of which has not been known in Toronto for very many years. As a matter of fact there was weeping and wailing in some homes, so great was the fear of disaster produced.

With the lightness of the sky, which was lit up as with one uniform conflagration reflected through dense clouds, was a degree of darkness which compelled the lighting of gas lamps all over the city long before the sun went down. Within half an hour after sunset the last trace of orange or red had disappeared, and the usual darkness of a cloudy, moonless night had set in.

## The City in Darkness
### A Bonus Held Out to the Burglar and Footpad

The question most commonly asked on the street last night, as citizens and visitors groped around in the darkness, was "Where are the lights?" and many denunciations were uttered against the authorities who were responsible for the want of light. Not alone to the belated traveller did it fall to be inconvenienced from the want of gaslight. From the peculiar state of the atmosphere the streets were in utter darkness at six o'clock, and not a single lighted gas lamp was to be seen. Throughout the whole evening this state of things continued, not even a lamp having been lighted at any of the principal corners till long past midnight, and the result was that only those who were forced to do so went out at all, and that at great inconvenience and hazard to themselves. An enquiry into the matter elicited the fact that the police authorities applied to Mr. Ashfield, Chief of the Fire Department, to have the lamps lighted, and that Mr. Ashfield applied to Ald. Adamson, Chairman of the Fire and Gas Committee, without any result. The authorities are well aware that at the present time the city has received a large accession to its usual number of thieves and footpads, and such an opportunity as last night afforded them of pursuing their nefarious calling would not be likely to be lost by them. To think that our city should be left in Stygian darkness on the first night of the Industrial Exhibition, when of all times the public should have the convenience and protection of lighted street lamps, is a reflection on the powers who have so ordered, and leaves them virtually responsible for whatever mishaps it may have occasioned.

# Thick Darkness

What is called "daylight darkness" settled over the town of Goderich, a port on Lake Huron, Ontario, on 5 September 1881. It is well described in this account, which like the previous account refers in passing to the English prophetess Mother Shipton. "Thick Darkness" appeared in the *Winnipeg Daily Times*, 15 September 1881.

◆ ◆ ◆

*THICK DARKNESS*
*The Strange Occurrence of the 5th Inst.*
*Special Correspondent of the London Free Press*

Goderich, Sept. 6.—Yesterday will be long remembered in Goderich. It was, in fact, the most remarkable day in its history. For several days past the atmosphere has been full of smoke, presumably from bush fires, although there have been no very large ones in the immediate vicinity; and the thermometer has mounted up among the nineties— something rather unusual in this cool lake town. Rain has been wonderfully scarce all summer, and of late the ground has become completely parched. There is no such thing as grass to be seen; pasture fields are dry and almost as dirty as the road bed. For a week or more—

"All is hot and copper sky,
    The bloody sun at noon
Right above the earth did stand,
    No bigger than the moon."

But yesterday afternoon it disappeared altogether, as effectually as though it had dropped out of the heavens. About noon clouds were observed gathering in the west and south. At one o'clock those who lunched at that hour found no little difficulty in distinguishing articles on the table, and shortly thereafter lamps had to be brought into requisition. From this hour the gloom thickened; at two it was with great difficulty one could read large print out of doors. Three gave every appearance of midnight, and half an hour thereafter the entire town and surrounding country was veiled in inky gloom. "No sun, no moon, no stars, no noon; no proper time of day." The blackness of midnight reigned supreme. The hand held before the eyes within three inches of the face could not be seen. To lend awe and sublimity to the scene, the intense blackness was ever and anon lit up by blinding flashes of lightning; and the reverberating thunder alone broke the painful stillness. In short, the scene was one never to be forgotten by those who saw it. The weak and the ignorant were of course terrified, and thought that at last of a certainty Mother Shipton's prophecy was about to be fulfilled to the letter. And others who would be insulted, and with reason, at being termed either ignorant or weak, were beginning to ask themselves and each other what it all meant. Little groups gathered here and there about the square and watched in wonder and awe for a termination of the phenomenon, but it was a long time ere the darkness was sufficiently dissipated to see to move about outside the range of street lamps and shop windows. At last the darkness in the east gave place to a red gleam, as though from a huge fire, and the reflection from this somewhat relieved the gloom and enabled people to see as well as upon an ordinary moonless night—but no better. And there it remained through the remainder of the afternoon and night, and not till the following morning, when Old Sol put in an appearance as usual and in his usual place, were apprehensions entirely removed and the alarmed ones really convinced that all was, indeed, well. During the continuance of the darkness a small quantity of rain fell, but it was so combined with ashes, cinder and dirt that to expose one's self to it for a few minutes was to have the face and hands blackened. The next morning the whole countryside was covered with a coating of dirt and filth—so much so that it was impossible to come in contact with a fence, tree, or, in fact, any exposed surface, without becoming soiled. The phenomenon is now of the past, but it is not forgotten, and is not likely to be for many a long year. And it is quite safe to say that every time the 5th of September rolls around the thought of the inhabitants of Goderich will revert back to the year eighty-one. Lake captains say the entire shores of Superior and Huron are in a blaze. The smoke from these and other fires are no doubt brought together by the wind, and floated over in dense masses, hemming us in on every side, and as completely shutting out the sunlight as though Old Sol had dropped entirely out of the sky. This is the first time night has ever set in here shortly after noon and lasted until next morning. May it be the last.

# Dazzling Flash

The following description of the passage and descent of a meteor might not be monstrous, but it does bear a sense of menace and magnificence that is decidedly unearthly. The sighting was "only five or six seconds in duration," yet what an impression it created on its witnesses! Note also the psychologically charged vocabulary: sudden, fearful, startled, burst, descended, spectacle, fiery, whirring, terrible, boiling, noise, terrifying, sudden, etc. This was an event to be associated with the end of days.

"A Remarkable Meteor" appeared in the *Daily Colonist* (Victoria), 2 October 1887. It refers to the meteorological event that took place in the night sky over Barrington, Nova Scotia, the evening of 15 September 1887.

◆ ◆ ◆

## A REMARKABLE METEOR
### Brilliant Spectacle Witnessed by Nova Scotians
### Wonderful Phenomenon

Halifax, N.S., Sept. 16.—A special from Barrington says a wonderful phenomenon occurred there last night, about 8:20. A luminous body, looking as large as an elephant, with a long tail attached, suddenly appeared in the southwestern sky and shot out of sight in a southerly direction. The night was cloudless and without moon, but the stars were out and a strange soft blue and white light lit up the whole firmament as bright as day. The light was only five or six seconds in duration, when all became suddenly dark again. No matter in what part of the city, no one could help noticing the sudden illumination. To a person at the south end it appeared like a frightful explosion in the vicinity of the northwest end, in which direction the light was brightest, but the noise supposed to accompany most explosions was absent. A reporter was crossing the north end of the common when he was startled by a sudden burst of fire lighting up the whole neighbourhood. The meteor descended like a shot out of the misty air. It looked like a large electric light, and a long tail of sparks trailed behind, the whole presenting a beautiful spectacle. To the reporters the fiery visitor seemed to strike the ground a short distance away. Afterwards a low shirring sound was heard in the direction where it had disappeared. The sound kept increasing in volume till the power was terrible. It seemed as if the bed of the ocean was a huge pot of water boiling over. The noise, which was terrifying, lasted fully a minute and a half. What was doubtless the same meteor was seen in Halifax last night, but the time was 9 o'clock. Its fall was accompanied by a most vivid illumination of the entire city. There was a sudden and almost dazzling flash, then all was over.

# Gravity-Defying Meteors

"Meteors that Defied Gravitation" appeared in the *Ottawa Journal*, 4 July 1894. The celestial event—a particularly bright meteor that apparently zigzagged in its course—was observed the evening of Wednesday, 28 March 1894.

◆ ◆ ◆

*METEORS THAT DEFIED GRAVITATION*
*Such Were Those Seen during the Past Week*
*Phenomena that People Are Talking about—*
*What the Dominion Astronomers Says about the Matter—*
*A Letter from Mr. H.B. Small*

"Meteor's" letter in last evening's issue has brought news of other meteoric phenomena.

A gentleman living in Central Ward writes to say that on Wednesday evening last about 11:30 while looking out of a western window he witnessed a peculiar action on the part of a falling star or meteor. The star appeared just south of Arcturus and proceeded very, very slowly in a northern direction till it disappeared about 20 degrees above the horizon. The peculiar feature of the meteor was the zigzag motion it took. It was not bright and did not leave a trail behind.

On Thursday night between nine and ten o'clock several ladies and gentlemen who went out near the Exhibition grounds saw a bright meteor, which started from the same locality as the one described above, and which also pursued a zigzag course. This meteor, however, left a trail of light behind, which was visible over five minutes.

Mr. D.D. Keenan of Coohe Bay, above Sturgeon Falls, who was in the city yesterday, informed *The Journal* that Saturday night about six o'clock he saw a bright meteor disappearing in the direction of the northern horizon.

Mr. W.F. King, Dominion astronomer, seen about the above, said it was not an uncommon thing for a meteor to leave a trail of light behind it, but he never knew a meteor to take a zigzag course. It was against the laws of gravitation for a falling heavenly body to take a course other than straight or slightly curved. He could give no explanation of the phenomena. It might, however, be that the zigzag course was produced by the meteors giving off gasses that forced them out of their direct line, as "snapper crackers" (fireworks) jump in a zigzag way under the effect of the exploding powder.

The unusual motion might also have been caused by some peculiar atmospheric condition that pressed the meteor out of its course. Outside of these surmises he had no explanation to offer.

The names of the people who saw the phenomena will be given to any persons specially interested.

Editor *Journal*:—As regards the peculiar meteor seen by your correspondent "Meteor" on Saturday evening last, he asks for some reason why the luminosity of its "traject" should have been apparent for some minutes after its explosion, I have heard the accounts of several eye witnesses of this meteor and all agree that the light remained for several minutes. This can only be accounted for by the supposition that the smoke of the explosion reflected the light of the sun, then below the horizon, the smoke itself being several thousand feet above the earth, just as the rays of the sun are seen on mountain peaks after the sun itself has disappeared from operation on the earth's surface. I some years ago witnessed a similar occurrence about eight o'clock on a June evening when an exploding meteor threw off a ring of white smoke which was visible several minutes, and before disappearing a rumbling sound reached the earth. It would be very interesting if other spectators of the Saturday meteor would give through your columns their account of this unusual display.

H.B. Small.
Ottawa, July 4

The meteor Saturday evening was also seen in Montreal. Of it, Walter H. Smith, the well-known meteorologist, writes:

"The evening was clear and calm, except for a few very black clouds in the north. At 8:53 my attention was drawn to a luminous object which slowly emerged from behind a cloud, about forty-five degrees above the northwestern horizon. It pursued its way quite slowly, emitting, as it went, smaller luminous bodies—like knots of light—as it descended in an oblique direction. Passing behind a detached cloud, it reappeared and, still descending, exploded, emitting rays in all directions, just as it neared the edge of another cloud. The meteor and its train were of the softest golden hue. The train was plainly visible until 9:03; the residue of the head for a few minutes longer. As a light breeze in the upper strata of the atmosphere divided up the train, it gradually assumed a serpentine appearance, very beautiful.

"The meteor was one of the largest it has been my privilege to witness. The fact that it passed behind the cloud strata showed it to be pretty high up. Several other meteors fell later, but none of them were of the magnitude or beauty of the larger one."

# Fireships

The lore of French Canada is replete with stories and songs about "flying canoes." Maritime traditions are enriched with innumerable descriptions of "phantom ships," deserted or "hoodoo" vessels like the *Flying Dutchman*, and "fireships," vessels visible on the horizon, generally at dusk, that glow as if aflame. Could these traditions be anticipations of flying saucers or UFOs?

This article appeared in the *Daily Colonist* (Victoria), 8 August 1897. There are varied explanations for the appearances of fabled "fireships" (which are more often associated with sunrises and sunsets over Maritime waters than with the waters of the Pacific coast). The reference to Toper's Tint has not been explained (except as a topical description of the ruddy colour of the face of an imbiber).

◆ ◆ ◆

### THE RUDDY MOON
*Late Hours Prove Too Much for the Monarch of the Night*
*Its Toper's Tint Causes Many Friends to Repudiate an Old*
*Acquaintance*

If the man in the moon is provided with a moderately good telescope, he must certainly have swelled with conceit last evening at the spectacle of the many faces upturned to him. His customary aristocratic pallor had been replaced by a ruddy blush, an extremely intemperate shade of red, which unhappily betokened at a glance that the moon was half full. At first glance many believed it was not the moon at all that they gazed upon, but the mysterious fireship.

The last persons reported as having been privileged to see this fireship were firemen North and Swain, whose story was printed yesterday morning. The two firemen said in recounting their experience that they would give a good deal to have the mystery explained. Now comes forward Mr. J.G. Elliott, secretary to the board of fire underwriters, who undertakes to wipe the veil away and set at rest the evaporating uncertainty as to this strange illumination in the heavens.

"What has been seen by so many people of late," says Mr. Elliott, "is very simple of explanation. The phantasmagoria is nothing more nor less than the fire raft made and sent out by the campers at Cordova Bay.

"During my stay out there this summer, the youthful element constructed no fewer than four or five, towed them out to sea a considerable distance, and when darkness set in applied a match to the pile. And there you had your mysterious light in the air—in the reflection.

"I have often thought how much the burning rafts must have resembled ships on fire, as they floated forth and back on the waves as the wind blew and the tides carried them. I have myself seen them just as described by the two firemen, burning through the night until close to the break of day, and lo, when the dawn appeared, disappearing as if by magic. The firemen described what they saw very accurately, but with one natural mistake. What they took for the object was in reality nothing more than its reflection on the sky; while what they took to be the reflection in the water has been the fire raft itself."

The firemen are not yet convinced, however. As North puts it, "That light was altogether too bright to be reflected, and it did not come from the water, but from the sky."

# PART II
# STRANGE CRAFTS

*I was an early Kellogg's Cornflakes Tom Corbett Space
Cadet, and have only taken to exploring Planet Earth as a
feeble substitute for genuine instantaneous intergalactic
teleportation, which I think is our destiny.*
—Robert Hunter, author and activist, *On the Sky: Zen and
the Art of International Freeloading* (1988)

With the approach of the twentieth century, sightings morphed from "mystery lights" to "strange crafts." Daniel Cohen has written about this era in his book *The Great Airship Mystery: A UFO of the 1890s* (1981). "I would suggest that the actual sightings of strange or unexplained things in the sky remains fairly constant over the years," he said. "It is only when these sightings get a focus, or are given a name—airship, flying saucer—that an apparent 'sighting wave' develops."

There have been various "waves" or "flaps" over the skies of Canada. Until the modern period, the most widely reported series of sightings were those of August Andrée's balloon. But it is now known that the explorer's balloon was nowhere near Canadian air space. The question then is the following: If the observers had not spotted the balloon, what had they seen?

# Sightings of Andrée's Balloon

In the summer and fall of 1897, the Swedish aviator and explorer August Andrée was very much in the news. Nine days before the following news story was written, he had set out in a free balloon. His destination was the North Pole. There were innumerable "sightings" of Andrée's balloon across Canada. The problem was that Andrée's balloon drifted eastward, not westward, and went down before it could attain the Pole. Only in 1930 was the crash site located and the brave balloonist's fate determined.

So no Canadians saw Andrée's balloon, yet many believed they had. In a similar way, Kenneth Arnold's widely reported 1947 sighting of a saucer-shaped object was followed by a "rash," "wave," or "flap" of similar sightings... sightings that have continued to this day.

"That Pillar of Fire" appeared in the *Daily Colonist* (Victoria), 18 July 1897. The headline writer recalled the Biblical "pillar of fire," but the contemporary reader may imagine an early "airship" or pre-1947 "flying saucer."

◆ ◆ ◆

*THAT PILLAR OF FIRE*
*The Mysterious Visitor Seen Again*
*Drifting over Northern British Columbia*
*River Inlet Fishermen Watch for Two Hours*
*the Powerful Moving Light*
*Visible by Daylight as Well as before Dawn*
*and Mistaken for Andrée's Balloon*

Evidence accumulates as to the existence of a great balloon-shaped body, powerfully illuminated, drifting over this continent, but the latest report as to its movements leaves the mystery as to the nature of the visitor and its mission—if it has any—as far from solution as ever. Just about a year ago it was reported from two points in the northern interior of British Columbia, by Indians who had no possible means of communication with each other before making their almost simultaneous reports to the Indian agents, but who claimed to have seen it at points not too far distant to make it probable that it was the same object both had seen. The Indians had all been warned to look out for Professor Andrée's balloon, and they supposed it was this balloon that they were reporting. The fact that they had received this warning caused the sceptical to aver that the Indians' imagination had been at work, and that there was no balloon or other aerial visitor about.

Now the report comes from a source not open to such suspicion, though, strangely enough, the witnesses again supposed it to be Andrée's balloon which for two hours they watched passing from rift to rift in the clouds a mile above their heads. The letter below has been addressed to the *Colonist* by a reliable man employed at the Wadham's Cannery, and speaks for itself as follows:

On the morning of July 10, about 2:30 or 3:00 a.m., my fishing partner and I were drifting for salmon out at the mouth of River's Inlet. Being both wide awake, and happening to look up towards the mouth of the inlet we saw over a lofty mountain peak what at first appeared to be a fire such as would be caused by the burning of a tall, dry cedar. Looking more closely, however, we saw that the light was at least a mile above the highest peak, and was soaring smoothly along in boundless space above the sea of mountains beneath. It couldn't be a fire, we knew, nor a star, nor yet the moon, and all at once the thought burst upon us that it was a balloon, and none other than Andrée's, we thought, would be touching in these regions. The night was dark and overcast and when it first came into view it was through a rift in a black mass of clouds.

There seemed to be, besides the powerful light, a large pear-shaped body attached and rendered luminous by the reflection of that light. We determined to watch it in its progress, and saw it pass through rift after rift in the clouds. It was evidently moving in a different atmosphere, or current of air, than we felt below at the time, for whereas on the water there was a nasty, squally wind blowing, it seemed to glide majestically along without so much as a tremor. Then daylight dawned and we discerned it plainly for another hour, but only the naked, powerful moving light now was visible, until, finally, it disappeared behind a huge mass of dark clouds, and we saw it no more.

It appeared to be moving in a southerly direction, perhaps some westerly, but always on the same plane. It was indeed a novel sight, and as we watched it we could not but feel proud, after all, of the puny race of man, that with all its weakness could conceive and execute such a deed of skill and daring.

W.S. Fitzgerald,
River's Inlet, July 14, 1897

Another letter received in this city yesterday from Mr. A.R. Langley, of the Wadham's Cannery, corroborates the statements made above, and says that the men who tell of having seen the strange visitor are in every way trustworthy.

# Aerial Mystery

"Aerial Mystery" appeared in the *Free Press* (Winnipeg), 20 July 1897. It evokes, again, the image of the balloon that carried August Andrée on his passage of exploration.

◆ ◆ ◆

*The Wonderful Sight Witnessed by Two Fishermen in British Columbia*
*Strange Story that Recalls the Report Made by Indians a Year Ago*
*Truthfulness of the Narrator is Vouched for*
*Positive that He Was Not the Victim of Imagination or Optical Delusion*

Vancouver, July 19.—Just about a year ago a great balloon-shaped body, powerfully illuminated, was reported from two points in the northern interior of British Columbia, by Indians who had no possible means of communication with each other before making their almost simultaneous reports to the Indian agents, but who claimed to have seen it at points not too far distant to make it probable that it was the same object both had seen. The Indians had all been warned to look for Prof. Andrée's balloon and they supposed it was this balloon that they were reporting. The fact that they had received this warning caused the sceptical to aver that the Indians' imagination had been at work and that there was no balloon or other aerial visitor about.

Now the report comes from a source not open to such suspicion, though, strangely enough, the witnesses again supposed it to be Andrée's balloon which for two hours they watched passing from rift to rift in the clouds a mile above their heads.

The letter below is from a reliable fisherman named W.S. Fitzgerald, employed at the Wadham's Cannery at River's Inlet, and speaks for itself as follows:

"On the morning of June 10th, about 2:30 or 3:00 a.m., my fishing partner and I were drifting for salmon out at the mouth of River's Inlet. Being both wide awake, and happening to look up towards the mouth of the Inlet, we saw over a lofty mountain peak what at first appeared to be a fire such as would be caused by the burning of a tall, dry cedar. Looking more closely, however, we saw that the light was at least a mile above the highest peak, and was soaring smoothly along in boundless space above the sea of mountains beneath. It couldn't be a fire, we knew, nor a star, nor yet the moon, and all at once the thought burst upon us that it was a balloon, and none other than Andrée's, we thought, would be touching in those regions. The night was dark and overcast and when it first came into view it was through a rift in a black mass of clouds.

"There seemed to be besides the powerful light a large pear-shaped body attached and rendered luminous by the reflection of that light. We determined to watch it in its progress and saw it pass through rift after rift in the clouds. It was evidently moving in a different atmosphere, or current of air, than we felt below at that time, for whereas on the water there was a nasty, squally wind blowing, it seemed to glide majestically along without so much as a tremor. Then daylight dawned and we discerned it plainly for another hour, but only the naked, powerful, moving light was now visible, until, finally, it disappeared behind a huge mass of dark clouds, and we saw it no more.

"It appeared to be moving in a southerly direction, perhaps some westerly, but always on the same plane. It was indeed a novel sight, and as we watched it we could not but feel proud, after all, of the puny race of man, that, with all its weakness, could conceive and execute such a deed of skill and daring."

W.S. Fitzgerald
River's Inlet, July 14, 1897

# Could It Be Andrée?

"Could It Be Andrée?" appeared in the *Free Press* (Winnipeg), 31 July 1897. As mentioned above, thirty-three years would pass before the Swedish balloonist's fate could be determined. Andrée and his two companions survived the crash but not the overland trek to civilization.

◆ ◆ ◆

### COULD IT BE ANDRÉE?
*A Large Balloon Seen by a Whitemouth Farmer*
*It Was Moving Northeasterly and Had a Large Boat Attached*
*Other Andrée Items*

Whitemouth, Man., July 30.—At sunset on the 29th, Andrew Henderson, a farmer who lives three miles from Whitemouth, saw a large balloon slowly drifting in a northeasterly direction. The balloon seemed to him to be twice the size of his house, and had a large boat hanging from it. Could it be Andrée?

It is quite possible that Andrée's balloon might be driven to these latitudes, but if Mr. Henderson was not mistaken, it would have to have come farther south than Winnipeg, and then have taken a turn northward to pass over Whitemouth in the direction stated. If the balloon continued its northeast course for any length of time, it would be driven to James's Bay.

Prof. Andrée's ascent was made from Davis Island, Spitzbergen, at the northern extremity of Norway on July 11, at 2:30 p.m., in the midst of strong wind. He shook hands heartily with those who were a-ssembled in the balloon house, nodded to the astonished trappers who stood watching him, and addressed warm and heartful words to all whose hands he could not reach. Then the trio, Andrée, Strindberg and Fraenkel, standing in the car, severed the ropes holding the balloon, while Andrée counted "One, two, three." The balloon rose majestically, while Andrée gazed in happy confidence upon those who remained behind. Then all three waved their caps and shouted, "Greetings to all at home in Sweden." After the narrow escape from being driven against the rock in Sweerinburg Sound, the balloon was soon moving northward easily, as Andrée wished, over the flat peninsula of Hollaendernaes.

### Expert Comments

Stockholm, July 29.—Dr. Ekholm (Ekhola), who was associated with Herr Andrée in his projected balloon voyage last year, writes in the *Aftonbaladet* that he declined to join in the present attempt because the impermeability of the balloon was unsatisfactory. He says it lost 51 cubic metres of gas daily from the time of inflation. In his opinion, it would not float longer than from 22 to 24 days.

Paris, July 30.—M. Machuron, who superintended Herr Andrée's preparations for the expedition in search of the North Pole, has returned here. He says all the preparations were entirely successful and it is impossible that Andrée's balloon could have fallen into the White Sea. Herr Andrée, M. Machuron adds, regarded it quite possible that he might not be heard from for a year.

# More on Andrée's Balloon

"Again the Airship" appeared in the *Free Press* (Winnipeg), 9 August 1897.

◆ ◆ ◆

*Can Andrée's Balloon Be Visiting These Parts?*
*North of Douglas Mysterious Moving Lights Are Observed*
*in the Northern Heavens*

Some mysterious airship is evidently floating about north of the international boundary, and naturally Andrée's balloon first comes to the mind of those who observe signs of it. First reports came of strange lights being seen off the British Columbia coast; then a statement reached the *Free Press* from Whitemouth that an aerial traveller had been noticed in that vicinity. All these reports have emanated from reliable parties and now comes a letter from a well-known young Winnipegger at present in the west on the same subject.

Douglas, Aug. 6, 1897
To the Editor of the *Free Press*,

Sir,—In case some of your numerous readers may have noticed something similar at some other point I would draw your attention to a peculiar matter noticed on the night of the 5th. About 11:00 p.m., just before retiring, a something that at first looked like a falling star appeared directly north of the residence of Mr. John Kyle, some four miles northeast of here. The person first to notice the strange object was led to call the attention of all in the house to the matter. For over half an hour we watched the strange visitor as it seemed to rise and fall and sway from east to west, but gradually travelling farther and farther northward, until about 11:45 it disappeared from view. At times several of those watching the peculiar object, which all the while shone brightly, thought they could discern the shape of a massive balloon just above the light. It would be interesting to know if the circumstance was noticed by any others, and if so, what the impressions conveyed were.

R.M. Scott

Any who have noticed similar objects are asked to inform the *Free Press*. If Andrée persists in floating above Manitoba barnyards, let us find him.

# Another Aerial Visitor

"Another Aerial Visitor" appeared in the *Free Press* (Winnipeg), 10 August 1897. The nature of the sighting remains a mystery, but not Andrée's involvement in it, as his expedition went nowhere near Manitoba or the Canadian Arctic.

◆ ◆ ◆

*ANOTHER AERIAL VISITOR*
*A Strange Object Seen Passing Over the City*

The family of W.J. McLean, who live in Point Douglas, had a novel experience on Saturday night. At about half-past twelve, Miss Eliza McLean observed a ball of fire over the southeastern part of the city. Miss McLean called to the rest of the family, who watched the aerial flight for three-quarters of an hour until it had disappeared in the north-west. The light was apparently suspended from a balloon, and naturally the name of Andrée associated itself with the strange object. Whether or not this was Andrée of course remains a mystery for the present.

# A Mysterious Luminous Body

"That Fiery Mystery" appeared in the *Daily Colonist* (Victoria), 14 August 1897. No attempt is made to link these strange sights with Andrée's balloon; fifty years later the "mysterious luminous body" and the "luminous ball of fire" would be described in terms of flying saucers.

◆ ◆ ◆

*THAT FIERY MYSTERY*
*Viewed by Thousands in Vancouver*
*Moving Swiftly across the Southern Sky*
*Rossland Also Reports the Strange Sight*
*Speculation as to Its Meaning*

Vancouver, Aug. 13.—Thousands of Vancouver citizens tonight viewed with the greatest interest and curiosity a mysterious luminous body believed to be that which has been seen in many parts of British Columbia during the past month. At nine o'clock it was travelling with tremendous rapidity in the same direction as the earth, and at a speed which would circle the globe in 24 hours. It is low down on the horizon, just skimming the mountain tops in the southern sky. It is travelling with a slightly rising and falling motion. It is extremely brilliant, red in the centre and surrounded by a luminous diaphanous mist. As seen tonight it would appear to belong to the stellar system, perhaps a mighty meteor running amuck, a strayed star erratically jolting across the heavens. It is strange that the observatories have reported nothing of the mysterious skylarking of this nondescript luminosity.

Before tonight this stranger had been seen by many Vancouver folk, including Reeve Schou, who was on the steamer *Rithet* on Monday last, and one of the many passengers who watched the object for hours. Mr. Schou gives the most exact description yet published. It moved parallel to the sea far below the star line. It looked like a very bright red star surrounded by a luminous halo, cigar-shaped. It travelled slowly, as appeared from that distance, and occasionally there seemed to drop from the bright red star a shower of sparks like the spluttering of an arc light.

◆ ◆ ◆

Rossland, Aug. 12.—A luminous ball of fire that glowed amidst a halo of variegated colours hovered over Rossland for a time last evening and was seen by several well-known citizens, among whom were: Major Cooper, J. Wilson, Magistrate Jordan, Andy Revsbeck, Alderman Fraser, Inspector Barr and others. When first observed it was hull down on the horizon, but approached with the swiftness of light, and after hovering about for over a quarter of an hour poised in mid-air, surrounding itself the while with flashes of colours, it streaked off in a southerly direction and soon faded from sight. At first it was supposed to be a shooting star, but as it approached nearer it gleamed like a great ball of fire and poised itself directly above Red Mountain. Although the moon shone quite brightly, it did not seem to dull the lustre of the stranger. Those who were watching saw a weird sight. Little patches of fire seemed to shoot out from the main ball and then a flash of red followed. It looked for all the world like a lighthouse with a revolving flashlight of colours. No doubt if it had been dark enough the thing could have been observed more closely, but as it was, it was a sight never to be forgotten. After showing its respects to Rossland, the wonder made several wide circles, like a bird undecided what course to pursue, and then struck an air line and passed rapidly away towards the south.

# The Appearance of an Airship

Around the turn of the century, the subject of aviation was much in the news, if not in the air. Yet it was not until 1903 that powered flight in a heavier-than-air craft was achieved at Kitty Hawk, North Carolina.

Yet the first person to fly a heavier-than-air craft may have been an anonymous Canadian, rather than the Wright Brothers at Kitty Hawk. If so, the Canadian made the world's first flight six years earlier than the Wrights. Yet the Canadian inventor achieved no fame but "came to grief in the wilds north of Lake Superior."

"The What Is It" appeared in the *Daily Colonist* (Victoria), 7 October 1897. The article seems to have been taken from the *Canadian Engineer*.

◆ ◆ ◆

### THE WHAT IS IT
*A Learned Publication Deals with the Aerial Mystery*

The *Canadian Engineer* says:

"On the 13th of August, at Vancouver, an object was seen in the sky travelling eastward, which had all the appearance of an airship, and what was said to be a balloon was reported at two or three different points in Manitoba and the Territories.

"At 12:40 on the morning of the 16th, C.W. Spencer, superintendent of the Eastern division of the C.P.R., was sitting with Thos. Hay, his assistant, in the observation car of the train, which had left Port Arthur for Sudbury, and as they were approaching Gravel River, and sat admiring the clear starlit heavens, they saw, in the words of Coleridge, "a something in the sky." There was a large white light, and at an angle above it on the left a red light and at a like angle on the right a white light. The object appeared to be about half a mile above the earth, and when first seen was at an angle of 30 to 40 degrees above the horizon. It seemed to be moving with the wind about 30 miles an hour, as the train was running at 45 miles an hour, and the object appeared to all in their wake. When they had watched it about three minutes the train turned inland from the shore at Lake Superior, and before it was hidden behind the bluffs it tilted and turned inland, apparently following them up the valley. As it turned, the red light became blue, and there was disclosed in line with the main headlight a row of four lights terminated by a circle or ellipse of a dozen lights, in the midst of which was the dark body of an air ship. The light had the steady clearness of electric or acetylene light, and Mr. Spencer and Mr. Hay could form no other opinion than that it was an airship, and if the object seen at Vancouver was the same, it must have travelled to this point, 2,100 miles, at the rate of about 700 miles a day. It is quite possible that some inventor has set to work quietly and unostentatiously, and thus put his theories into practice before announcing his discoveries to the world; and if he has not since come to grief in the wilds north of Lake Superior, we should soon know that air navigation was first accomplished on Canadian territory."

# Intense Brilliancy and Short Duration

This article, "Peculiar Light in Northern Sky," appeared in the *Yukon World*, 5 May 1905.

◆ ◆ ◆

Vancouver, April 12.—A peculiar light, of intense brilliancy and short duration, illumined the entire heavens to the gaze of the officers of the steamer *Cassiar* who happened to be on duty at 1:45 o'clock yesterday morning when the steamer was running down Johnston Strait. None of those who saw the light are able to account for it, and their experience never before permitted them to witness a similar phenomenon.

The illumination lasted for fully forty-five seconds, and during that time it would have been possible to read newspaper print distinctly. When the light flashed, those in the pilot house of the *Cassiar* thought that the steamer *Cottage City*, which had just been passed, was playing a searchlight on them. On looking out, however, it was seen that such was not the case. The watch on the *Cottage City* must have observed the light also.

Following the blaze a peculiar haze overspread the waters through which the *Cassiar* was passing, and this mist lasted for two minutes. The *Cassiar* reached port this morning with an account of the phenomenon.

# A Shower of Meteors

A shower of meteors is a celestial event, irregular in frequency, splendid to behold. Here is an account of just such an event that has been reprinted in its entirety from the front page of the *The New York Times*, Monday, 5 November 1906. An unidentified reporter interviewed Chief Officer V.E. Spencer of the steamer *St. Andrew*, who, off Cape Race, Newfoundland, beheld "a shower of meteors." One detail that struck Spencer has had special meaning since the flying-saucer flap of the late 1940s: "It was saucer shaped..."

◆ ◆ ◆

*A SHOWER OF METEORS*
*AROUND THE* ST. ANDREW
*One, Weighing Tons, Hit the Sea a Mile Away*
*A Great Show, Even By Day*
*Chief Officer Thinks Such Messengers from the Blue*
*Have Sent Many a Ship Down*

When the Phoenix Line steamship *St. Andrew* arrived from Antwerp yesterday Capt. Fitzgerald reported that the steamer had passed through a meteoric shower at 4:40 o'clock on Tuesday about 600 miles northeast of Cape Race. The largest meteor observed fell into the sea less than a mile away. Had it struck the *St. Andrew* all hands would have perished.

Yesterday afternoon Chief Officer V.E. Spencer, who was on the bridge when the meteors appeared, told what he saw there.

"On Tuesday afternoon the weather was clear and light, although there was little sunshine. Just after one bell, 4:30, I saw three meteors fall into the water dead ahead of the ship one after another at a distance of about five miles. Although it was daylight they left a red streak in the air from zenith to the horizon.

"Simultaneously the third engineer shouted to me. I then saw a huge meteor on the port beam falling in a zigzag manner less than a mile away to the southward.

"We could distinctly hear the hissing of the water as it touched. It fell with a rocking motion, leaving a broad red streak in its wake. The meteor must have weighed several tons, and appeared to be from 10 to 15 feet in diameter. It was saucer shaped, which probably accounted for the peculiar rocking motion.

"When the mass of metal struck the water the spray and steam rose to a height of at least 40 feet, and for a few moments looked like the mouth of a crater. If it had been night, the meteor would have illuminated the sea for 50 or 60 miles. The hissing sound, like escaping steam, when it struck the water, was so loud that the chief engineer turned out of his berth and came on deck, thinking the sound came from the engine room. I have seen meteors all over the world, but never such a large one as this."

Asked what would have happened if the meteor had tumbled onto the *St. Andrew*, Mr. Spencer said:

"The ship would have been burned out immediately and every soul on board destroyed. I have no doubt that many of the vessels which have been lost at sea in apparently fine weather have been destroyed by falling meteors."

Capt. Russ of the Hamburg-American steamer *Brazilia*, which arrived yesterday about the same time as the *St. Andrew*, reported having seen a large meteor at 7 p.m. on Tuesday, October 30, in latitude 47 degrees north and longitude 48 degrees west. This is believed to have been a part of the intermittent meteoric shower observed by the *St. Andrew* earlier in the evening.

# A Blazing Star of Great Magnitude

"The strangest part of the story is the unannounced approach of this terrestrial wonder," wrote the reporter about the sudden appearance of a comet in the evening sky. His article "Winnipeg Startled by Blazing Comet" appeared in the *Winnipeg Free Press*, 21 January 1910. It vividly describes a celestial event that took place the previous day, Thursday, 20 January 1910.

The article is the first of three stories that appeared in the same newspaper. All three appear here. "Mysterious Comet Puzzles the World" appeared on 22 January 1910, and "Comet Alarms St. Peter's Indians" appeared on 7 February 1910.

◆ ◆ ◆

*WINNIPEG STARTLED BY BLAZING COMET*
*Heavenly Body of Extraordinary Appearance*
*Becomes Visible in Western Sky*
*Observed by Citizens*
*Believed to Be of First Magnitude—*
*Astronomers Are Mystified at Sudden Apparition*

About six o'clock last evening the people of Winnipeg were startled to observe in the western sky a blazing star of great magnitude, and many conjectures as to its identity were offered. In appearance it was similar to the traditional conformation of Halley's comet, a reddish coloured head with a streaming tail. Portage Avenue seemed to point due towards it, and it was low on the horizon. For some time afterwards the Free Press was besieged with telephone enquiries, and from places in the west came telegraphic communications reporting its appearance and position. The consensus of opinion in town and country seemed to be that it was Halley's comet, but those versed in astronomy repudiate this. The first communication received was from the men at No. 5 Fire Hall. They had seen the phenomenon out in the west and were anxious to know if the long-looked-for comet had arrived, and whether Halley's prediction had been fulfilled. Then followed a telegram from Bossevain and in quick succession telephone messages, both on the local and long-distance phones. The observatory at the Free Press offices began to fill rapidly and the astronomer was kept busy answering questions, at the same time trying to make sufficient observations to enable him to calculate the identity and orbit of the new visitor.

According to his report the new comet followed the sun's course downwards, and was clearly visible to the naked eye for fully eighteen minutes. Though this period was much too short to enable the observer to make many calculations it was long enough for him to make an estimate of its size and shape. The nucleus, or head, was clearly formed and was of a reddish tinge. The colour may, however, have been due to the atmospheric conditions in the west caused by the setting sun. The tail he estimated to be 22 degrees long, or about 20,000,000 miles. The time it was in view was, however, much too short in which to make calculations as to its orbit, so its return or reappearance can not be definitely decided. If its orbit could have been obtained it would have been possible to calculate when it would be seen again and the length of its visits. It is most probably on its perihelion passage, that is, going towards its turning point round the sun. All comets travel to the sun and retrace in a parabola.

If the comet visible last night was near to its perihelion, it will be visible tonight and perhaps for some nights to come at the same time on its return journey, but if it is some distance from its perihelion it will be visible for some weeks. The strangest part of the story is the unannounced approach of this terrestrial wonder. The Free Press astronomer can offer no explanation beyond the supposition that its orbit is of such immense proportions that it was two or three thousand years ago since it last appeared, and hence there is no record of its prior appearance. It was thought at first that it might have been Halley's comet, for which astronomers all over the world have been seeking, but calculations made at the observatory last night as to the speed of that comet and the position of it at the last observation dispelled this idea.

When last seen, Halley's comet was in the constellation Pisces. To reach the position where last night's comet was observed it would have had to travel from the constellation Pisces into Aquarius, a distance of 55 degrees, which at the known rate Halley's comet travels would be impossible.

The comet was not seen until the evening, the reason being that it had been travelling close to the sun all day. As the astronomer was unable to calculate its orbit he cannot say definitely whether it will be visible for any length of time. It is almost certain, however, that it may be seen tonight, and for the purpose of enabling those who so desire to see it, the Free Press observatory will be open during the afternoon, as well as in the evening. It will be in view probably a little earlier, as it is evident that it is travelling faster than the earth. Had it been travelling at the same rate of speed it would have gone down with the sun and would hardly have been noticeable. This evening shortly after sunset, it will probably be visible in the western [sky].

## MYSTERIOUS COMET PUZZLES THE WORLD

Many Winnipeggers scanned the western sky last evening in vain to descry the new comet which appeared so suddenly at sunset on Thursday. The sky was overcast with clouds and though the Free Press astronomer swept the firmament with his telescope he was unsuccessful. Anticipating its reappearance, many who were anxious to see the brilliant phenomenon climbed to the observatory and searched the skies, trying to discover its position. The first man to report that he had sighted it was a fireman, Cameron, of No. 1 Fire Hall, who rushed into the observatory with the announcement that he had located it. He was immediately besieged with questions and following his directions those at the observatory had a fine view of the gilded ball which caps the flagstaff on the dome of the Nova Scotia bank building. The light from the streets below was reflected from the ball while the supporting pole was not noticeable. Later a report came in over the telephone from North Winnipeg saying that it had been sighted from there, but it was probably a similar error.

Venus, the evening star, was unusually brilliant last evening, a circumstance which led many people to mistake it for the comet. As the evening passed and the comet did not appear, it seemed as though the astronomer's prediction had failed, but the following telegram from Saltcoats, Sask., removed all doubts, and showed plainly that the only cause of its non-appearance had been the bank of clouds behind which it had gone down:

"Saltcoats, Sask., Jan. 21.—The comet was plainly visible here last night in the southwest and was seen again tonight in about the same place, but about half an hour later. It was visible only for a few minutes, owing to a bank of clouds obstructing the view."

The following message from the C.P.R. agent at Tache, Ontario, which is 260 miles east of Winnipeg, corroborates the statement of the western correspondent:

"Tache, Ont., Jan. 21.—Comet visible in western heavens at 6 o'clock here this evening. A telephone message was also received from Teulon, Man., saying that the comet had been sighted there on Thursday evening being at the time about 12 degrees above the horizon in the west, about fifty people seeing it."

Referring to the account which appeared in the Free Press yesterday morning, of the phenomenon, it may be noticed that the cabled reports received from London, England, fully bear out the statements issued by the Free Press astronomer. It is also noticeable that while the English astronomers reported a tail two degrees long, the measurements taken in Winnipeg gave it much larger dimensions. This would show that the people of Western Canada were much more favoured, as it appeared more distinctly here than anywhere. The secret of its identity has not yet been fathomed by any astronomer and the statement made by the Free Press that it is unknown to science is probably correct. Until further reports come from Greenwich Observatory nothing further can be stated as to its time of passage and its dimensions.

### COMET ALARMS ST. PETER'S INDIANS
*Older Members Think It Foretells Tidings*
*to Be Feared and Dreaded*
*Story of Centenarian*
*Tells What Happened to Tribe*
*When Other Celestial Visitors Appeared*

St. Peter's Reserve, Man., Feb. 5.—Many of the Indians of this district, especially the older ones, are mystified by the appearance of the comet. They believe that the comet foretells some bad tidings to be feared and dreaded. One old man interviewed on the subject said that he believed God or the Great Manitou had become angered at his race and had sent the fiery comet to show His wrath. He refused to comment much and keeps repeating that men dare not say much about this message.

Others say that it means sickness and sorrow should the comet last long.

White Owl, an Indian who is almost a centenarian, recalled and cited many incidents of past days relating to different periods in which comets appeared. He said long years ago when his race was scarcely molested by the white man, the appearance of a comet was always the cause of much sorrow and dread in the tribe. Games of all kinds would disappear, the weather would become disagreeable, great fires would drive the buffalo from the plains and enemies would be victors over his race.

Another noticeable fact is that many of them would refuse to be out of doors, or to enjoy the regular Indian amusements when the comet was in sight.

One thousand of the St. Peter's Indians or nearly all those now on the old reserve intend leaving it in the spring for the new reserve on the Fisher River, where they may enjoy the wilds unmolested by the white man. Fish and game are all more plentiful there and they will be able to secure their living much easier than in the old reserve.

Many of these Indians dread to leave their old home, and state that although they will enjoy more freedom their hearts will always be with the old reserve and their birthplace.

# Sailors Surprised by Phenomena

"Sailors Surprised by Phenomena that Accompanied Comet" was published in the *News Telegram* (Calgary), 25 May 1910. Such "falls" as this one were of interest to collectors of curiosities such as anomalist Charles Fort. When the news story appeared, it was followed by a shorter account, which went like this:

"Philadelphia, May 25.—Captain Anderson of the Norwegian steamer *Friea*, which arrived here from Port Antonio, reports that on the night of May 18, when abreast of Cuba, he witnessed the fall of a large meteorite, from the direction of Halley's comet, which was plainly visible at the time. Captain Anderson says he saw the shining mass fall into the water, and his story is corroborated by members of his crew who were on deck at the time."

The full version of this news story follows.

◆ ◆ ◆

*Showers of Substance,*
*Closely Resembling Sulphur,*
*Fell in Newfoundland—*
*The Sky Became Blood-Red—*
*Inhabitants Were Greatly Alarmed—*
*Big Meteorite Fall in Sea off Cuba*

Halifax, May 25.—Captains of vessels arriving in North Sydney from the southern sections of Newfoundland report an atmospherical phenomenon Wednesday last, the day the comet was supposed to pass between the earth and the sun. At Harbour La Cou, there was a shower of substance closely resembling sulphur, which covered the entire neighbourhood to a depth of about a quarter of an inch. The sky became blood red, and many of the inhabitants were greatly alarmed.

Captain Mouton, of the steamer *Victory*, which arrived at the same port today from Burin, a village about 200 miles east of Harbour La Cou, reports that at that place there was a heavy snow squall, followed by a shower of fine ashes or some similar substance. Clothing hung out on the lines had to be taken in and rewashed.

At both places the showers lasted about fifteen minutes.

A similar occurrence is said to have taken place at Burin three-quarters of a century ago, when Halley's comet was last seen here.

# Mystery Airship

Here is an unusual article that invites further research. It was titled "Mystery Airship Seized at Winnipeg" when it appeared in the *News Telegram* (Calgary), 23 October 1911. Does anyone know the fate of "the O'Hare flyer"? Does this constitute a "Canadian first"?

◆ ◆ ◆

### MYSTERY AIRSHIP SEIZED AT WINNIPEG
*Said to Be Most Wonderful Craft*
*Inventor Had No Money*
*(Special to the* News Telegram*)*

Winnipeg, Oct. 23.—The mysterious airship which has been seen by many Winnipeggers during the past few weeks was seized Saturday by bailiffs.

The inventor, it appears, failed to pay the two mechanics who constructed the air craft, and after many attempts to get their pay, they put the matter in the hands of a lawyer, who caused the final papers to be issued, and it is now attached in the Granite Curling Rink, where it was recently taken after several successful flights.

This airship is said to "have everything best" in the line of aerial navigation, for its motors are so constructed on a segment that they can be twisted at the will of the operator to make the craft go in any direction. It resembles a huge bird with wings which fold up, enabling it to be stored in a very small space, and those versed in aerial navigation say it is the most wonderful machine of its description ever perfected.

It was invented by William O'Hare and built from money supplied by A.R. Donaldson, and is the same machine which was seen floating over Winnipeg some two months ago, and was first seen by the police of the North End Police Station.

It was built in the north end a year ago, but at the initial trial, it failed to float through the air like well-behaved airships should float. Then improvements were made on it and finally it flew. Many flights were made during the night time, for the inventor did not wish his unique invention to be seen.

Then the airship was taken to a barn, where it was kept and taken out for trial spins, making several trips to Winnipeg, Selkirk and other places no great distance from Winnipeg. So careful was the inventor of his machine that he would not let even his closest friends see it, and some of them learning of its whereabouts caused its removal to another barn, out in the northwestern portion of the city not far from the Exhibition grounds.

Then it was taken still further northward and later across the Red River into Kildonan East. This week it was removed to the Granite Curling Rink, where it was seized.

# A Celestial Neon Sign

"Mystery lights" that appear in the sky by day and by night, especially at dawn and at dusk, have been subjects of discussion and debate since time immemorial. Until the modern period, no consensus emerged as to the importance or the nature of such sights in the heavens; indeed, anyone who took such matters seriously was considered somewhat unserious.

"An Amazing Sky Spectacle" appeared in the *Calgary Herald* on 12 January 1934. It was written by Margaret Somerville McDonald. The last paragraph of McDonald's article poses a rhetorical question that may be answered in one of two ways: It seems no one else observed the "celestial" spectacle that she witnessed; and it seems countless millions have observed the spectacle of "mystery lights" in the heavens.

◆ ◆ ◆

Tuesday night in Macleod was mild with a chinook wind blowing. The stars were bright and numerous as they are before a storm. I turned my bed in front of a west window, and let the soft chinook wind come into the room. I noticed the stars were unusually bright.

Sleeping soundly after midnight I seemed to either dream or see a bright light. I realized this sensation three times before waking. The fourth time the light came, I was sure it was a flashlight and wakened quickly and with some alarm.

There was no one stirring in the house. Nor were there any lights, so I laid down to sleep again. Again there came the flash. It came out of the western sky. It was gone instantaneously. I thought I was mistaken. I watched the spot where it had appeared—about one third (or a little more) up to the zenith of the western sky. The stars were very bright, but none seemed to be shining below the spot where I had observed the light.

It was a little past 2:00 a.m. I noticed a small cluster of dim stars— so small one could hardly see them. Then suddenly they began to blaze like rockets—reddish coloured, quite large, and in a shape such as would be if one tied a piece of string to a circle and let it fall to the floor. I counted eight stars—and with the same flash which had wakened me they disappeared. Thinking I must be mistaken I got out of bed and sat by the window, where I watched this strange dimming and glowing and flashing till after 3:00 a.m. There were more than eight stars in the constellation—I never got it counted past eight on account of the strange flash which appeared about the size of a man's handspread, fingers touching. The flash was like a flashing flash in colour, but one would almost think it was a piece of metal.

The constellation (if such it was) moved towards the north very slowly, but the flashes became much dimmer as the group moved from direct west.

Certainly I have never seen anything so strange in the sky. I have never heard of a group of stars appearing dim and waxing to great brilliance and then disappearing again. Nor of a flash accompanying the maximum brightness of a star or group of stars.

The nearest one could liken this strange spectacle to was a celestial neon sign. The hour—between 2:00 and 3:00 on Wednesday morning—makes it improbable that many persons saw it all. Though it may have been visible earlier in the evening as the travellers journeyed from the south along the western trail.

Did anyone see this most peculiar phenomenon?


# Like a Low-Flying Plane


Mollie M. Bennetto, who served with the Royal Air Force during the Second World War, is a resident of Sarnia, Ontario. She was listening to CBC Radio's popular *Radio Noon* program one day in October 1991 when I was the guest on the program and chatting about UFO sightings. She accepted the general invitation to listeners to respond with accounts of their own sightings by sending me the following letter, which I have reproduced in its entirety.


◆ ◆ ◆

Oct. 16, '91

Dear John,

I was intrigued with the discussion and call-ins today on the subject of
UFOs. I was in the RAF for four years during WWII (WAAF section)
and worked on early radar and special duties. I remember one night we
had a strange object on the screens and our plotting board, which came
in at a terrific rate and then disappeared, but that was not a UFO, that
turned out to be the Vice-Chancellor of the German Reich (Rudolf
Hess). But there were many strange happenings, and stories from the
pilots of most unusual events.

That is not what I am wanting to tell you today.

A few summers ago... could be eight or nine... my daughter and her
husband were visiting from Scotland and were standing on the shore of
Lake Huron at the bottom of our garden. Suddenly they rushed up to
the house and called me to come and look. When I went down, whatever it was had gone... but I have never seen my practical daughter and
her very practical husband so excited. They said the object looked like
a low-flying plane with all the inside lights on and possibly people
inside. They thought it was going to crash, but there were no crashes
that night and nothing at the Sarnia Airport. They are not easily excited,
as people go, but they talked for hours and days of what they had seen,
and I still remember vividly the feeling of strangeness on the beach.
The "plane" was travelling very fast and very low; they thought they
could almost reach it. If there are other sightings of something of this
nature I could check the year with her. It was a summer dusk... probably July. I have had a lot to do with aircraft over the years, and wish I
had seen this.

Good luck with your work,
Mollie M. Bennetto

# Part III
# SIGHTINGS

*It has been frequently proposed to invest enough
capital to signal Mars, and it is ingeniously suggested that
the signals should be sent in six languages.*
—Stephen Leacock, "The Outlines of Everything,"
*Winnowed Wisdom* (1926).

As noted earlier, the modern era of "saucer sightings" began with the report of civilian pilot Kenneth Arnold, who was flying in the vicinity of the Cascade Mountains in the state of Washington when he was surprised to observe not one but nine "flying saucers" proceeding in formation. Arnold carefully observed their flight patterns but attached little (if any) importance to the direction of their flight. The saucers were headed in a southwesterly direction. From their flight path, it would seem the point of origin of the saucers was the province of British Columbia! (Is there a "nest" of flying saucers somewhere in the wilds of the interior of B.C.?) This chapter includes numerous sightings made in the wake of Arnold's catchphrase "flying saucers."

# I Saw It, and I'm Not Sorry

Eleanor Todd is a local historian who makes her home in Goodwood, Ontario. On 2 April 1996, she sent me a letter that includes the following item of information: "I took a writing course last year, and to celebrate the finish we had an informal party where we were each to read a short story none of us had heard before. I wrote about my UFO experience, for what it was worth, and I enclose it for your perusal. I rather expect you will be disappointed, since there was nothing dramatic about it—for anyone but me."

Ms. Todd is too modest. She is a smooth writer and the author of a fine local history, *Burrs and Blackberries from Goodwood* (1980). As well, her account of a sighting of something unidentified in the sky is a fine medley of everyday life and something that may not be everyday at all!

◆ ◆ ◆

I once had an experience that made such an impression upon me that I know I shall never forget it to the end of my days. But it was a non-event really. It couldn't have lasted more than a minute at most, and I know that as soon as I tell you what it was, your previous opinion of me will be altered, and not for the better. Unless...unless you've secretly experienced a similar event, perhaps?

I saw a UFO!

No, wait! Hold that thought, please! Before I tell you about it, I have to remind you that UFO doesn't necessarily translate into aliens and flying saucers. It simply means unidentified flying object and *that's* what I saw.

The actual sighting is as clear to me today as it was the day it happened, one of those "Where were you when you heard that JFK had been shot" sort of things. Yet everything else surrounding the sighting is vague, a blur, much altered by guesswork, reconstructive surgery if you will.

Okay, here goes. I was driving to Stouffville to buy groceries, and the back seat of the car was full of kids. That means it must have been about 4:15 on a Friday afternoon, unless it was a Professional Development day, which could make it earlier by half an hour. It had to have happened after 1974 or my mother would have been in the car too. She was always with me when I went to buy groceries before she moved to Kirkfield. Of course, I could be wrong about going to buy groceries...

Well, at least I know that I was alone in the front seat and the kids were laughing and giggling in the back. I was driving west and had just passed the last farm on my left before reaching the Lincolnville corner where I would turn south. There wasn't a cloud in the sky, and the sun was somewhere above or behind me.

I saw my UFO through the windshield first, and I slowed the car to watch, but I didn't stop. I don't think I even pulled over, because there was no other traffic on the road. I soon had to look at it through the driver's window because it was moving east as I was moving west. I told the kids to look, too, but if they saw it, it couldn't have made much impression upon them because to this day they don't remember the incident. They were too busy laughing and giggling.

I watched my UFO move steadily east in a straight line until I had to turn my head too far left for safe driving. Then I concentrated upon the road until I'd turned the corner to go south to Stouffville. When I looked again, it was gone.

Now what I saw could only be described as a large silver disc, the size of a harvest moon when it is close to the horizon. I think if I'd held a quarter in front of my UFO at arm's length it would almost have covered it. It didn't dart about erratically at impossible speeds, the way some people have described their UFO encounters. It had no windows, lights, landing gear, no external features of any kind to break its smooth, silvery surface. But it shimmered. Or maybe my eyes were playing tricks as I watched, but while it was moving east on its steady, deliberate course, it was almost imperceptible and I thought I could detect the same sort of shimmering that accompanies heat waves rising from the highway on a blistering summer day. Was my UFO merely a mirage?

My children don't remember my unforgettable experience, but they do remember two or three highly significant incidents which followed when we all piled into the car to chase moving lights in the night sky; lights which turned out to be aircraft, or when we drove to the gravel pit and waited. Waited while Mother watched the distant stars...looking, expecting, waiting...for what? They didn't know. I didn't know either.

# An Excellent View of a Flying Object

On April Fool's Day 1997, I received a long-distance phone call from Rob Sheppard, a gentleman otherwise unknown to me. All I know about him is that he has a fine taste in reading matter. I know that much because right off the bat he mentioned that he had enjoyed reading my book *UFOs over Canada* and that he wanted to add to it.

He explained that he was calling from Lower Prospect, Nova Scotia, and that a number of years earlier he had experienced an excellent UFO sighting. I listened to him tell his story, in synopsis form, and asked him to write it out in more detail and send it to me. This he did by email the following day, 2 April 1997.

How do I know the phone call and the exchanges of email are not an elaborate April Fool's Day joke? I have no such assurances, but I have no reason to doubt Rob's word. After I read the first part of the account that appears below, some questions occurred to me. That is why there is a second account, dated 4 April 1997. I checked my files and books, but I was unable to find a record of anyone else reporting the early spring 1974 sighting that Rob had observed. Innumerable sightings were reported in the 1950s; the so-called Sudbury Incident took place on Remembrance Day, 11 November 1975, when the radar screens at the NORAD base at Falconbridge responded to UFOs. Here is Rob's account.

◆ ◆ ◆

Back in the early spring of 1974 I had an excellent view of a flying object that has always held my interest in more ways than one.

At the time I was living just north of Sudbury, between Val Caron and Hamner, Ontario. I was busy outside, when for some strange reason I felt compelled to look up and far over to my right. Perhaps what caught my attention was the absence of sound of the flying object that I saw, with the Sudbury Airport being so near and my experiences flying around in bush planes and the like.

The object was cylindrical, although somewhat squat or pinched on its ends, kind of blimp-shaped, but the ends looked peculiar. It was about 150 feet long, with 9 or 10 segments which divided its length. The time was about 4:00 in the afternoon, and sun shone on the surface, which appeared like burnished aluminum. It flew directly over Hwy. 69 going north at approximately 60 kph. While I watched, it slowly stopped and turned 90 degrees to the east, and just as leisurely it carried on at the same pace directly towards CAFB [Canadian Air Force Base] Falconbridge, part of NORAD's old Pine Tree line. For the period of time that I witnessed the craft, it was a ¼ mile away, till it went finally over the horizon and the altitude remained constant at about 400 feet. For the most part, the craft appeared rather featureless, except for what I described with the bottom being flatter leading up to those peculiar ends.

Another thing that was strange was that not long after that thing was gone (out of place) a four-engined turbo-prop airliner came hustling right along the previous flight path of that strange object like there was no tomorrow. I often wonder what that was all about. It would really be great to be able to read more about it, where it went and what it did.

Well... let me tell you a little about myself. I'm employed as a marine engineer in the Navy, and perhaps I should direct my questions to a higher authority in my outfit. Scary thought! I face the bureaucracy every day just trying to get my job done, and I think I know the reason why they won't come or be more forward in explaining these occurrences. Nobody wants to be guilty! Oddly enough, I think that whoever is up there has appreciated that fact.

An old buff and sailor...

Thanks, Rob

◆ ◆ ◆

Twenty-three years ago does make it hard to be specific. The time of day I can only approximate as 3:30–4:00 p.m. Initially I was facing north, but the craft caught my attention on my right or due east. It was flying from south to north directly over Highway 69, paralleling it. I was only a quarter mile from the Highway. When it stopped and turned to head due east, I believe that its new course was directly over a township road that also headed due east, providing a direct line of sight to the NORAD radar station at Falconbridge.

The exact time of year is a tough one, but the best I can manage is the first week in May. Damn it all! It was all so casual and so quiet. It never occurred to me till much later (years later) that I had seen a UFO.

It's kind of hard to talk to somebody out of the blue, but through the early stages of my childhood, and as I grew older, I think I have been closely scrutinized by some thing or body up there. What scares me is that I may know the reason why. Talking like this is rather difficult but what the hell. Just for fun (no, this is not fun!)... here goes.

I would just like to rattle off some instances from my youth and up. Running to Father with bloody noses late at night. Sitting up in my bed in total darkness and seeing a bright, shining, yellow, round window with a face looking back at me. Being literally flung from my bed to the floor and pretending to be dead. A young lady in a skirt (blue with flowers) that strangely caught my attention (the way she looked at me was as if she knew me)... she was there one minute, gone the next. Sitting in class and feeling compelled to look out the window, only to see on a rock outcrop a small gold sphere (about the size of a basketball) that had the strangest protrusion. It was about the length of a cane, all black in colour that sort of "melded" into the top of the sphere with the black fading halfway down the sphere. I quickly looked around in the class to see if anybody had noticed and looked back and it was gone!

This is quite personal, and I hope you can appreciate that. I also think it is quite evident that I have to maintain a sense of humour to ward off any anxiety (which is great!) that is the result of "their" sense of humour. As for my rattle, there is a bit more, but when I read what I have just written and put myself in somebody else's shoes, it's time to stop! I hope you can help me with that UFO.

Thanks again, Rob

P.S. Sorry but I had little time to finish my email last night as a friends outboard motor needed a new drive shaft. Something sure is afoot!

# In the Awesomeness of the Moment

The Roselawn Centre is a community centre for the arts, education, and business that is housed in an historic mansion in Port Colborne, Ontario. I was pleased to be invited to speak in its parlour in the Doane Raymond Canadian Writers' Series, and I did so on 22 February 1996. As part of the presentation I invited members of the audience to share their unusual experiences. One member, Leslie A Turvey, a journalist and photographer, agreed to do so. In a manner all the more dramatic for being straightforward, he told the story of his sighting of a UFO. Then and there I asked him to share it with the readers of my books. Three days later he wrote up the account and sent it to me, adding, "Nothing spectacular, but you're welcome to use it." Here it is.

Leslie A Turvey and Harry S Truman share the absence of periods in their middle names. Turvey wrote, "I do not use a period following my middle initial A. Not a big thing, but can you imagine the keystrokes saved over a lifetime!"

◆ ◆ ◆

It was a frosty January night about 1:30. The year, 1959—possibly '60—I've forgotten.

I locked the doors of the C-HOW radio transmitter and left for home. The route to Port Colborne took me across a large peat bog.

To the east I saw what appeared to be a ball of fire the size of a basketball. As it approached, not fast yet not slow, the music on my car radio turned to static.

I stopped and got out. Soon it was in front of me, about twenty feet in diameter and maybe thirty feet from the ground.

A ball of fire it was, but it radiated no heat. It continued travelling west across the bog and eventually disappeared. My radio was playing music again.

I returned to my car to continue homeward. There on the seat was my camera: in the awesomeness of the moment I had not thought to take a picture.

Human nature being what it is, when we reported the story on C-HOW's morning news, it seemed like everyone in Welland County had been up at 1:30 that frosty January night. We had about a hundred calls from people claiming to have seen my UFO.

# Three Extraordinary Experiences

H.R. Stevens, a native of Cameron, Ontario, wrote an account of an unusual experience that he had during World War II. I included it in my book *Mysterious Encounters* (1990). It seems Harry Stevens' life has been characterized by a series of unusual experiences—from his early years to the present. The following "extraordinary experiences" were described in the letter he sent to me on 16 April 1990.

◆ ◆ ◆

1.

I believe wholeheartedly that there are unknown beings in our midst. I have had many small things happen in my life that lead me to believe in the supernatural. Or whatever. Who knows?

I will tell you of some of them.

When I was three years old, my two sisters and I lost our mother. Consequently our dad hired a lady to look after and raise us children. This lady was named Mrs. Nel La Pierre. She was well known among our friends and neighbours as a teacup reader. She was so good with her predictions that many people came to her for teacup readings. Her predictions were accurate, and it was uncanny how they frequently came to pass.

The most memorable thing about her was the following incident, which happened one winter's evening in the kitchen of our farmhouse at Highland Creek, Ontario. The kitchen windows were almost completely covered with frost. Mrs. La Pierre was sitting and staring at the frosted window. She jumped up quickly and remarked to my dad that her close friend Helen Reid, who lived on a farm a mile away from us, was calling out to her. She said she had just had a vision of Helen's face, which was peering at her through the small opening in the frost on the window.

Dad tried to calm her down and convince her that she had been dreaming. This took some time and much conversation. The conversation was interrupted after a short period of time by the ringing of the telephone. It was Mr. Reid, who was calling to inform Dad and Mrs. La Pierre that his wife, Helen, had just passed away, and that her last words were "Nel, Nel, I need you."

Now, that story is as true as my name is Harry Stevens.

2.

I am an enthusiastic fisherman. One day, while fishing with Steve Bainbridge, formerly of Willowdale, Ontario, but now living in Cameron, Ontario, we were on a river that had never before been fished. After about two hours of no luck, I pointed to a spot at the edge of the river and told Steve to cast his line at that point. I told him that there was a big fish waiting for him there. He then cast his lure to the exact spot that I had pointed to and, sure enough, he pulled in the one and only muskie of the day.

Call it a fish story, call it fisherman's luck, call it experience or a quirk of fate, or anything you like. But something told me, without question, there would be a fish there.

Another time, Steve and I went to a lake that neither of us had ever before been on. We got the map of the lake, and while sitting on shore, we looked at the map. I placed an X on a certain spot and remarked that there were fish waiting for us right there. We then proceeded to fish as we made our way across the lake, trying various likely looking locations, without results. We arrived at the spot where I had earlier placed the X on the map. As we approached, I said, "Here is our spot." And sure enough we caught several pickerel (walleye). We did it only in that area. We caught no fish anywhere else that we tried that day.

Again, I ask: Fisherman's luck? Or was something watching over me?

3.

While fishing with my brother-in-law, George Mattison, late one evening, we were out in the middle of Buckhorn Lake. Buckhorn Lake is in the Kawartha Lake chain. The sun had gone down and the stars were beginning to show in the clear, cloudless sky. While I was staring at the beauty of the sky, I happened to look to the east. Now, keep in mind the fact that while on a lake the horizon is a long way off, and it offers a person an unobstructed view.

I noticed a bright light appear over the eastern horizon. It was brighter than any star I had ever seen, and it was brighter and larger than any aircraft light I had ever observed. So I remarked to George, who had his back to the east, that there was something very unusual out there. Before George could turn his head to look, it was over our heads. As fast as I could swing my arm to point it out to George, that light was disappearing over the western horizon.

I have never in all my life seen anything travel that fast. In a matter of seconds, it had travelled from the eastern to the western horizon. I would estimate the distance to be a hundred miles or so. It covered that distance in a matter of seconds.

It was not a falling star, because falling stars always appear in the sky and then fall towards earth. I have never known one to follow the curvature of the earth.

What else could it be but a UFO?

# Knowledge Far Superior to Ours

Here is the account of three sightings that were made over the period of some sixty years. The observer was Maria Herzog of Toronto. Under the title "Who Says UFOs Are Mysterious?" her account appeared on the reader's "Have Your Say" page of the *Toronto Star*, 19 August 1990.

◆ ◆ ◆

I think that it is an insult to our mind, and an utter naïveté, to suppose that our Earth is the only inhabited planet in that vast universe. There might be countless heavenly bodies with intelligent life on them, with knowledge far superior to ours.

And I do not think that UFOs are so mysterious. We just cannot explain them on our present evolutionary level, with our science and technology. But we're certainly improving! Not long ago, people who saw UFOs were considered as drunks, being under the influence of hallucinatory drugs, or just simply demented. But when a U.S. military expert, a U.S. president, and many other prominent persons have seen UFOs, we have to think more seriously about that controversial subject.

Our present knowledge of Matter, Time, and Space might be totally different from an extraterrestrial's; so complex and seemingly so paradoxical for our way of thinking that we should not even contemplate understanding it, yet. Could we make a person who lived, let's say, in the 17th century, understand our TV and computer system? Of course not! Can we imagine the marvels of our science and technology at the end of the next century, or in later centuries? Hardly!

I have seen UFOs three times in the last sixty-one years, and I hope to see more of them, for it is really a wondrous experience, and the emotional impact they created in me was profoundly uplifting and fulfilling.

The first time, I was ten years old. It was in December, just before Christmas, so I was convinced that I was witnessing the flight of some kind of an angelic vehicle that carries the decorated pines and presents to peoples of far-away lands. (That was in the '30s, in the age of innocence and make-believe.) It was on a moonlit night, with just very small fleecy clouds in the sky, and a silver gondola flew silent under the clouds, about twice the size of a crescent moon; and when it reached the full moon, it disappeared.

The second time was right here in Toronto, about five years ago. The *Star* announced that a Soviet space station, *Mir*, would cross our skies at a given time, in an east-west direction. I was standing on our balcony, enjoying a very rare clear night with perfect visibility for stargazers, when right above our building a bright orange-coloured sphere flew silently from north to south. It could not be *Mir*, for it was much bigger than a star (it seemed to be the size of a cantaloupe), and although it did not emit sparkles, it was a very dense, brilliant light. I followed its flight with wide-open eyes until it reached the CN Tower, where it suddenly disappeared.

My third sighting was this year, in late January. I was standing by my window, stargazing as usual, when out of the dark a very bright, orange-coloured column appeared suddenly under the stars. It was motionless, the length of my arm, and just about as wide. It was visible for about a minute, and just as suddenly disappeared, like a switched-off light.

What I felt during those sightings was a mixture of amazement, wonder, joy, hope, and an infinite inner peace and tranquillity. But most of all, I felt privileged.

# I Saw a Big Round Dome

"A tiny minority of sightings, perhaps one in 1,000, seems genuinely mind-boggling in their implications, providing one can assume the honesty and stability of their witnesses. One such case, not previously published, is especially interesting because the observer was a newsman who did not tell his story for several years because he was afraid it wouldn't be taken seriously."

So wrote the journalist Jon Ruddy in his article "Look, There's a Flying Saucer" which appeared in *Maclean's*, November 1967. Ruddy continued, "Jerry Boileau is the chief photographer at Hamilton's CHCH-TV, a hard-working, matter-of-fact cameraman with no axe to grind. Here is what he told *Maclean's*."

◆ ◆ ◆

In September 1960 I was on a holiday with my family at my father-in-law's farm at Wanup, about sixteen miles east of Sudbury. On this night at about 9:30 p.m. we were sitting in the kitchen. My wife was feeding the baby. My brother-in-law was outside. He came in and said, "Want to see something funny?" So I went outside and looked up at this thing, a big ball of light, that was up there, pretty high at first. It was dark on the farm. There is no hydro and it was overcast. This thing seemed to light up the whole countryside. I was standing there, and it came down closer and closer, making a winding, whipping noise, so loud it hurt your ears. My wife had come out with Timmy, who was three years old then, and he started screaming. The noise really got bad. I told them to get in the house. I opened the door and sort of pushed them in, and then I turned around and got my last good look at it. I saw a big round dome, about the size of three cars, and it seemed to have a second stage above the first—it was as if the second stage was revolving the other way. Then it sort of took a sudden glide on an angle and—whoosh!—up it went. It disappeared so fast—not like a jet. You could hardly follow it. I noticed separate white lights on it before it took off. Later, my wife said she thought some of them were coloured—we could never agree on that. The noise was sort of like when you year a big jet winding up. It was really whistling.

I got in touch with the Falconbridge Radar Station—I had a younger brother on the air force there. I even saw the C.O. and told him about it. They said, no, they hadn't picked up anything on the radar. My wife and my brother-in-law, we talked about it for a while and made an agreement not to say anything else to anybody. I didn't want to be made an ass of, and I didn't want people to think that I was another bloody crackpot. We kept it quiet for five years. Then one night at a party my wife joked about it. I told the story to a friend of mine, and it got around a little bit because *Seven Days* got wind of it and wanted to interview me. I said, no ice. They were trying to put words in my mouth. I know what I saw. Whenever I'm up north now, I sit and I look.

# UFO Sighting in Caledon

"The following is a UFO report that was submitted to *The 'X' Zone Radio Show*, Research/Investigation Section. I would appreciate any assistance from members of this selected mailing list and the mailing lists that this will appear on throughout the Internet.

"My sincere thanks and appreciation in advance."

So wrote Rob McConnell, host and executive producer, *The "X" Zone Radio Show*, NewsTalk 610 CKTB / Affinity Radio Group, 12 Yates Street, St. Catharines, Ontario L2R 6X7, Canada.

"The 'X' Zone—where people dare to believe and dare to be heard," exclusively on NewsTalk 610 CKTB, Friday, Saturday, and Sunday evenings.

◆ ◆ ◆

| | |
|---|---|
| Name: | Don C. Male, 36 years |
| Address: | Withheld by X |
| City: | Caledon |
| Province: | Ontario |
| Country: | Canada |
| Postal Code: | L0N 1C0 |
| Tel #: | Withheld by X |
| Employment: | Sales Representative |
| DOB: | 1962—36 years of age |
| Education: | Some college |
| Military: | None |
| Special Training: | None |
| Date of Observation: | November 2, 1998, between 17:53 hrs and 17:56 hrs Eastern |

Weather conditions:                      "Clear sky"

Position of Sun or Moon in               Not known—the subject was "too
  relationship to subject:               caught up in observing objects."

Was there wind:                          "Yes"

Approximate direction                    "I believe a north wind on the right
  and speed:                             side of my face looking west."

Were the objects observed                "No"
  through an optical instrument
  or other aid, a windshield, a
  window pane, storm window,
  screening, etc.?

Did the objects have                     "No"
  any sound?

Please tell if the objects were:

Fuzzy or blurred                         "No" .

Like a bright star                       "No"

Sharply outlined                         "No"

Was the object:

Self luminous                            "Yes"

Dull finish                              "No"

Reflective                               "No"

Transparent                              "Yes"

Tell the apparent size of the            "A dime"
  objects when compared with
  an object in your fingers
  pointed straight out in front
  of you:

How did the subject happen               "We were driving north on Highway
  to notice the objects:                 10 and my girlfriend was driving and
                                         I saw two objects in the west sky
                                         through the windshield. I asked my
                                         girlfriend to stop the car and she did.
                                         We got out of the car and observed
                                         the objects for three minutes."

Describe the movement of the objects:

"We observed in the west sky two objects that hovered side by side for 30 seconds (not moving) just strobing lights. Then one object moved across the sky, many times faster than a plane, still with the strobe effect. Then the moving object disappeared for a few seconds and reappeared in a different part of the sky with the hovering object remaining motionless, strobing in its original position. Then the moving object came back across the sky and made a right-angle turn, then, while moving away from us, lost altitude—at least half its altitude in a second or two. Then the object disappeared and a few seconds later reappeared beside the hovering object in its original position. At this point the hovering object did similar manoeuvres as the first object and then returned to the now hovering first object. They hovered together for a few seconds and disappeared before our non-blinking eyes instantaneously."

How did the objects disappear from view:

"They simply vanished, disappeared before our very eyes, without a blink. These objects could hover, turn at right angle and travel at speeds at least 10 times that of a normal air craft (approx)."

| Were there any conventional aircraft in the location at the time of the sighting or immediately afterwards: | "Not that I noticed, but we were two miles north of the Brampton Flying Club at the time of the sighting, near our home, where we observe planes of all sizes every day." |

The subject contacted the local CTV affiliate CFTO in Toronto, who disagreed with the subject when they found out that he did not have any photographic evidence. The subject did file a report with the National UFO Reporting Center on or about the first part of December 1998. The subject has checked subsequently and has not seen his report listed.

This is not the first UFO sighting the subject has had. About 20 years ago, the subject observed a UFO over a power station on the shores of Lake Ontario.

The subject stated that during this sighting, he remained calm but was in awe. He believes that he saw extraterrestrial devices—UFOs.

After his sightings, the subject did not notice any changes in his sleep patterns, his dream patterns, his work habits, his eating habits, was not ill during the sighting or after the sighting. The subject did not develop psychic abilities after his sighting.

The subject has showed similarities to others who we have investigated for UFO sightings. He is attracted to water, is artistically inclined, he likes children, is concerned with the state and the care that the elderly receive, is concerned with the ecological state of the world; he likes animals and believes that we are not alone in the universe. The subject said that it was a "tough call" when he was asked about having psychic abilities or if he has had a spiritual or religious growth in his life after his sighting.

The only airport that the subject stated was close to his sighting was the Brampton Flying Club. However, a check with Transport Canada ATC sources showed that, on occasion, the area over the flying club is part of a final approach pattern to Pearson International.

Signed January 26, 1999

# A Most Spectacular Sight

Lucie Romanycia is an excellent observer and investigator. She is also a fine correspondent, so it is a simple matter for the reader of the letter she sent to me to visualize the sight in the night sky that she and other members of her family saw from the patio of the family home in St. Louis, Saskatchewan. The letter also conveys a sense of excitement at the "spectacular sight," a sighting that lasted only four or five minutes but that will remain with her for the rest of her life.

Accompanying the letter was the correspondent's sketch of what she saw in the sky, in four colours: cadmium red, light pink, light blue, and dark blue. The left-hand side of the disk, ball, or sphere appeared in red with some purple highlighting, whereas the object's right-hand side appeared in blue with some purple highlighting as well. The UFO emitted red, blue, and white sparks, a most wondrous sight to behold!

It is difficult to know what to make of the object or image. It was moving too slowly to be an airplane. Perhaps it was a helicopter, but it seems unlikely that there are helicopters with bright, multi-coloured searchlights. Could it be connected with the northern lights? Maybe it was an alien spacecraft. It is possible—indeed, likely—that we will never know the real cause of the "spectacular sight." In the meantime, we should be grateful to Mrs. Romanycia for taking pains to recall what she and her three sisters saw that night and then deciding to share it with us.

◆ ◆ ◆

August 19, 2000

Dear Mr. Colombo:

It was good talking to you last night and to know that you are still interested in supernatural experiences.

The first time that I wrote to you, on September 6, 1990, I mentioned that eight people witnessed a UFO on June 29, 1974. This time four of us witnessed a UFO on July 31, 2000.

On Monday, July 31, 2000, at approximately 11:25 p.m., I was sitting outside on the patio gazing east at a dark sky. All of a sudden my eyes saw a most spectacular sight. Shaped like a volleyball, it was the most beautiful display of red and blue bright sparkling lights that shone like gems with rays darting out like shooting stars. It was travelling from east to west, at a speed of about 15–20 miles an hour. The bright pulsating ball was approximately 400–500 feet from the house and at approximately 80–90 feet in the air. It shone so brightly that it left me mesmerized. A sight to behold like you should expect to see upon entering Ali Baba's cave. Only this was not in a cave but red and blue sparkling jewels in a dark sky.

The patio door was open so I called my oldest sister, Blandine, who was finishing her lunch in the adjoining kitchen. I told her to hurry if she wanted to see something beautiful sparkling in the sky. My sister immediately came out. The two of us admired the bright coloured object. On the outside left of the ball, the cadmium red was darker in colour. On the outside right the sparkling blue was darker in colour. Lighter red and lighter sky blue, almost like diamonds, glowed in the middle. The blue side of the ball was pulsating a bit more than the red side. I do not know if the muffled purring sound came from the UFO or from the noise caused by cars on the No. 2 Highway.

Knowing that my two other sisters, Monique and Colombe, would enjoy looking at this bright coloured phenomenon, I ran upstairs to get them. They both followed me outside. Behind the pines and the maples only the bright red sparkles could be seen. The object had now become smaller as it sailed away towards the southwest. The four of us watched until the ball finally disappeared in the dark behind the trees. The spectacular sight lasted for approximately 4–5 minutes.

*Aftermath*

On August 1, at 7:50 a.m., I phoned 306-763-7421—CKBI radio station in Prince Albert. This city is approximately 30 km from St. Louis. I explained everything to Mr. Wade Custer, after I had asked him if someone had reported a UFO sighting. No reports had come in, so Wade said that he would call me back after he'd made a phone call. Mr. Custer phoned at approximately 9:04 a.m. and told me that he had contacted the airport. The personnel there had no knowledge of planes or helicopters flying the night of July 31. They did not know what the object could be. "Who should I call?" I asked. Wade suggested that I contact the Saskatoon weather bureau. At approximately 9:15 a.m. I phoned 306-975-6906 and explained once again about the spectacular sight to Don Ryback. He could not help as he had no knowledge as to the identity of this round sparkling object. Mr. Ryback advised me to call the RCMP. I did call 306-233-5810 at approximately 9:30 a.m., Got Regina headquarters twice instead of the Wakaw detachment. A lady at the Regina office listened to my story. She found it mighty interesting, so she helped me connect with the RCMP in Wakaw. I left a message at the Wakaw Depot to call me—Lucie Romanycia. Sergeant Scarf called me at approximately 12:50 p.m. He thought that I had an interesting story. He said that an officer from Wakaw had been in St. Louis on July 31, at about the same time that my sisters and I had spotted the UFO, but this officer hadn't reported anything about a sighting. To this statement I answered, "The officer who was in St. Louis would have probably been in his car with his eyes on the road—not looking at the sky like I was." Sergeant Scarf retorted, "Oh well, that's right!"

On this same day, at approximately 2:20 p.m., I saw an army plane flying south to north on the west side of the house. Whether this had any connections to the sighting, I do not know.

Lucie Romanycia

# Some New Answers to Our Questions

George W. Beck is a retired aviator who lives in Duncan, British Columbia. A number of unusual events and experiences occurred to him during the course of an adventurous life. Born in Victoria, he served with the 5th B.C. Coast Artillery. Part of that time he was an instructor in signals and radar. Reading of my interest in "mysterious matters" in the pages of the Duncan *Pictorial*, he kindly wrote to me. We exchanged a number of letters, and from his correspondence I gleaned accounts of some of his experiences. The following details about aerial observations come from Beck's letters of 14 August and 24 August 1990.

◆ ◆ ◆

1.

About mid-January of 1947, a doctor of astrophysics at the Dominion Observatory on Little Saanich Mountain, near Victoria, B.C., was being interviewed on the radio about Comet Kohoutek, which was at that time visible in the southern sky at about 15 degrees above the horizon. He said that with binoculars or telescope we might see it best between 23:00 and 01:00 hours.

So, with my 8 x 50s in hand, I went out in the backyard and began to scan the sky in that area. Sure enough, there was the little "fuzz" ball, complete with skimpy tail, a very unspectacular object, to say the least.

Then a new light moved into my field of vision. I dropped the binoculars down to look at this with eyes only. At first, I thought that it was an airplane flying a westerly path over the city. Although there was a light breeze from that quarter, I didn't hear the sound of a motor. Then I brought up the binocs and refocused. But I could not pick up a starboard wing-tip light. Nor could I see a blinking red tail-light. There was no sound at all, only a steady white light steadily moving west.

It then passed from sight, behind a nearby house, so I moved around to our front porch. The light had now taken up a northwesterly heading. When I got the glasses on it again, I was in for a big surprise. Suddenly it was gone. Adjusting the lenses, I could now see a faintly elliptical shape with a series of brighter, "port-hole"-like apertures running the length at the mid-line. "Hmmm, what's this, I thought to myself?" Then a light was seen to issue from the end opposite the one into which the light had disappeared. Soon it was lost behind some trees.

I went into the house and then to bed. Next morning, as I came out the front door to go to work, I glanced up to the place where I had seen the disc in the sky the evening before. There, on a tall mast, was a long boom, a yagi-type TV antenna, the "port-holes" were obviously the loop-ends of the director-bars. The moving light? Well, I guess, it was a plane all right, even if I couldn't see the proper nav lights.

Next, on a camping trip to a provincial part on Buttle Lake in central Vancouver Island, the family group were sitting around the dying campfire on a mild but very damp evening. It was not raining, but the air was soggy with 100 per cent humidity. As I glanced up to a distant hillside, I could see a bluish-white glow that irregularly strengthened and faded. It was not moving, only pulsing very slowly. Not wanting to "start something" by pointing and shouting "Whatzat?" I decided to keep quiet and watch. Finally, we all turned into our bunks and enjoyed a good night's sleep in the fresh outdoor air.

Next morning, I ambled over to the block of wood I'd been sitting on last night. I lifted my glasses to see the hillside where the "little pulser" had been. Now I could see the Hydro transmission line that feeds the pulp mill at Gold River. What I'd seen last night was most likely the coronal glow around the insulators holding the conductor wires.

These two experiences have taught me to be aware and observant of what is around us. But most importantly, they taught me to keep cool and analytical. Many things that "go blink" in the night can be logically explained. Yet there are some very well-publicized sightings that so far have remained unresolved.

So keep an open eye and an open mind. Someday we may get some new answers to our questions.

2.

To the best of my recollection, the following events occurred late one afternoon in August of 1970.

A friend and I arrived at the Victoria Flying Club at the Pat Bay International Airport, where I had reserved a Cessna 150 for a little sightseeing fun. Everyone in the office was "babbling" about the UFO that had been seen earlier in the afternoon. From what they told me, it happened this way.

The CFI [Chief Flying Instructor] was up with a student and they were doing "circuits" for "touch and go." They were flying west at about 800 feet ASL [Above Sea Level], when Noel, the instructor, looked to the north and saw an intense bright "light" that was moving very fast. His estimate was Mach 2. (As he was a former Air Force pilot, I would accept his word for the speed.) The speeding "light" passed in front of and below the top of Mount Maxwell on Salt Spring Island. That would give it a height of about 1000 feet and a line-of-sight distance of approximately eight miles. The object then made a

60-degree change of direction, not a turn, without any change in velocity. It now had a SE heading.

Noel called the Tower to advise them of what he saw; they acknowledged. Then other people on the ground, who often monitor the Tower talk, rushed out to have a look, too. Noel and his student watched as the "light" made another right-angle change of direction, over the City of Victoria. This brought it to a NE heading, which would bring it over East Vancouver, B.C. Then it disappeared in the distance.

Later, while I was sitting on the porch of our home on North Pender Island, in the gathering twilight, enjoying the pleasant view over Swanson Channel, my thoughts went back to the account of that flying "light." Glancing to the west, I could see the winking red lights on the B.C. Telephone Company's wave-guide telecommunications towers on Mount Bruce, also on Salt Spring Island, but about two miles south of the summit of Mount Maxwell.

That's when a few things began to fall into place. Noel had seen the "light" just before it did that 60-degree change of direction to a SE course. In downtown Victoria, the B.C. Tel, at that time, had radio-wave guides on top of their office tower. One set of dishes faced NW (to feed the Mount Bruce tower); the other set of dishes fed directly NE to their terminal on Capitol Hill, near Burnaby (East Vancouver).

So, it seems the speeding "light" was flying in the wave-guide beams of B.C. Tel's VHF radio link with the mainland. "But," I said to myself, "those signals are zipping along at 186,000 mps, whereas the 'light' was dragging along at only Mach 2. Could it be some sort of an electromagnetic phenomenon? Or was it something else entirely?"

One thing is sure. It was not likely a rigid structure. A 60-degree change in direction, with no loss of velocity, would set up centrifugal forces that I would shudder to contemplate. (The speed of sound near sea level is plus or minus 760 mph. The "plus or minus" bit relates to the air temperature and density. So the estimated Mach 2 at 1000 feet ASL would be a little over 1500 mph.)

Anyway, there it is, just as unanswered today as it was then.

# All of This Sounds
# Very Weird

Lorraine Warmington, a resident of Mississauga, Ontario, is of Celtic background, with an Irish mother and a Scottish father. She works as a training administrator. Mrs. Warmington's son is a newspaper reporter in Toronto, and he brought us in contact after I discussed UFOs on Radio Station Q-107's popular open-line show *Barometer*.

Mrs. Warmington experienced a series of strange sightings. I encouraged her to write an account of them. She did so, and on 14 July 1992 I received this account of her experiences. It has been slightly edited for publication. In a subsequent letter, dated 24 July 1992, Mrs. Warmington noted: "Most of my three brothers and two sisters have had UFO sightings. Most sightings are high up in the sky, except for the experiences of my sister Heather, who has had closer encounters.

"Because my daughter, Dana, and I often talk about our experiences, we have met many, many people who have had sightings. Just the other day I was talking to a woman whose boyfriend had this encounter: He and his brother were lying in a field and a UFO—a metallic, saucer-shaped object—hovered low in the air directly over them. Unfortunately we were interrupted when she was telling me about this and I don't have any more details."

◆ ◆ ◆

Years ago, when we were just tiny girls, my sister and I saw something that didn't make sense, at least from an adult perspective.

In the summer of 1944 or 1945, when Heather and I were three and four years old respectively, we were playing in our backyard in Woodroffe, a suburb west of Ottawa, now annexed to the city. Our backyard was small and fenced in, like all the others in the suburb.

What we thought was an airplane swooped down slowly in front of us, about ten feet over our heads. It did not make any noise. We do not remember seeing wings or propellers. The "airplane" was kind of egg- or oval-shaped, and I guess it was about five feet high and four feet wide. Sitting inside it were two men. They smiled at us and I think they talked to us, or at least they reassured us and told us not to be afraid. I recall that the man on the side near to us cautioned the man on the far side not to frighten us. This "airplane" did not land. It just flew away.

I remember that afterwards we ran into the house to tell our mother. She did not believe us. She said it was just our imagination.

Whenever my sister and I recall this event, we are certain that it was not an airplane. If it had been an airplane, it surely would have crashed. At the very least its occupants would have been afraid that they might crash. The occupants, who looked like regular people, were clearly smiling and happy. The memory has stayed with us all our lives. I cannot swear that what we saw as not some kind of airplane, but my sister thinks it most definitely was not.

The next occasion on which I saw something strange was early one evening, around September 26, 1975. This occurred in Blackburn Hamlet, a suburb east of Ottawa. We were driving home from my daughter's ballet lesson around 7:10 p.m. on a bright, clear, still-sunny day. As we drove east and came around the curve on Orient Park Drive, we saw, just hanging in the air, lamp-post high, a hamburger-shaped metallic object. The object was silver in colour and had portholes. Beautiful coloured lights were swirling around, beaming from the craft. The lights were colours we had never seen before or since.

This craft, just hanging there in the air, was about fifteen feet from the ground and about a yard or so in from the curb. No houses yet stood on that side of the street. It was an open field, except for the presence of lamp-posts.

By now my memory of the sight has somewhat faded, but I believe the object was hovering. There was no sound. At least we could hear nothing from inside our car. I am sure that we had the windows of the car open, as there was no air-conditioning in the little Vega I was driving at the time. The hamburger-shaped object was close to the size of the car, but not quite, perhaps two-thirds as large.

My daughter and I both witnessed it. Dana was seven years old at the time and got very excited. She jumped from the front seat to the back seat. Neither of us saw any people or beings inside or around the vehicle.

I was driving slowly while staring at the thing, but another car was gaining on us from behind. I decided to drive around into the development so I could turn around, park, and have a better look. I did just that, but by then the thing had disappeared.

If I could do things over again today, I would just have parked the car then and there and not have worried about the car behind us. But at the time I remember that I thought the car was going to hit us, which is why I sped up. Although we were curious, we were also very frightened of this object. I tried to find the car later, to find out if the occupants saw what we saw, but I could not locate it.

The strange thing is that about five years later, when we were visiting my brother's house at Christmas, another guest told us about a UFO that he and a friend had seen in Toronto. I recall that the guest was a scientist. It turned out that they saw exactly the same thing that we saw on the same night. They saw it around 7:30 p.m., about twenty minutes later than we did.

His description was identical to mine, right down to the swirling, coloured lights, except for one detail. In his account the object was much higher in the sky than it was in ours, and it was travelling, not just hanging there. He had not previously heard about our sighting, and I deliberately waited until he finished his account before telling him about ours.

In the late spring or early summer of 1985, my daughter and I witnessed yet another strange occurrence. In the evening we were driving west down the Queensway, near Stittsville, Ont., when all of a sudden Dana yelled, "Look, what's that up there?" I looked up towards the area of the sky she was pointing at, and there was a huge, strange machine above the treeline. This was right near the highway. It was difficult for me to drive the car and at the same time to watch this thing or things. I wanted to park the car, but there was nowhere to do so. Dozens of cars were parked along the highway, as well as on the bridge, the Terry Fox Drive overpass. Their occupants were sitting and standing outside alongside their cars, watching the sight.

I will try to describe what we saw. Sometimes the thing looked boomerang-shaped. There were round, white lights on the wings. Sometimes they would change from white to blue, or blink out altogether. The boomerang seemed to move in a backward direction. The machine flew low, directly over our car, very slowly, so we had a good look at the bottom of it. There seemed to be many pipes running up and down all over the bottom. I think the paint was camouflage—green, brown, and pewter-coloured. At times the object was gigantic in size, just unbelievably huge.

We did not hear any sound. The machine seemed to turn itself inside out and take on different shapes. Then all of a sudden it turned into a bright light and swooshed across the sky towards the west. It seemed to hang there while. Then it disappeared.

There were a lot of people looking at these things, and cars were parked all along the highway and even on the overpass. But for some strange reason nothing was reported in the newspapers. Not one word. Believe me, if you know the Queensway in Ottawa, nobody in his or her right mind would park there and watch an airplane or a helicopter pass overhead. This had to be something really unusual. And it was.

A policeman gave us a UFO hotline number to call and report what we had seen. We did call, but when they wanted our names and addresses, we thought the better of it. They would think we were crazy people, so we just told them to never mind. If they keep records of anonymous calls, they should still have a record of this one.

I know all of this sounds very weird, but I also know what I saw. Although my memory of all these events is starting to erode, I have described them to the best of my recollections.

# Like an Electric Light Bulb

Mildred (Millie) Young Hubbert is a retired teacher who lives in Markdale, Ontario She heard me discussing UFOs on Q-107's *Barometer* and sent me the interesting account that appears below. Her account bears the date 28 October 1991.

The event she describes took place over four decades ago, yet the memory of the experience of seeing the "mystery light" over an arm of Great Slave Lake in the Northwest Territories remains as vivid as ever. There are two reasons why the sighting is of particular interest. First, it took place early in the era of flying saucers, so early that such sights were not being widely or commonly reported. Second, although the sighting may not be unique, it may be linked with the one mentioned on the television program seen by the author.

◆ ◆ ◆

The UFO sighting that I experienced took place in September 1948, outside Yellowknife, in the Northwest Territories, where I was teaching.

Four of us were crossing an arm of Great Slave Lake in a large canoe with an outboard motor on it after visiting a tiny, unmanned Signal Corps station in the bush. Two of us were teachers, one a civil servant and one the Signal Corps man in charge of the station.

As we were crossing the lake, we noticed a small light, like an electric light bulb, appear above the trees far behind us. We were assured that this had no connection with the S.C. station. Very slowly the light grew larger, drifting across the tops of the trees along the far shore of the lake, its reflection visible in the dark water.

It was a beautifully clear night full of stars and, I think, a full moon. All around us was total darkness, except for some indication of the lights of Yellowknife in the opposite direction of the sighting.

Whatever it was, it grew very slowly larger, until it was perhaps a little smaller than a full moon, bright orange and with a sharp circular outline. The other teacher said it was jagged at one side, but it looked just like a sharp circle to me. At that point it suddenly stopped, almost as though it had either become aware of us or had seen the lights of Yellowknife in the distance. It hovered a few moments, then shot off at right angles and disappeared among the distant stars. We had spent about twenty minutes crossing the bay and had observed it almost the whole time.

I don't think any of us had, at the time, heard of UFOs or flying saucers. We were totally perplexed by what this might be. When we reached Yellowknife, we asked those we met if they had seen the object, but no one had. Actually, no one else was interested, their concerns being involved in more important things, like the price of gold or who had made the latest strike.

The next summer, when I returned to Toronto, I visited the David Dunlap Observatory to ask for some scientific explanation of what we had seen. The people there were of no help whatever, just remarking, "If you had been a trained observer, you would have known what you were looking at."

Many years later there was a program on television that re-enacted reports of UFO sightings that had been reported to the U.S. government. One of these programs featured a reported sighting in the Yukon that took place about the same time as our experience. The object that was depicted looked exactly like the one I remembered.

Since this happened over forty years ago, I have to acknowledge the possible vagaries of memory, but this is how I remember it. I have no further explanation of this experience, nor have I seen anything like it since.

# Two Incidents

Arlene Smilovitch of Montreal wrote to me on 8 November 1990, sending me brief accounts of two experiences. They are reproduced below. The first experience involves "mystery lights"; the second, a "strange sensation."

What prompted Mrs. Smilovitch to write to me was seeing a notice in a Montreal suburban newspaper that I was collecting stories of the supernatural for use in a book. It is interesting to note that the episode with the "mystery lights"—unidentified flying objects—remains so clear in her memory after the passage of a quarter-century.

◆ ◆ ◆

Two incidents happened to me in my life that I will share with you.

Approximately 25 years ago I was sitting in the living room of my parents' home when I glanced out the window and saw six objects, which were lit up and slowly flying through the sky in formation. I watched them from my seat as I was too frightened to actually get out of my seat to take a really good look at them. To this day I regret that enormously. I will draw the formation as I remember it.

Another incident happened to me just this year. This I believe was a friendly spirit, as I did not have any threatening or ominous feeling when this occurred. This happened to me during the early morning hours while I was in the washroom putting on my makeup and preparing for work. My husband had already left for work, and my daughter was sound asleep as she did not have to arise for a while yet. Suddenly I felt someone playfully (I felt that it was actually playful) tap me on my buttock. I thought it was my daughter who had got up without my knowing and was playfully trying to trick me. I turned around, expecting to see her standing behind me, but she was not there. I quietly went into her room, and there she was sleeping like a log. This event really jolted me, but in a positive way. I felt that we had a friendly little spirit with us, a young spirit.

This was my first, and to date, only experience with a "spirit."

I hope that this will be useful to you and would very much appreciate hearing a little about your research and any personal experiences you have had that you might be able to share with me.

# I'd Say It Was the Size of a Barn

This letter, signed Mrs. Marjorie Brignall, appeared in *Canadian UFO Report*, Issue No. 2-2, 1971. Only one section of the long letter is reproduced here, the one that records the appearance of "a huge cone-shaped object."

◆ ◆ ◆

Sir:

March 1968. A regular night passed by. I was on duty in a small hospital and did the records on the hour, 3:00 a.m. All was quiet. I had returned to the nurses's station when I thought, "Oh, oh, the lights are burning out!" I glanced up. The lights appeared all right, but where was all this other light coming from? I looked out the window, and there was a sight to behold, and no camera!

A huge cone-shaped object was hovering above the ground. There was illumination all around. The treetops were visible; an aluminum storage bin in a field was like daylight in one area. It was weird. Many thoughts raced through my mind while I stood rooted to the spot fascinated. Scared—no—it was a distance away from me and it didn't hug the window or move in any closer. Only one thing very clear came to me—"In my house there are many mansions," etc.

Trying to describe it, I'd say it was the size of a barn and appeared to have three large rocks suspended from its undercarriage—could it have been the landing gear? The light was a vivid orange, luminous, the rocks underneath were dark in colour. It rose a little higher, just above the treetops and disappeared into the black night.

Regarding this sighting, I phoned Dauphin radio station and they announced it, as they did other sightings. Of late I don't hear [such announcements] any more. Sorry about this for many people listened and were interested. A comment I overheard was, "Just like everything else—they get something good on and then take it off."

From this experience I know there is a world of worlds way out there—a very highly intelligent world—so who am I…?

Mrs. Marjorie Brignall
Elkhorn, Manitoba

# I Had Seen a Flying Saucer

The well-known UFO personality Betty Stewart was the studio guest on an open-line radio program on CFRB Toronto the evening of 21 February 1992. Betty talked about her experiences as an abductee. By telephone I contributed some comments of my own. There were many callers, as there always are for programs about UFOs, and Betty encouraged callers with particularly interesting stories to tell to contact me directly, as my phone number was (and is) listed in the Toronto telephone directory.

As a result of this appearance, I received a most interesting letter from Arthur Zutis, a barrister and solicitor and notary public in Toronto. He wrote on 24 February: "I was listening to your program on CFRB a few nights ago, which you gave together with Mrs. Betty Stewart, and found it most interesting, the more so because I, too, have had this experience.

"I have enclosed with this letter a copy of my account as to what I saw and experienced on August 5th, 1968. You are welcome to make any use of this story in your unfettered discretion. It has never been used before, although I have told many of my friends about this experience; some of them believed me, some others laughed, one woman remarked that the UFO crew must have been interested in my car. No matter what, I believe I saw the real thing.

"P.S. At the time, I was driving an Aston Martin DB6."

◆ ◆ ◆

November 5, 1968

## *Sighting of a UFO*
## *on King's Highway No. 69, in Ontario,*
## *on Monday, 5 August 1968*

I had gone to Sudbury over the long weekend and was returning to Toronto on Monday, 5 August 1968. I was driving my car on King's Highway No. 69, which covers a stretch from Sudbury to Parry Sound. It was a very hot and humid day (later I learned that both the temperature and the humidity had been in the nineties), otherwise very bright and sunny. It was early in the afternoon, and I had covered about two-thirds of the distance from Sudbury to Parry Sound. I was alone on the road and was going through a wooded area at the time. (The stretch from Sudbury to Parry Sound is largely forest.) Presently I felt that there was a shadow behind me, but I thought nothing of it, and did not even look in the rear-vision mirror. A few seconds later I heard bzzz... bzzz... bzzz... a sound resembling the hum of a heavily overloaded electrical circuit that is about ready to blow a fuse. The buzzing sounded as if it first came from the back of the car, then from the right-hand side, and then again from the back, and strangely, it seemed as if it was both in and outside the car at the same time. It occurred to me that it may have been a signal from another car trying to overtake me; I looked back but saw nobody behind or ahead of me. Then I got the feeling that something round was alongside or above my car, but since my car was not fitted with a side mirror, I couldn't see. Whatever it was, the object swept upwards and I could no longer feel the shadow. The next thing I noticed was intense heat coming from the left side of the road, such as you would feel standing in front of an open fire or stove with the door open. I looked to the left but there was no campfire or people to be seen in the clearing. (Later it occurred to me that a campfire at that time of the year would have been an impossibility. I reached out to change the air conditioning from "medium" to "high," and at that point I noticed the object. It looked like a pot with a mushroom-type lid on top of it. Its colour was slate grey with undertones of brown, but the top of it was much darker. It appeared to be about five feet in diameter; its height, less the conical roof, about three to four feet. It moved silently, and when I saw it, it was ahead of my car and just clearing the treetops on the right-hand side of the road. I observed it for about three or four seconds and in that period the object maintained its straight and regular course, i.e., it was moving south. (Highway 69 runs in a south-easterly direction.) What impressed me was the bleakness of the object: It was all enclosed with no openings or windows. Assuming that the speed of my car was from 60 to 65 mph, the speed of the object, while I observed it, was about 60 mph. It was moving rather slowly and downwards. As it was about to disappear, a thought flashed through my mind that I had seen a flying saucer. The whole episode had lasted from ten to fifteen seconds. The object had demonstrated some curiosity, but there was nothing dangerous or ominous about it, and at no time was I afraid of it or its intentions.

# Yes, It Really Scared Me

W.K. Allan is an investigator of UFOs and a contributor to *Flying Saucer Review*. In the 1970s he was a regular UFO commentator for the Calgary radio station CFCN.

"Car Levitation on the Blackfoot Reserve" is the title of Allan's taped interview with Rosalin and Wilton Raw Eater. The couple are residents of the Blackfoot Indian Reserve in Alberta. The transcript of this interview was originally published in *Flying Saucer Review* in its August 1971 Supplement.

In the editorial note that precedes the taped interview, there is a reference to the "Craigmyle experience." This refers to an earlier report of a levitating vehicle. In this incident, also investigated by Allan, an automobile being driven by Barbara Smyth, a teacher from the Alberta community of Craigmyle, was apparently levitated and propelled along the road. Allan reported on this case ("A UFO and the Car Which 'Floated Along': School-teacher's Unnerving Experience in Alberta, Canada") in *Flying Saucer Review*, August 1971, Supplement.

With the present case, Allan put the Raw Eaters at ease by playing the Smyth tape before commencing his interview.

◆ ◆ ◆

*The following is a transcript of a taped interview with Wilton Raw Eater and his wife, regarding an unusual levitation, which is said to have taken place on the Blackfoot Indian Reserve near Gleichen, Alberta, Canada, on May 14, 1971. Mr. Raw is driver of the local school bus.*

*These people were very reluctant to speak until we played them the tape of the interview with Barbara Smyth about her Craigmyle experience. In passing, I should add that it is apparently Mr. Raw's custom to visit the bar at the end of the working week.*

Mr. Raw: Well that's pretty hard to start with. Well... I went to the bar, had a few beers, and when I start coming home it was night like... then I saw these four houses just up the hill here, and as soon as we passed the houses, all of a sudden we seen this bright light, like, just hit us like lightning.

Allan: Was it ahead of you or to one side?

Mr. Raw: It was sort of on the right side of the car, you know. It just happened for a few seconds, and the car... we didn't notice it till after, oh, about a few yards, and the wife told me: "The car's off the ground." I kept steering the car while we stayed on the side of the road and went for about a quarter of a mile... it didn't bother me none. Had my lights on. All of a sudden my car hit the ground...I could feel the wheels when they hit the ground, and we just drove home right away and went to my brother's place [where we] talked to his wife about it. I waited for my brother and I told him about it.

Allan: You say you kept steering the car. How if you turned the wheel? Just kept to the centre of the road, did it?

Mr. Raw: Oh, yes.

Allan: You didn't steer it to either side?

Mr. Raw: No, I had my steering steady like, you know. Like I said before, I didn't steer it actually; I was just holding my steering [wheel] when I stay in the centre of the road [from], just before going down the hill, until we hit the gravel road again on this hill coming down there. Well, it didn't actually scare me then, but the wife must have been scared.

Allan: Could you tell by the headlights on the road ahead that the car wasn't in the normal position?

Mr. Raw: Well actually the car was running...was going about 40–50 [mph]. I was looking at the speedometer sometimes, but it didn't bother me, like you know.

Allan: But you still feel sure the car was up?

Mr. Raw: Oh yes, you could tell it.

Allan: Because you looked out the window?

Mr. Raw: I was looking down the side, you know.

Allan: Did it feel any different? You didn't feel the little bumps?

Mr. Raw: I didn't feel nothing, just floated, like.

*That completed the interview with Wilton Raw Eater, and his wife now kindly allowed me to ask her a few questions.*

Allan: Now Rosalin, Mrs. Raw Eater, could you tell me what you saw, you noticed it first, didn't you?

Mrs. Raw: Yes, I noticed it because we have rough roads here. At first I didn't really care, I thought first he was just speeding, because he always speeds. But this time it was just like driving a new car, and our car isn't that new; could feel the bumps with it, but then I looked down and the car was off the ground.

Allan: How high do you think it was off the ground?

Mrs. Raw: Oh, about two feet, or something like that.

Allan: How long do you think it stayed that way; can you tell?

Mrs. Raw: Well, I was really scared, I couldn't very well remember.

Allan: Did you notice the bump when it was back on the road? There was no mistake about that?

Mrs. Raw: Yes, we can tell when we're on our gravel roads, especially the roads we've got, they're real bad.

Allan: Now this light, did it continue with you all the time you were off the ground?

Mrs. Raw: Yes, it did until it... it just went off.

Allan: The light went off and then your car went down.

Mrs. Raw: Then I told him to drive a little faster so we could get home. I wanted to come home to my kids because I thought that was the last time I was going to see them.

Allan: You must have been very frightened.

Mrs. Raw: Yes, it really scared me, so we took the kids in the car and I told him, "Let's go over to your brother's," and that's when we went over to his brother's place.

# Then I Saw the Ship

Researcher John Magor noted in the *Canadian UFO Report*, Vol. 3, No. 6, 1975, that the Georgian Bay area of Ontario experienced a mini-"flap" during the winter of 1973–74. The UFO sightings centred around Boshkung Lake. Magor credited the UFO investigator Henry H. McKay with drawing attention to the "dramatic encounter" that occurred on 7 October 1975.

The sole witness was Robert A. Suffern, a carpenter, twenty-seven years old, a resident of Utterson, near Bracebridge. Suffern filed a statement about the sighting with the Ontario Provincial Police. That statement is reproduced here. McKay investigated the sighting and added the following details about the ship and the alien that were reported by Suffern: "He estimated the size as 8–9 feet top to bottom, and a width of approximately 12–14 feet. The ship appeared to look like the dull side of aluminum foil, wrinkled and displaying a narrow dark band around the edge of the clam-like portion of the structure. He indicated the ship had rested on or close to the gravelled road surface.

"Robert Suffern is engaged in the building trade as a carpenter and would be familiar with aluminum foil for its insulation qualities, and a good judge for estimating the relevant dimension."

◆ ◆ ◆

At about 8:30 p.m. tonight I got a phone call from my sister Shirley, who lives about 300 yards northeast of my house. She said it looked like a fire at my barn. I went out, and at first I couldn't see anything, but then I heard the cattle rustling, but told my sister I couldn't go out because I was looking after the baby. She came down to the house and I took her car and went to the barn and saw nothing. I went out the lane and drove down the road and then turned down a sideroad.

Then I saw the ship in the centre of the road. It was the colour of the dull side of aluminum foil wrap and the surface was irregular and crinkled. I could not hear any sound other than the motor of my car. I only saw it momentarily and then it went straight up to a fast speed and disappeared. There were no lights.

I turned around and started for home, turned onto Three Mile Lake Road, and then I saw the thing on the side of the road. It was on the grass shoulder of the road and was about to cross from my right to my left. It suddenly pivoted and turned towards the pasture and vaulted over the fence and out of sight.

It appeared to be short and had very broad shoulders which seemed to be out of proportion. The movements were similar to an ape or a midget, but it was very agile. It reached up with its hands, grabbed the fence post and vaulted over with no effort. The head portion was covered in a globe and I couldn't detect any mask or face portion. The suit was a silver colour, and one piece—the globe—was a contrasting white or light colour.

I returned home and had time to get the kids to bed. The T.V. was on and suddenly the sound stopped and when I looked it had blacked out for a matter of seconds. I went to the door, and out behind the barn in the pasture I saw an orange fluorescent light that was not flashing. The light seemed to follow the contour of the land and headed out over Three Mile Lake.

I debated for some time who to call, and then I called the O.P.P. in Bracebridge.

About 10 years ago in the same area I saw a similar ship in flight over my barn.

# Director Has Close Encounters

Lawrence J. Fenwick is one of the country's knowledgeable UFO investigators. He attended McMaster University and is a graduate of the Ryerson Polytechnical Institute. At the time of these reports, he worked in credit assessment; he now works in telemarketing. In 1977, with fellow investigators Joseph Muskat and Harry Tokarz, he founded the Canadian UFO Research Network (CUFORN).

Fenwick is widely read in UFOlogy. He favours the Extraterrestrial Hypothesis; he argues that crash/retrievals are solid evidence that alien craft and their occupants have come down to Earth; and he seems drawn to the Conspiracy Theory, which holds that the U.S. government, despite denials, possesses knowledge of alien visitations and at top-secret bases has undertaken "reverse engineering" of the alien craft in its possession.

Such views have little to do with the detailed investigations of other people's sightings that he has conducted. Indeed, they have little to do with these two conscientious accounts of his own sightings. The reports are reprinted from *CUFORN Bulletin*, June–September, 1982, when Fenwick was the group's director and editor of its *Bulletin*.

◆ ◆ ◆

1.

The date was November 16, 1977; the location, the northwest corner of Bathurst and Glencairn in Toronto, Ontario. The observers: Your Editor, Lawrence Joel Fenwick, age 41 at the time, and a Metropolitan Toronto Police Officer, name and badge number not obtained, age about 35. The incident began when I got a phone call from Ero Talvila, Editor and Publisher of *Inner Life*, a magazine covering psychic matters. It was 10:45 p.m. Ero said he had received a telephone call from an aged couple who lived directly south about four miles at Bathurst and Dupont. They told him they had seen something unusual in the sky that was moving slowly northward up Bathurst Street. He immediately called me and told me about the report. I walked out to the corner previously mentioned and noticed a police cruiser parked on the gas station lot at the corner. I asked one of the two officers if anything unusual had been reported in the sky in the last few minutes. The younger of the tow officers said they had heard nothing on their police radio.

It was now 11:00 p.m., and I was about to go home when I looked up to my left (southwest) and saw a softly glowing oblong or cigar-shaped object moving very slowly north. I tapped on the police car's window and the officer rolled down his window. I said, "Come on out and look at this." The policeman got out of the cruiser and stood beside me as we watched the object moving just beyond the 50-foot-tall tree on the gas station lot. It was silent and had a diameter of a baseball held at arm's length. It glowed evenly all over in a sort of soft, white-yellow colour. The edges were simply fuzzy, although there was no glow surrounding the object. It seemed to have a glow of its own rather than reflecting the street lights. It was moving at an estimated 5 mph on the west side of Bathurst Street.

The police officer stood, as I did, open-mouthed for a moment. Then he ran back to the cruiser, said something to the other officer, and the other officer started up the car motor and they headed off the lot and south on Bathurst. The officer seemed rather frightened when I looked at him heading back to the cruiser. He was in the car before I had a chance to get his name or badge number. I neglected to get the number of the cruiser, so I could not get confirmation of the sighting from him. I had my Instamatic Kodak camera with me and was so taken aback and astounded that I completely forgot I had it with me and did not take a photograph.

I had been looking up at the object at a 45-degree angle during the observation, which lasted for the officer about five seconds and for me about 12 seconds. The object headed north, and I did not try to follow it as it was a very cold night, about 20° Fahrenheit, and, since I was not dressed very warmly, I headed home, and wrote down a description of what I had seen. It was five years before I told anyone about this incident. This is the first time it has been in print. I recall that it was a clear night, but I do not remember seeing the moon. The lights of the city were obscuring most of the stars. I was wearing eyeglasses, which I need for distant viewing. The policeman was not wearing glasses. Ero Talvila does not recall the names of the two elderly people who first reported the object. At the time of the sighting, I was living on Bathurst Street in an apartment that faced away from the street. My only frame of reference during the sighting was the tree, and we saw the object pass behind it briefly. I felt no heat and there was no odour in the air. I do not drink or take drugs. There was negligible wind that night. I would estimate that the object was no more than 75 feet from me at its closest point. There was very little traffic at the time, although I did not pay a great deal of attention to that aspect.

My observation was continuous, and I kept my eyeglasses on during it. I had been in UFOlogy research for 27 years prior to my sighting. I do not recall calling the airport or any other authorities other than speaking to the police officers. The object moved in a straight line throughout the observation. As it moved north, it was lost to my sight when several apartment buildings obscured it. There were no other reports of the object made that night, as far as I know. I did not sense anything in the way of communication from the object, but I did feel that the object was surveying the urban area at its leisure. Bathurst Street is a very heavily populated street in a residential-commercial area of north-central Toronto.

*CUFORN*'s conclusion: Genuine CE1 [Close Encounter of the First Kind], multiple-observer case.

## 2.

A second observation by Your Editor occurred on November 16, 1981, at 8:56 p.m. The location of the observers (there were four in one place and more persons in other areas of the City of Toronto) was 457 Marlee Avenue. The observers whose names are known are Lawrence Joel Fenwick and Mitchell Sparks. The duration of the sighting for Your Editor was six seconds; for Sparks, five seconds; for two others whose names are not known, five minutes; and for others the duration is unknown.

This turned out to be a coincidence as it was Fenwick's sister's birthday, the *same date* as his CE1 of 1977. His sister lives in California. He was not celebrating the birthday in any way on either occasion.

Fenwick's occupation is that of a credit reporter. He is educated in psychology, having attended McMaster University in Hamilton, Ontario, and has a degree in journalism from Ryerson Polytechnical Institute in Toronto. He has not attempted to profit in any way from his experiences from a financial standpoint.

It was a clear night with many stars visible. He lives in a residential area in a four-storey apartment building, with a view to the east. It was a cold night. The temperature was 25° Centigrade with a humidity at 84%. There was no wind. He was wearing corrective eyeglasses for distance viewing at the time. He was inside his apartment during the observation. The sighting occurred during the peak of the Leonid meteorite shower, as did his previous encounter.

He was looking out his apartment window to see who had left a car motor running. As he did, he noticed an aircraft heading north on a flight path which would have been ten minutes to the east. At that time, something impelled him to look in the direction from which the aircraft had come, i.e., the south. He thought he was looking at a twinkling star, when he saw the "star" moving. He immediately began counting "1,000... 2,000," etc., military style, so that he could time whatever it was as it moved. He was not thinking of UFOs at the time.

As it got closer, he could see that what he was watching was three lights, one blue, one red, and one white. Each was blinking on and off like a strobe light, and they all blinked on and off at the same time. The object moved directly from east to west at a very high rate of speed. There was no way in which he could determine what the object looked like except that the three lights must have been synchronized. There could have been three objects, or one rather large one. The object moved out of his line of sight after six seconds had passed. The apartment building obscured the object at that point.

The lights were about the size of a pea held at arm's length. It moved ten miles at an estimated elevation of 3,000 feet, which meant that its speed was about 18,720 mph. Twice during the observation the three lights went out for about one second. They did this simultaneously. There were no apartment buildings in the line of sight which could obscure the lights and make it appear as though they had turned off momentarily. The lights were not blinding, but the observer was impressed with their beauty, since he is of a somewhat artistic bent. The blue, red, and white were average in intensity and were medium in hue. The observer was looking at the lights at angles varying from 25° to 45° at various during the observation. The lights turned off at a regular interval of two seconds, and then on again simultaneously. Its trajectory seemed level.

When the sighting was over, he called out to his wife and daughter, who were busy in other parts of the apartment, but it was too late for them to see anything, or so we thought. Months later, we knew that if we had returned to the window we would have seen the same object heading back to the east and then north. The next thing he did was phone Downsview Air Force Base, or CFB Downsview as it is designated by the military. A captain who answered the phone asked Fenwick some questions from a sighting form. He said he would send a filled-out form to the Herzberg Institute of Astrophysics. This is a division of the National Research Council in Ottawa.

He called Harry Tokarz and Joe Muskat next, and the next day at work he called the University of Toronto's Department of Astronomy. Three professors there were asked separately by Fenwick whether this was part of the Leonid meteorite shower, and each said it was not a meteorite, and that they did not know what it was. He called two radio stations a few days later. They said they had had a few calls about an object that night, but that they attributed the calls to "cranks." Fenwick did not ask anyone in the apartment building if they had seen anything that night, but on May 7th, as he was entering the apartment building lobby, a first-floor resident, Mrs. Mitchell Sparks, complimented him on his appearance on CUFORN's Rogers Cable TV show. He asked her if she or her husband had ever seen anything unusual in the sky, and she said her husband had seen something the previous November. He realized that that was around the time of his sighting and brought a sighting report form to Mr. Sparks that night.

The following is Mr. Sparks's report: He had a five-minute sighting of three lights, red, white, and blue on November 16, 1981, at 9:00 p.m. They were heading slowly towards the east and turned north. He had just got out of his car at the front of the building, where he parks. He looked up and saw the lights. He noticed two teenage boys watching it. They later walked on, talking, and he did not think to ask them their names. He continued to watch the lights. He could not tell what shape the object or objects were. He is 36, an upholstery repairman, married with four children. He has good hearing and does not wear eyeglasses. He said he saw many stars that night but did not notice the moon. He said it was mild for November. He said the edges of the lights were fuzzy. He said the one light was yellowish-white, the others being red and blue. He said the lights went on and off in a sequence, although he couldn't recall what the sequence was. He had no frame of reference during the sighting. The lights moved at about the speed of a jet aircraft. The turn the object or lights made to the north was gradual. He said they reminded him of a neon sign. At first, he thought it was an aircraft, then he realized it must be a UFO because aircraft do not carry blue lights. The investigator had not mentioned his own sighting to him until he had completed filling out the form. His knowledge of the regulation against blue lights on aircraft was confirmed for him by the investigator. He said the lights were the size of a 25-cent coin held at arm's length.

Comment: The returning object, if it was the same one, seems to have been at a lower elevation and at a slower speed than the lights seen by Fenwick.

CUFORN's conclusion: Genuine NL [Nocturnal Light], multiple observer case.


# They Were a Little Bigger than Stars


The abbreviation ET stands for extraterrestrial; it also stands for Etobicoke. The two letters are the official abbreviation of this city in the west end of Toronto, part of the Municipality of Metropolitan Toronto, now the Greater Toronto Area (GTA).

Tony Allison, who lives in Etobicoke, sent me this letter. He was twenty-eight years old at the time he wrote it, and his letter tells of an odd sighting that took place over fourteen years earlier. After phoning me about the sighting, he attended the UFO Symposium held on 12 March 1992 at the Metropolitan Toronto Reference Library, where he heard me discussing the subject of UFOs and alien contact with Betty Stewart, the well-known abductee from Bond Head, Ontario. Then I received his letter.

◆ ◆ ◆

March 16/92

Dear Mr. Colombo,

Hello. My name is Tony Allison and I talked to you at yours and Betty Stewart's symposium a little over a week ago. I originally phoned you a few months ago and told you about my mother's UFO or "mystery lights" experience.

You told me to write up my own experience, so I decided to do so.

My experience happened back in 1977–78. (I don't recall the exact year.) I was 14 or 15 at the time.

The time was approximately 10:30 or 11:00 p.m. My father came home and I heard him say to my mother, out in the living room (we live in an apartment), "Have you heard what they're saying on the radio?"

My mother said, "No, what?"

"Well, apparently there have been sightings of UFOs in Etobicoke."

I heard this and rushed out to the living room, quite excited. My excitement was brought on partly because my father is a very serious man and he tends to be quiet and subdued. So I realized he wasn't joking.

After that we all went out onto the balcony. (We live on the 5th floor, overlooking the 18th hole of a golf course.)

We were out there no more than 5 minutes or so when we noticed 3 small white balls of light on the northern horizon.

My father called up a friend of his who lives down on the 3rd floor (just 2 below us). He came out with his daughter and watched this all with us.

Within the span of about 10 minutes, I would guess, there were anywhere from 4 to 6 people who came out onto *their* balconies and watched the event.

As we all kept a close eye on the objects, I can recall a lot of discussion and excitement amongst the spectators. Comments such as "Those aren't helicopters!" "Aren't those strange!" etc.

The sighting lasted about 20 minutes, as I remember.

The objects moved from right to left, all together, in a group of 3. They would stop and hover, then split up and join back together again in a group, not into one. They were a little bigger than stars and moved very fluently. However, when they would stop, they stopped suddenly.

The weirdest part of the sighting was their departure. They seemed to just split up or splinter at a very high rate of speed.

Needless to say, it was something I will always remember. As a result of that night, I have had an extreme interest in the so-called UFO phenomenon.

Sincerely,
Tony Allison

P.S. I really enjoyed *UFOs over Canada*. I look forward to your next one.

# It Looked Like a Star

Paula Tomei, a resident of Islington, Ontario, heard me talking about UFOs on the radio. On Saturday morning she telephoned me and related an account of her own experience with a mystery light, an incident that had taken place in rural Italy some years earlier. At my request she typed out her memory of that experience and sent it to me. Here it is, from her letter, which I received on 15 November 1991.

◆ ◆ ◆

For my vacation I was sent to Italy to visit my grandparents. They were living in the town of Limano, which dates from the fifteenth century. The town is located in the Tuscany region.

I was there a couple of months when one of my girlfriends introduced me to a young man. At the time he was eighteen and I was sixteen.

One evening, after we had been dating for a few weeks, I waited for him at my girlfriend Rita's house. He arrived around 8:00 p.m., as he always did. Rita decided she did not want to go out that evening.

So the young man and I decided to go to a restaurant in the next town. It was the gathering place for teenagers. On that particular evening we decided to walk there the long way. Instead of taking the usual cable stone road, the one that most people used to get to the piazza of the town of Gave, we would walk along the side road, the one that is usually travelled by cars.

The dirt road was void of streetlights. It was made for romantic walks! The distance was longer, too. We started walking. It was very dark. All we could see were the bright stars. We walked hand in hand for about ten minutes. Then all of a sudden we noticed a bright light in the sky. It looked like a star. But it suddenly started moving. Then it came to a stop. A flash of light appeared and seemed to turn upside-down. The light was as wide as the road. It slowly descended onto the dirt road and moved along it towards us. It stopped about two or three feet ahead of where we were standing.

At this point we were both in a state of terror. We stood there, paralyzed, unable to move. Finally we turned towards each other, trying to understand what was happening. Then the enormous light started drifting towards the neighbouring town.

A car was travelling on the other road. The light moved from the original position in front of us over to the car that was on the other road. It followed the car for a few minutes, then the light disappeared. The bright light in the sky moved very fast to one side. Then it was gone. We started talking. We were no longer fearful. We decided between us not to talk about what had happened to us.

At our destination, one of our friends mentioned the time. We were both surprised that it was so late. I recall that it was 9:45 p.m. We had set out at 8:00 p.m. Both of us were surprised at the amount of time that had elapsed. The walk on the long road would normally take about twenty minutes.

The walk that night took much, much longer.

# Something Was Unusual

Kevin Unger is a Toronto member of the Canadian UFO Research Network (CUFORN). He wrote this account of a sighting of a daylight disk, and it appeared in the July–August 1992 issue of the *CUFORN Bulletin*.

Lawrence J. Fenwick, a CUFORN founder and director, gave it the title "Witness Recalls Daylight Sighting." Perhaps one of the hot air balloonists will read this account and contribute his or her own comments.

◆ ◆ ◆

How many sightings have you heard or read about in which the witness has three full minutes to study a UFO in broad daylight? I am one such witness.

It was three years ago this past winter that I found myself in between jobs, so I took up making deliveries for my brother-in-law's business: importer and wholesaler of fine gourmet foods.

I remember Friday, March 17, 1989, well. It was a beautiful winter's day, the air was crisp and fresh, the sun was shining gloriously, and the sky was stark clear blue against a fresh clean white snowfall.

It was rush hour, approximately four o'clock in the afternoon, and I was travelling south down a residential side road towards St. Clair Avenue, a couple of blocks west of Avenue Road. Two blocks north of St. Clair Avenue is an elementary school with an accompanying football field.

As I was slowly passing the field on my left, I was admiring four hot air balloons crawling southbound through the air in a square formation: two in front and two behind, from my perspective. I would estimate the height of the balloons to have been 500–1,000 feet. While I watched, I noticed an object coming towards the balloons from the southwest. At first, because of the distance, I couldn't make the object out, but as I got closer I had a feeling that something was unusual.

I stopped the van and walked across the street to the field and stood at the edge of the clearing, accompanied by some evergreen trees. The closer the object got, the more excited I became. It was travelling from southeast to northwest. From my perspective, it slipped right between the four hot air balloons. It was triangular in shape with the top pointing towards the sky. The colour was metallic grey and the sun gleamed off its shiny, smooth surface. I estimated the height to be approximately 1,000 feet.

As the object travelled towards me, I looked for any telltale sign that would identify it as a conventional craft. I looked for wings, I looked for propellers, I looked for blinking lights and markings. Nothing. As the object travelled away from me towards the north, I again looked for the same telltale signs of conventional aircraft. There were none. The object moved through the air so silently, and so perfectly, that I couldn't tell if it was spinning or not. I stared at it clearly for a full three minutes and still couldn't tell if it was spinning!

Once the object had passed, I was so excited over the possibility that I had witnessed a daylight sighting of a UFO that I began to look around for others who may have seen what I saw. It was rush hour. Surely at least one other person had seen it too. I found no one near me. But what about the people in the hot air balloons? They would have had an unbelievably close look. Unfortunately, I'll probably never know.

Later on that evening, I received confirmation from nearby Downsview Air Force Base that there was, in fact, aircraft in the area at the time of my sighting.

I'm no fool. I know what I saw. On March 17, 1989, I witnessed a daylight UFO sighting that I will never forget.

# I Couldn't Believe
# My Eyes

I received the following letter from Mrs. Janet Allison, who is a resident of Etobicoke, Ontario. She had heard me discussing UFOs on a radio talk show, so she contacted me and told me her story of the strange "ball" she saw. The experience took place in her home on Markland Drive, Etobicoke, on a Tuesday afternoon in November of 1989.

I urged her to write out her experience. Here is her account of the sighting, in a somewhat edited form.

◆ ◆ ◆

November 14, 1991

Dear Mr. Colombo:

I have finally found a few moments to put my story on paper for you. I only hope you're able to read my writing. So here goes!

It was one of my usual restless nights. I went to the kitchen to get myself a glass of juice, went to the bathroom, and before returning to bed looked out of the bathroom window. I always did this (perhaps to see how many other people were up like me).

I saw this rather big, hazy "ball" in the sky. It was nestled between two apartment buildings. At first when I saw it, I thought of the airplanes we see so often and of lights from buildings. All of these I am used to seeing, but this "ball" seemed to draw me to keep an eye on it. I stood very still and stared at the glow, scared that if I blinked it would disappear. I was experiencing something very different from what I usually experience and was filled with many feelings that I find hard to explain.

After a few minutes passed, I took a quick glance at my bedroom clock. It was 1:20 a.m., and the "ball" still had not moved. I ran to my living room and opened the blinds to make sure I had enough room to see the "ball." By now I was very excited, and was very tempted to wake up Tony, my son, but I wanted to be sure of what I was seeing.

Still it did not move. It just sat there. Fifteen minutes passed. Then very slowly it started to move. It went in a straight line, heading south, and as it passed over to the side of the building, it took on the shape of a large, long object. In fact, it looked like a long cigar. I guess I was looking at the side of the object.

Something else was strange to me also. There was no sound at all. I knew in myself at this point it was not a plane. The lights on it did not flash or blink at all.

When it had gone, I felt angry, upset at myself for not going over to the other side of the building to see where it went. I was also upset that Tony had not seen it.

I still stayed at the window, with mixed feelings, and I tried to gather myself and concentrate on going back to bed. But when I got there, I couldn't sleep. I struggled for fifteen minutes. So I got up again, and I went back to the bathroom window.

I couldn't believe my eyes. It was back again, and in the very same place. I was so excited that I went to Tony's room and woke him. I was faltering so fast, he said, "Okay, Mom!"

But when I told him it was there the second time, I'm sure he was feeling all the excitement and curiosity I had felt and was still feeling. It repeated the procedure I had witnessed earlier. It came back the second time at 1:50 a.m., and it went out of sight at 2:10 a.m.

So to this day I still look, again and again, for a repeat performance, but I haven't been lucky. Not yet, anyway.

Janet

# Wheel of Colourful Lights

Paul Shishis, who lives in Scarborough, Ontario, heard me discussing UFO sightings across Canada on Q-107's popular *Barometer* phone-in show. He did not try to phone the show while it was on the air; later he contacted me and told me of his unusually vivid sighting. He agreed to write out an account of his experience and send it to me.

Here is Paul Shishis's account. It is taken from his letter dated 6 November 1991. The account is interesting, especially for the "so-called wheel" and for the reactions of others to the sighting, which was clearly seen by those who cared to look up into the sky. The account has been slightly edited for presentation here.

◆ ◆ ◆

Date: Between spring 1977 and summer 1978
Time: Approximately 8:30–9:00 p.m.
   It was a Thursday night.
   The sky was dark, with very few clouds.
Location: Scarborough, at Neilson and Ellesmere

That night I was working at the plaza. I had a part-time job at Dominion Stores Ltd. I was working outside, at the car pick-up, serving customers.

While I was serving a customer, a man, plus or minus 55 years old, with a pipe, sitting in a car, said, "See that funny object up there? Do you know what it is?"

I was busy serving. I said, "It's a plane." I continued working until I had finished with the customer. And the man in the car asked again. I hardly took notice, saying, "If it's not moving, it's a helicopter."

The man looked serious and said, "It's not moving." Then he added, "Look at the lights!"

Now, not having to concentrate on work, with no cars left to serve, I paid more attention and looked up into the sky—at the object.

This man was right. There was something strange about this object. At first, from where I stood, the object looked quite distant. But it now had my full attention and I was very curious about it. I started to walk towards it. I walked faster, right out of the parking lot and across the field adjacent to the store.

Before I realized it, this object seemed closer. My guess was that it was approximately one-eighth to one-quarter of a mile above the ground. I had a full view of this object. I suddenly felt very excited, but disconcerted that I had a job back there. I stared with amazement at it, and pointed up and then pointed down and yelled, "Come on, down! Land!" Or words to that effect.

This object may be described as a craft, silver or grey, with no markings, except at the back of the craft. Here there was a wheel of distinct colours. I remember there was flashing around the perimeter of the back end. The colours it flashed were blue, green, yellow, and red. I am sure the rotation was clockwise. Within the perimeter of this so-called wheel of colourful lights was an orange-yellow glow. The glow was like the light of a light bulb, not fiery at all. In size, from what I could make out, I saw something as big as a Mack truck. The shape looked cone-shaped, rounded. (It could be described as capsule-shaped. The object appeared like the final stage of an Apollo space capsule—when it returns to the Earth for splashdown—except that in the air it was horizontal, not vertical.)

I was alone in the field, staring at this object for probably 15–20 minutes. This was an incredible sight! I had to show this to my fellow employees. So, turning around but still having an eye on it, I started to run back to the parking lot. The man who had pointed it out to me did not accompany me into the field, nor did he stick around the parking lot.

When I was halfway across the field, the object started to move, slowly. A sound came from the object, nothing I've ever heard before. No pattern of lights changed; just a weird pattern of sound.

I ran into the store to tell a workmate who was unloading a 45-foot trailer. He laughed and said, "I'm busy."

I ran through the store and back outside again and yelled to another workmate across the parking lot who was collecting buggies. I urged him to look up and see this object. He ran over and just caught the end of the sighting. It was now moving, quite slowly. Its speed had to be roughly 20 mph. Then it went out of our line of sight.

The workmate was as fascinated as I was, so we both looked around elsewhere in the sky. After ten minutes of endless searching to no avail, we resumed our work outside. Suddenly, we heard an unusual sound coming from above us. As the sound was streaking by above, the other guy, the one I had tried to show it to, heard and saw the end of the craft. He yelled, "Yeah! Did you hear that?"

Again we were together. What I could make out was that there was a stripe of cloud, anywhere from one-quarter to one-half a mile in width, running directly above us from west to east. At this time, with eyes searching to the east, we could see a distant light. It was shining. First it was a bright white light, then it was a red bright light, and so forth. It would go out but reappear shining. It was approximately 2–5 miles across the sky in seconds. It looked like it was near the Lakeshore, possibly above Pickering. Minutes later the light was gone.

Now the cloud business might be explained naturally, and the distant shining, red-white lights might possibly be a distant aircraft. But this object that I clearly saw when I was standing underneath it could in *no way* be so explained. No way was it a large balloon or an earth craft. There was no sound of engines or propellers.

The sense I received, while standing under this object, was that it was studying/surveying something or other. It seemed futuristic.

Thereafter this object up there was on my mind, and it still is.

Over the years I told people of my experience, but they laughed and didn't take me seriously. Silence about my experience has played its part for quite some time. It seemed the best thing at the time. Since the time I experienced this sighting, I have always been interested in the subject and feel like I always will be.

I really would appreciate some of your time to help me collect any material of the precise date and data. Thanks for your time.

One footnote: Occasionally I dream of saucer-shaped disks hovering in groups, quietly, with a single low-beaming red light on the top.

The description may help if I draw a diagram of the craft's precise location.

# A Black, Oval-shaped Object

As mentioned, Q-107 is a Toronto hard-rock radio station with a wide and devoted listenership. Listeners are especially devoted to *Barometer*, the station's early afternoon chat and phone-in show with its talkative host Bill Carroll. Once, when Bill and I were on the air discussing the subject of UFOs in Canada, the telephone lines lit up with calls from listeners anxious to share their sightings. There were a lot of calls and a lot of sightings.

One listener who responded to my invitation to write out a full account of her sighting was Rita Hooper of Newmarket, Ontario. Ms. Hooper prepared her account in the form of a statement, which is printed below. The account is dated 11 October 1991. Accompanying her account was a rough sketch she prepared of the "black, oval-shaped object" that she and her husband saw, with an indication of its size: 20 feet high, 100 feet long.

Who knows what it was or is that the Hoppers saw that night while driving for hours on the lonely, dark highway between Prince George and Vancouver?

◆ ◆ ◆

This is my statement about a sighting by myself and my husband in the year 1974.

It was about the middle of August. My husband and I were travelling by car from Prince George, B.C., to Vancouver. Around 11:00 p.m., my husband noticed an object following us. It was travelling at the height of the treetops.

At the time I was asleep in the back seat of the car. As I awoke, I heard my husband ask, "Rita, what's that look like following us?" I looked behind, trying to focus my eyes on the object, thinking that my eyes were playing tricks on me.

What I saw was a black, oval-shaped object following us at treetop height. Whenever we approached a town, or lights of some sort, the object disappeared. As soon as the area was dark again, again the object was back.

I described what I saw to my husband. He said it was exactly what he had been seeing for about an hour prior to my waking up. We both continued in silence, observing this object for approximately another thirty minutes. It always stayed some distance behind the car. After some time the object slowed down its speed, stayed stationary for a couple of minutes, then lifted up and disappeared.

The object was completely black. There were no lights or sounds of any sort. It followed us for about three and a half hours in all. Neither my husband nor I could relate this object to anything either of us had ever seen before. It definitely was not any aircraft that we had ever seen. Nothing that small, without lights or sound, that could travel so close to the ground, at that slow rate of speed, could feasibly be from Earth in our comprehension of air travel.

# They Were Changing Colour

Robert Ritchie, a resident of Toronto, heard Betty Stewart, the UFO abductee, being interviewed by Jim Carroll on Q-107's *Barometer* on 6 November 1991. Betty talked about sightings and abductions and Ritchie was fascinated. When Betty mentioned that I was collecting accounts of sightings and reports of contacts with alien intelligences, he phoned after the program and told me of two incidents that had occurred to him. I encouraged him to write out his experiences. He did so and that very afternoon faxed an account of them to me.

Ritchie's account appears below. The mushroom-like cloud is an unexpected touch. But then, as Ritchie mentioned in conversation, he saw the mushroom over the Caribbean and the Caribbean is near the Bermuda Triangle, and anything is possible in that zone of wonders!

◆ ◆ ◆

I'm a firm believer in UFOs, or is it ghosts?

Many things have happened in my life that I have dismissed as ghosts. Having heard you and other speakers talking about UFOs, I'm beginning to think that, maybe, I've been visited by extraterrestrial beings.

My first experience came at the age of twelve years. My parents were out at a party. I had just gone to bed and my dog was on the floor beside me. (She never leaves my side when I'm the only one at home.) All of a sudden my dog jumped up and ran out of the room. I thought someone must have come home. However, there was no sound of doors opening and closing. I lay there, waiting to hear something.

As I waited, the covers of my bed began to pulled away from me. I pulled them back, and felt them tug away again. I jumped out of bed and ran out of the room. I ran out onto the second-floor balcony, I was so scared. As I opened the sliding door of the balcony, I noticed that there was a dense fog swirling all around the townhouse complex. The fog was glowing with the colour red.

I felt like I was all alone. Normally there were signs of people either outside or inside the townhouses. It seemed that time stood still and no one at all was around. I went back into the townhouse and turned Johnny Carson on very loud and waited for my parents to come home!

I have seen what I think are ghosts many times. It makes me wonder if there is a connection with UFOs.

The next time I saw something strange was in Jamaica, on a holiday with my mother. It was late at night, and my mother and I were enjoying the beaches of Ocho Rios. We were stargazing, when I spotted six lights in the sky. They were arranged in two columns of three, one on top of the other, like this:

```
o   o

o   o

o   o
```

They were changing colours and moving up and down ever so slightly. My mother saw it too and confirmed everything I saw. It's hard to say how big or how far apart they were, due to the large expanse of the ocean.

I waited all night to see if they were going to go down or up into space. At two o'clock in the morning, directly underneath them, a cloud, like a gigantic mushroom, rose up out of the Caribbean Sea and covered them up. The cloud then drifted away and the lights were gone.

I don't know if they went up or down, but they were gone.

# We Decided to Call It the Floaty Ball

Catharine Côté lives in a charming house in a small community north of Toronto. It was while living in a friend's isolated country home that she and others saw a number of strange sights. She wrote about them in this detailed memoir, which I received on 23 November 1992.

Here, with minimal editing, is her account of these odd experiences. She refers in passing to the alien abductee investigator Budd Hopkins. The reader is left to make of Catharine Côté's experiences with the mystery lights and "the Floaty Ball" what he or she will.

◆ ◆ ◆

My two youngest children and I had moved temporarily into the home of a friend, so we had the good fortune to live in the country in the heart of a dairy farming district, with corn and wheat growing up everywhere.

My children are LeeAnne and Katie. We were assigned the largest bedroom in the house. This made it possible for the three of us to sleep in the same huge, well-lit room. The room was located over the double garage. I felt that this location was going to be my spiritual therapy, as we had faced several crises the previous year.

Smoking was not allowed in the house, so it became my habit to smoke while walking the spacious grounds and drinking in the tranquillity of nature. It was also my habit to go out every night for one last cigarette just before I went to bed. Not even rain storms prevented me from doing this.

One night, after we had been living in the house for about a week, the children and I were driving home up the long country road. The kids noticed a low-level, slow-moving light coming from the east across the field. I slowed the car down in order to get a better look. I could not believe how low the light was, as I was under the impression that it was the light of an airplane. But when it flew over the road just ahead of us, it did not continue to go west. Instead, it made a brief pause, and began going up the road just ahead of it. I felt that the only thing we could do was follow it.

The light moved ahead slowly, as did we. When we got to the driveway of the house and turned in, the light turned west over the field just north of the property. We leapt out of the car and ran round the side of the house to watch it. It made absolutely no sound. There was a casual, lilting bounce to its movement. We watched it till it was out of sight. We found we didn't really have very much to say about it.

About a week later, at about nine o'clock, I was standing at the end of the driveway. I was having my usual cigarette, thinking about nothing more important than the peaceful darkness. My children were in bed and the house was otherwise unoccupied. I found myself looking down the road. A few cars were approaching from the distance, so I thought nothing of the light that I saw until it was about three hundred feet away. I suddenly realized that this single light was not on the level of the road. It was at treetop level, and it was lighting up the tops of the trees as it approached. I turned and ran for the house without looking back.

I cannot say what it was, but I was later to learn something of interest from my friend's son. About a year earlier, he and others had been driving from the same direction as this light came, and as he slowed the car to approach the driveway, the light paced them at ground-level in the field on the east side of the road. When they stopped to take a look, the light also stopped, then took off at an angle at a fast rate of speed. Perhaps the light I was seeing was the same light the friend's son had seen.

A few weeks later, as I was speaking with my friend's daughter out front of the house at about 10:00 p.m., I saw a light approaching from the east. As we watched it, it moved noiselessly over us, with that familiar lilting bounce. We decided to call it the Floaty Ball, as if naming it would somehow help us to understand it and deal with it.

It was about this time that the teenage son of my friend told me of what he had experienced with the mysterious light. The previous summer, he had decided to ride his bicycle north on the country road to accompany a friend home. While they were biking, a light came into view just over them. They were too terrified to move, so they stood in the darkness and watched it. After a while, it moved on at an unbelievable rate of speed. The son of my friend said that they both felt that whatever it was that they were watching, it knew they were there.

At the beginning of November, we were entering the third month of our stay at my friend's country house. One night, as usual, at about 11:30 p.m., I went out for my smoke. I stood at the end of the driveway and drank in the peace of the surroundings. Eventually I went inside the house and saw that the bedroom light was still on. I knew that my eight-year-old was probably still awake, reading. The rest of the house was in darkness. I made my way to the room. My little one was closing her book and I walked past the window to turn off the light. I gave a quick glance outside. I could not believe what I was seeing.

A beautiful, soft, glowing light, pinkish-orange in colour, was sitting above the ground. I could see the soft edges of the furrows of the frozen field beneath it. I could see all around it, and I could see nothing else at all. No people. What was the most surprising aspect of what I saw was the knowledge that I had just been out there, probably no farther than from thirty to fifty feet from the point where this light was now positioned. I had just come in, and no more than five minutes had passed. I was left to ponder the implications of the fact that it had been out there. Maybe it had been watching me.

I needed another opinion. I called LeeAnne over, and casually asked her, "Do you see anything unusual out there?"

She immediately said, "Mommy, what's the light doing out there in the field?"

I turned out the light in the room and we watched. The sight was so beautiful; it had a certain tranquillity. The only thing of which we were aware was of Katie's peaceful breathing in the dark. After about twenty minutes, the light just disappeared. We waited to see if it would reappear. After a few minutes, a white light appeared in the field a fair distance away. It was halfway up a bank of pine trees. We spent quite a long time watching as this bright white light glowed and increased and decreased in size for quite some time. In time it winked out and we were left peering into the darkness. A few minutes later, however, a fast-moving, wildly spinning light went from left to right in our view. The next morning I was able to determine, using as reference points from the window, that the light had been spinning at the height of the hydro lines corridor.

At this point, LeeAnne made an interesting point. She said it was as if they were putting on a show for us. This comment became increasingly significant for us as we had one more visual treat in store. When the spinning light disappeared, we waited. Suddenly, a bright light appeared high above the horizon. It glowed and grew so huge so quickly that both LeeAnne and I instinctively dropped to our knees behind the windowsill. It seemed that my daughter felt as I did that something was coming to us, closing the distance between us. Nothing further happened that night. Then I realized that it was after 2:00 a.m. LeeAnne and I went to bed. I was more than a little ashamed of myself that I had not wakened Katie. To this day I cannot explain why I did not. It would have been more in my personality to have shared the experience with my children, particularly an experience so weird and wonderful.

I could not wait until the next afternoon to share this unusual story with my friend's son. We had become quite close, as he too had had an experience with the light. When he returned, about 4:00 p.m. the next day, I stopped him. I just had to tell him about the weird thing that had happened to LeeAnne and me the previous night. But he was more excited than I was.

He begged to tell what had happened to him the same night. He had been in the back of the darkened house, looking out the kitchen window, when he heard me return after smoking my cigarette. He didn't say anything to me because he was planning to go to bed. His little pet kitten Smokey was in its usual place, perched lovingly on its master's shoulder. He said that after he heard me come in, he was suddenly gripped with a terror for which he had no name or explanation. His vision was diminished. He could still see, but there was a general darkness, as if a filter had been put over his entire field of vision. He stated that he was paralyzed, and when he tried to move he was unable to move a muscle. He could not say how long he was in this state, but he did add that the kitten was also unable to move and sat motionless on his shoulder. He said that when he was released from this force and was finally able to move, so too was the kitten.

Little did he know what LeeAnne and I were going through. He said that when he was finally able to move, he ran down to his basement bedroom and locked the door. He and the kitten stayed under the covers all night long. Due to this nameless fear, he was unable to sleep. He felt that it was interesting that the kitten did not move during the night, as the kitten usually kept everyone up. It was a little terror with its all-night scampering.

It was about a year later, when I was writing up this account of the experiences, that LeeAnne's remark about something putting on a show for us to see took on a deeper meaning. Could it have been that something wanted the only other people who were awake that night to be kept busy? We were enthralled for two hours, and we did not even do what would have been a normal thing, that is, wake up other members of the household. This was odd, as Katie was sleeping only five feet away. Needless to say, I am even more puzzled today than I was a year or so ago.

This leads me to relate the most unusual experience that I have ever had in my life. It occurred around the middle of the month of November. I had my late-night cigarette as usual, and the children and

I went to bed. I cannot say when this experience began, but it must have been after 12:00 midnight and before 2:00 a.m. I was awakened out of my sleep by the incessant meowing of one of the numerous family cats. The cat would not let up. I finally got up and began to search for the rude kitty in the dark. After seeing its form dimly in the darkness, I basically told it to shut up before it succeeded in waking everyone up. Then I returned to bed, slightly annoyed, hoping to resume my sleep.

I have never in my adult life had a fear of the dark. Suddenly I became utterly terrified. It was as if the very hairs on my back were standing on end. I have never known such a nameless, unprovoked terror in my entire life. What I said to myself was that I knew if I were to roll over at that moment, I would see something. And the thought chilled me to the bone. Never before had I had such a feeling in my life. Then I had an even more scary realization. I tried to move my body but I could not. My eyes were wide open and I could not close them. I attempted to move the most easily moved part of my body, one of my fingers, but I could not budge it. Now I was really frightened. I knew something was right behind me.

What happened next is completely unbelievable, but it happened the way I am going to describe it. I felt what seemed like an arm slip under my shoulder, and another slip under my leg. I was still lying on my side and I still could not move. It seemed I was screaming in my mind, "What are you doing?" and I was stunned when an answer came back directly. I was told, "Don't worry, we won't hurt you."

With that, I watched my visual perspective change, as I began to rise in the air. It was wild, because everything I could see was changing in my view, the way the view changes when I rise from a chair. Before long I could see the bedroom window, and I was slowly heading towards it. There was the most beautiful glow of light on the other side of the sheer curtains. As I seemed to float towards the window, I screamed out in my mind, "Please, I cannot go through a window. It's not possible. Please, let me pass out."

And that was the last thing I remembered until I was back on my bed. I still had the feeling of paralysis, and I still could not move a muscle. But now I was totally fixed on a beautiful white ball of light that was hanging suspended in the air on the other side of my bed. It was about five feet in height. I said, in my mind I assume, "What just happened here?" I was told that there was something about my mind that amazed them. And then they said something to me that was very personal, a message that only this year acquired a deeper significance.

With that, the beautiful light began slowly to shrink in size, and then it just winked out. With the light gone, my body was released and I could move. My body and its movements felt bizarre. I looked at the clock. It was just after 2:00 a.m. I have no idea how long this thing went on. After puzzling it out for a while, I was finally able to go back to sleep.

When I awoke the next morning, my children knew that there was something wrong with me. I told them that I had had a rough night. They had to get themselves ready for school, as I was physically quite out of it. During the course of the day, I alternated between feeling "wow" and "I think I must be losing my mind."

But something else was about to happen. It occurred when the children returned home from school. It put a whole new complexion on what had happened the night before. When the school bus brought Katie home, she told me something that gave me the chills. She said that one of her school friends, who lived on a farm property about a mile down the road from us, had been at school that day, telling the teacher that she and her mom had witnessed a UFO appear over their back field. This had occurred the very night that I had had the experience. I later learned from my daughter LeeAnne that she had heard the cat meowing repeatedly that same night. She had heard me instruct the cat to shut up. She remembers nothing else happening that night.

There is one more part to the story. Approximately two weeks after the last incident, the children and I moved. But just before we moved out, my children and my friend's children watched across the field to the east, and on more than one occasion we saw fast-moving lights travelling at low levels across the field, with apparent disregard for wire fences and other things that were in the way. In one sense, I was happy that we were moving. I was not sure how much more of this we could take. In another sense, I was a little disappointed, as I had an understandable fascination with all of it.

But that was not the end of it. The night we moved into our new house, I looked out and saw once again the Floaty Ball. And since we have been living in our new house, I have seen it two more times. Last March, I contacted Budd Hopkins. I was having problems that I had never had before: unable to sleep, bad nerves, extremely emotional, low self-esteem. In addition, I was not handling it very well.

I have recently been in touch with a researcher in Montreal. He is going to arrange for hypnosis sessions, so I can begin to piece together what has probably happened to me and to my children.

# The Light Was Glowing

"Unexplainable Experiences" is the title given this letter by the editors of the American magazine *UFO Universe*, Winter 1988. The letter was contributed by Janet Reynolds, of Burnaby, British Columbia. It touches upon the touchy business of reporting and interpreting strange sightings.

◆ ◆ ◆

My first actual sighting of a UFO was in June of 1983. I was driving home from Bellingham, Washington, that night. There was nothing unusual about the night until I got close to home. (I was about one mile away.) I had stopped at a 7-11, looked up in the sky and thought to myself what a beautiful night. It was at that point I decided that I'd drive down and park by the river, and just take in the sky. (Ever since I was young I'd always been interested in sky watching.)

As I was driving down the hill towards the river, I noticed my radio was really getting a lot of static. When I got near the river, I stopped in a gas station parking lot. The radio station I was listening to, at that point, went right off the air. It was a regular night for air traffic over the river. (This is part of their flight path to the Vancouver International Airport—one of the reasons I didn't report this sighting as the authorities would put it off to be a plane.)

It was about twenty minutes after having parked that I saw in the distance about five miles down the river a bright, glowing object which was at a resting point. It was not low to the ground but quite high up. It seemed to stay in one spot longer than a circling plane would sit until it gets its signal from the airport to land. I figure that it had only rested long enough to catch my eye. It then started rotating in a circular fashion, lights rotating in colours of bright red and blue. As it shot off across towards the horizon. I was overcome or mesmerized by a feeling of deep amazement, feeling as though I had witnessed a thing of beauty. At that moment in time I felt as though the occupants had picked up on some of my emotion and I had shared something special of theirs. I possessed no fear of the object at all. I will mention that the object shot off at incredible speed, it was gone in a matter of ten seconds. As I started to speed off, I tried to follow it in my car, but it was useless.

I could offer you an explanation of the interference with my radio, as Delta has a lot of radio towers in the vicinity of where the UFO was sighted. If they were tracking me, somehow the interference of their vehicle could have gotten picked up by my radio. Or do these visitors interfere with our radios on purpose?

During the next two days, I felt like I was in a daze (stunned by this encounter). I did not sleep or eat much at all. But, because I had to rationalize this encounter with myself, I tended to bury it in the corner of my mind, basically out of protection against public ridicule. But, as the years went by I did not forget this encounter, as I sort of kept it for evidence (maybe for the shape of things to come).

I'll just mention another encounter; this was in '66. Our family was coming home to Canada from Seattle. It was just outside of Seattle that my dad noticed that an object was following the car. It had to be highly unusual, because nothing disturbs my dad. He stopped the car to take a closer look, and I knew right away when he got back in that he had seen something highly unusual. He seemed to stay outside for a while and study the object. Getting details about this encounter has become difficult. My dad is now claiming it was a weather balloon. Also some of the other facts do not coincide with mine. My dad does work at a job that would not take kindly to him talking about his personal UFO experiences. You see, one has to understand that Canada is not that open to UFO encounters. Most people here believe that other civilizations are so far away in an unknown galaxy that they could never travel here.

I think, though, you Americans and the British are more open to UFO theories, experiences, etc. I recently telephoned the observatory on a recent sighting of a light in the sky. I explained to the astronomer that this was a light that came down slowly, vertically from the sky, leaving behind it a small mushroom cloud about three feet wide. The light was glowing, and translucent. The astronomer said, "You must have seen a seagull." Well, it's because of that sort of ignorance that I've kept silent about my encounters. But I've decided to open up and share some of my experiences with a magazine that does believe in this phenomenon.

# This Something in the Sky

The following letter came from Mrs. J. Robinson, who is a resident of Bramalea, Ontario. In this letter, dated 2 November 1991, the correspondent describes an unusual sighting that took place on Airport Road, a scenic, north-south highway that takes motorists into "cottage country" north of Toronto.

Her letter makes or raises a number of interesting points. Two people, seated side by side, may have different reactions to the same sighting. UFO imagery is familiar from popular movies like *Close Encounters of the Third Kind*. Airport Road, as its name suggests, leads to Pearson International Airport, the country's busiest air terminal. People who wish to describe sightings are often reluctant to report them to just anyone because they may be labelled a "UFO nut."

Mrs. Robinson mentions Betty Stewart, the articulate UFO abductee. When Betty was the guest of Bill Carroll on Q-107's *Barometer*, she mentioned my own work, which involves collecting and publishing accounts of sightings, contacts, and abductions. That was probably the program Mrs. Robinson heard. It is possible that she also heard a portion of the late-night talk show on CFRB-FM that featured Betty and me discussing the broad aspects of the UFO phenomenon.

Mrs. Robinson included with her letter a pencil sketch of what she saw in the sky that rainy morning in summer 1991. "I'm not an artist, but it was something like this," she wrote. "It happened so fast, by the time I realized what I was looking at, we were down a hill and it was gone!" Her sketch depicts the side view of an elongated saucer with a somewhat irregular outline and five thin-lined markings, or perhaps portals, positioned around the rim of the saucer.

◆ ◆ ◆

Dear Sir:

I heard part of a radio program this past week (CHUM-FM, I think), on which Betty Stewart was a guest, speaking about UFOs. At one point she mentioned your name and that you had written a book entitled *UFOs over Canada*. That is what has prompted me to tell you about an experience my husband and I had this past summer, for what it is worth.

On Monday morning, September 23rd, 1991, my husband I were heading south on Airport Road from our cottage. We had spent the night at the cottage, deciding to head home early in the morning. I don't enjoy doing this because it makes for such a long workday, but nevertheless, there we were.

It was raining. Quite hard, actually. I was just watching the wipers and listening to the radio, and suddenly I said to my husband, "Look at that—isn't that beautiful?"

He looked and said, "What is it?" and I replied, "It looks like the sunrise through the clouds."

I was tired, and I just stared at it a bit, but then all at once I realized it couldn't possibly be the sunrise! This light in the sky was in the south. Didn't the sun always rise in the east? I looked at the clock; it was 6:40 a.m. Didn't the man on the radio say that sunrise this morning would be at 7:10 a.m.?

I said to George, "That can't be the sunrise; it's south." He said, "Then what is it?"

I said, "I don't know..."

But as I stared at it, I suddenly realized that I was looking at an enormous, gigantic, saucer-shaped "thing" with red blinking lights; this "thing" was so huge, it was absolutely awesome!

What I had thought was a cigar-shaped line of clouds with holes that the sun was shining through was, in fact, this dead-on view of a saucer!

I remember that when we saw that UFO movie with Richard Dreyfuss about *first encounters*, or something like that, anyway, when this huge thing came over his head in one scene, and it was so incredibly big, right out loud in the theatre I said, "Oh, my God!"

And that's exactly what I said when I realized what I was looking at on this occasion... "Oh, my God!"

I think we were somewhere between Hwy. 89 and Hwy. 9, as I said, travelling south on Airport Road. The road is very hilly, and we started down another hill, and when we got to the top again, it was gone! We never saw it again.

I realize that we were tired; the vision was blurred because of the windshield wipers. My husband didn't see it as well as I because he was driving and had to keep his eyes on the road. Nevertheless, I asked him, "What do you think it was?" and he said, "I don't know."

My husband and I have always been very sceptical about things like this. I was tempted to write to the *Toronto Star*'s "Have Your Say" page to ask if anyone else had seen this "something" in the sky that morning. There was lots of traffic, so maybe someone else did see something. But I didn't want to be labelled as a "UFO nut." Sorry if I offend—but that's what sceptics think.

The whole thing probably sounds pretty "nothing," but I just thought I'd let you know.

Yours very truly,
J. Robinson (Mrs.)

# PART IV
# CONTACTS

*I should like to extend the greetings of the government and*
*people of Canada to the extraterrestrial inhabitants of*
*outer space.*
—Audio message preserved in digital form on the Voyager
Interstellar Record, affixed to the *Voyager* spacecraft,
launched in 1977, now entering interstellar space; the mes-
sage was recorded in English by Robert B. Edmonds,
Canadian Delegate to the United Nations; quoted by Carl
Sagan, et al., in *Murmurs of Earth: The Voyager*
*Interstellar Record* (1978).

UFOlogy took a dramatic turn when sightings of strange lights or craft
in the day or night skies were followed by communications between
alien beings and human beings. The contact seemed at first to be telepathic; then it was face-to-face. The interesting fact is that the
communication between selected individuals—contactees—and alien
entities was not just one-way (alien to human) but increasingly two-
way (alien to human, human to alien). The messages that were being
conveyed were often less meaningful than the fact that the commu-
niqués were getting through. Here was an epochal event: interspecies
communication. There are, inevitably, many other interpretations of the
nature of the transfers of information.

The passages in this chapter begin with the celebrated Falcon Lake
encounter, a sighting and landing and takeoff that lacks only the physical appearance of the alien entities. The passages become increasingly
concerned with the conveying of meaningful messages—often warnings to mankind to mind its errant ways.

# The Falcon Lake Encounter

The Falcon Lake Encounter is the name given to the sighting of two unidentified flying objects from Manitoba's Falcon Lake Provincial Park on 20 May 1967. More information is available on this incident than on any other UFO sighting reported in Canada. There is about the episode the suggestion of lingering menace.

The sole observer of the two UFOs was Stephen Michalak, a fifty-one-year-old Polish Canadian. Later that year Michalak offered the following account of himself: "In 1949 I came to Canada, and some years later, settled in Winnipeg, Manitoba. I live with my wife, two sons and a daughter in a modest home. I have a steady income from my job as a mechanic at the Inland Cement Company. Two of my children attend the University of Manitoba. We live a happy, satisfied life of average Canadians, fully enjoying all the blessings this country is offering us."

It was Michalak's passion for amateur prospecting that took him that weekend to Falcon Lake. What he saw that Saturday is open to interpretation. What is laudable and sincere is his desire to tell others what he witnessed and what he felt about the experience. His account appeared in a privately printed forty-page booklet titled *My Encounter with the UFO* (1967). Michalak wrote about his experiences in Polish; the manuscript was translated and printed for private distribution by his friend Paul Pihichyn.

There were unexpected consequences from the sighting. The encounter left Michalak, as he wrote, "desperately in need of medical attention." He suffered nausea and first-degree burns on his chest. He was admitted to the Misericordia Hospital in Winnipeg, his first hospital treatment for recurring, sighting-related health problems. This did not deter him from leading investigators to the exact spot where the sighting had taken place. "Landing traces" were found there. Earth analysis showed "some radiation but not enough to be dangerous."

The case was widely reported by the media. There were investigations by the RCMP and the RCAF, by representatives of the National Research Council and the Atomic Energy Commission, as well as by the Aerial Phenomena Research Organization. A question about the government's silence connected with the case was asked in the House of Commons by Ed Schreyer, then a Member of Parliament, not yet the Governor General. The Minister of National Defence replied, "It is not the intention of the Department of National Defence to make public the report of the alleged sighting."

The full story of the Falcon Lake Encounter will not be known until Chris Rutkowski, the Winnipeg-based UFO researcher and investigator, publishes his study of the episode. Even then aspects of the encounter will never be explained to everybody's satisfaction.

◆ ◆ ◆

It was 5:30 a.m. when I left the motel and started out on my geological trek. I took with me a hammer, a map, a compass, paper and pencil and a little food to see me through the day—wearing a light jacket against the morning chill.

The day was bright, sunny—not a cloud in the sky. It seemed like just another ordinary day, but events which were to take place within the next six hours were to change my entire life more than anyone could ever imagine. I will never forget May 20, 1967.

Crossing the Trans-Canada Highway from the motel on the south side, I made my way into the bush and the pine forest on the north side. After travelling some distance I got out my map and compass and orientated myself.

By 9 o'clock I had found an area that particularly fascinated me because of the rock formation near a bog along a stream flowing in the southward direction. I was searching for some specimens that I had found on my earlier expedition.

My approach had startled a flock of geese, but before long they became accustomed to my presence, quieted down and went about their business.

At 11 o'clock I began to feel the effects of the breakfast I did not eat that morning. I sat down and took out the lunch I had brought with me. Following a simple meal of smoked sausage, cheese and bread, an apple and two oranges washed down with a couple of cups of coffee, and after a short rest, I returned to the quartz vein I was examining. It was 12:15, the sun was high in the sky, and a few clouds were gathering in the west.

While chopping at quartz I was startled by the most uncanny cackle of the geese that were still in the area. Something had obviously frightened them far more than my presence earlier in the morning when they gave out with a mild protest.

Then I saw it. Two cigar-shaped objects with humps on them about halfway down from the sky. They appeared to be descending and glowing with an intense scarlet glare. As these objects came closer to the earth they became more oval-shaped.

They came down at the same speed, keeping a constant distance between them, appearing to be as one inseparable unit, yet each one completely separate from the other.

Suddenly the farthest of the two objects—farthest from my point of vision—stopped dead in the air while its companion slipped down closer and closer to the ground and landed squarely on the flat top of a rock about 150 feet away from me.

The object that had remained in the air hovered approximately fifteen feet above me for about three minutes, then lifted up skyward again.

As it ascended its colour began to change from bright red to an orange shade, then to a grey tone. Finally, when it was just about to disappear behind the gathering clouds, it again turned bright orange.

The "craft," if I may be allowed to call it a craft, had appeared and disappeared in such a short time that it was impossible to estimate the length of the time it remained visible. My astonishment at and fear of [the] unusual sight that I had just witnessed dulled my senses and made me lose all realization of time.

I cannot describe or estimate the speed of the ascent because I have seen nothing in the world that moved so swiftly, noiselessly, without a sound.

Then my attention was drawn back to the craft that had landed on the rock. It too was changing in colour, turning from red to grey-red to light grey and then to the colour of hot stainless steel, with a golden glow around it.

I realized that I was still kneeling on the rock with my small pick hammer in my hand. I was still wearing goggles, which I used to protect my eyes from the rock chips.

After recovering my composure and regaining my senses to some degree I began watching the craft intently, ready to record in my mind everything that happened.

I noticed an opening near the top of the craft and a brilliant purple light pouring out of [the] aperture. The light was so intense that it hurt my eyes when I looked at it directly. Gripped with fear and excitement, I was unable to move from the rock. I decided to wait and watch.

Soon I became aware of wafts of warm air that seemed to come out in waves from the craft, accompanied by [the] pungent smell of sulphur. I heard a soft murmur, like the whirl of a tiny electric motor running very fast. I also heard a hissing sound as if the air had been sucked into the interior of the craft.

It was now that I wanted a camera more than anything else, but, of course, there is no need for one on a geological expedition. Then I remembered the paper and pencil that I had brought with me. I made a sketch of what I saw.

By now some of the initial fear had left me and I managed to gather enough courage to get closer to the craft and to investigate. I fully expected someone to get out at any moment and survey the landing site.

Because I had never seen anything like this before, I thought it may have been an American space project of some sort. I checked for the markings of the United States Air Force on the hull of the craft, but found nothing.

I was most interested in the flood of lights that poured out of the upper reaches of the craft. The light, distinctly purple, also cast out various other shades. In spite of the bright midday sun in the sky, the light cast a purple hue on the ground and eclipsed the sunlight in the immediate area.

I was forced to continually turn my eyes from the light, which made red dots appear before my eyes every time I looked away.

I approached the object closer, coming to within 60 feet of the glowing mass of material. Then I heard voices. They sounded like humans, although somewhat muffled by the sounds of the motor and the rush of air that was continuously coming out from somewhere inside. I was able to make out two distinct voices, one with a higher pitch than the other.

This latest discovery added to my excitement, and I was sure that the craft was of an earthly origin. I came even closer and beckoned to those inside: "Okay, Yankee boys, having trouble? Come on out and we'll see what we can do about it."

There was no answer and no sign from within. I had prepared myself for some response and was taken aback when none came. I was at a loss, perplexed. I didn't know what to do next.

But then, more to encourage myself than anything else, I addressed the voices in Russian, asking them if they spoke Russian. No answer. I tried again in German, Italian, French and Ukrainian. Still no answer.

Then I spoke again in English and walked closer to the craft.

By now I found myself directly in front of it and decided to take a look inside. However, standing within the beam of light was too much for my eyes to bear. I was forced to turn away. Then, placing green lenses over my goggles, I stuck my head inside the opening.

The inside was a maze of lights. Direct beams running in horizontal and diagonal paths and a series of flashing lights, it seemed to me, were working in a random fashion, with no particular order or sequence.

Again I stepped back and awaited some reaction from the craft. As I did this I took note of the thickness of the walls of the craft. They were about 20 inches thick at the cross-section.

Then came the first sign of motion since the craft touched down.

Two panels slid over the opening and a third piece dropped over them from above. This completely closed off the opening in the side of the craft.

Then I noticed a small screen pattern on the side of the craft. It seemed to be some sort of ventilation system. The screen openings appeared to be about $\frac{3}{16}$ of an inch in diameter.

I approached the craft once again and touched its side. It was hot to the touch. It appeared to be made of a stainless steel–like substance. There were no signs of welding or joints to be seen anywhere. The outer surface was highly polished and looked like coloured glass with light reflecting off it. It formed a spectrum with a silver background as the sunlight hit the sides.

I noticed that I had burned the glove I was wearing at the time when I touched the side of the craft.

These most recent events occurred in less time than it takes to describe them.

All of a sudden the craft tilted slightly leftward. I turned and felt a scorching pain around my chest; my shirt and my undershirt were afire. A sharp beam of heat had shot from the craft.

I tore off my short and undershirt and threw them to the ground. My chest was severely burned.

When I looked back at the ship I felt a sudden rush of air around me. The craft was rising above the treetops. It began to change colour and shape, following much the same pattern as its sister ship when it had returned to the sky. Soon the craft had disappeared, gone without a trace.

# They Belong to a Different Life Wave

I know nothing about Howard Brenton MacDonald except that he is the author of record of an attractively printed and smoothly written booklet, 32 pages in length. It is the source of the following extracts.

The booklet's title page reads as follows:

FLYING SAUCERS

AND

SPACE SHIPS

*AND THE UNKNOWN PLANETS*
*FROM WHENCE THEY COME*

*By Dr. Howard Brenton MacDonald, F.R.G.S.*

The initials F.R.G.S. stand for Fellow, Royal Geographical Society. The copyright page supplies a few more facts. It says that the booklet was printed by Provoker Press, St. Catharines, Ontario, and that its contents were copyright in 1970. Its cover price is one dollar.

It seems that Dr. MacDonald's text is the product of sessions with the pendulum. I have yet to set my eyes on the booklet titled *The Pendulum Speaks*, which is mentioned below, so I remain in the dark concerning its operation. Yet it is possible that the pendulum in question swings over the alphabet, spelling out words in the same fashion that the planchette seeks out and spells out words based on the alphabet printed on the familiar and popular Ouija board. It is an exasperating and time-consuming way to "take dictation," but the results are invariably revelatory.

Revelation is perhaps the right word to use for Dr. MacDonald's account of the two types of space vehicles from the two planets, Jokly and Millokkom. Sections of revelation are interspersed with sections of commentary. I have reproduced the novel passages. Perhaps one-quarter of the contents of the booklet appear here. In a section not reproduced, Dr. MacDonald notes that the standard interpretation of sightings of UFOs is that they signify the End of the World, they mark the start of a New Age, they post a warning "to us humans not to use the Atomic Bomb any more," or they monitor our progress in "the field of atomic fission" so that humans will not go "too far." He goes on to suggest there is a far simpler explanation—a non-catastrophic one. "Instead," he writes, "my spirit collaborators offered a more simple explanation, which is that the great Space Ships from Millokkom are merely coming here on sightseeing cruises!"

◆ ◆ ◆

*Exclusive Spirit Revelations*

As yet, I have not actually seen a Flying Saucer or a Space Ship; but I have received some exclusive information concerning them.

On the night of May 3, 1952, I discovered, quite by accident, that I possessed the gift of radi-esthesia, or the sensitivity to radiations, and could operate a pendulum. (The complete story of this discovery and my subsequent research in many unknown fields of radi-esthesia is told in my booklet *The Pendulum Speaks*.) And during the course of my early communications with the Spirit World I learned some interesting and exclusive facts about both Flying Saucers and Space Ships and the heretofore unknown planets from whence they come. It took me about five months to receive the entire story, word for word, thru the pendulum; but the results were worth every effort. The spirit people who supplied me with this information were Penjy, my pendulum guide; William Brenton, my late cousin, who was an amateur pilot during his

Earth Life; and my Mother. Frankly, I do not know whether these revelations are 100% true or not. They seem logical to me. Judge for yourself. I do believe they are genuine spirit messages from the Higher Planes of Life.

## What are Flying Saucers?

The first question I asked my spirit loved ones were: What are the Flying Saucers? How do they operate? Where do they come from?

In answer to the first two, I was told the following:

The Flying Saucers are genuine flying machines of a revolutionary type not known on Earth. They range in size from little ones approximately 25 feet in diameter to the larger ones of 200 and 300 feet across. They are made of a metal unknown to us. Definitely, they are physical objects and not "ectoplasmic ghost animals" or etheric materializations, as, perhaps, some other types of aerial phenomena may be. They are wonderful pieces of mechanism and incorporate in their design principles of aerodynamic engineering beyond our ken as yet. And they are run by a kind of "condensed energy" which not only can propel them forwards at unlimited velocity, but which can also "reverse gravity" and allow them to rise straight up from the Earth's gravitational zone into interstellar space, where they can, if they desire, join one of the cosmic currents which flow between the various heavenly bodies, and ride on this "magnetic river" to their home star or anywhere they desire.

## The Planet from Whence They Came

The answer to my third question came as a distinct surprise to me. I had assumed my spirit collaborators would mention Mars or Venus; but instead the pendulum spelled out: J-O-K-L-Y

I had never heard of such a planet before, but my guides assured me that this was its correct name. It is a most unusual place, they say. It is a globe, slightly smaller than our Earth, located in the heavens about as far away from us as the Moon. Curiously enough, it is constantly surrounded by a blanket of heavy clouds which make it invisible from the Earth. Thus our astronomers cannot see Jokly, or any evidence of it; nor can the inhabitants of Jokly see us.

Another strange thing is that because of this layer of clouds the rays of the sun cannot reach it. Therefore Jokly has no sunlight; but certain of the rocks scattered along its surface are radioactive and give out an effulgence of their own, which serves to illuminate the planet itself. Physically speaking, there are no great mountain ranges or continents or oceans on Jokly; merely one large land mass dotted with rivers and lakes. But it is a fertile place, with abundant crops, which get their nutriment from the radiations of the rocks; and this energy is stored in the plants and furnishes vitality for the people in the food they eat. The Jokly-ites subsist entirely on this vitalized plant food, and always enjoy radiant health.

The inhabitants of Jokly are little people, only about 4 feet tall on the average. They are of dark reddish-brown skin, male and female, very similar to ourselves. They are a highly advanced race, possessing a technical knowledge far outdistancing our own, and having a social organization that is interesting. The populace is divided into a number of small nations, all at peace with each other. The governments of these different nations are essentially the same, consisting of an Aristocracy of the individuals best fitted to rule. There are no wars, no crime, and no poverty on Jokly. They have a language of their own, of course, but in addition a few of the Jokly-ites, the ones who ride the Flying Saucers, can speak a few words of our Earth tongues, which, apparently, they have learned clairaudiently. There are modern cities and towns on this little planet, but no wheeled vehicles. For local transportation they use small flying saucers as we do automobiles. Education is universal and comprehensive, and there is one religion for all the people, based on a belief in One God.

## Giant Space Ships

So much for the Flying Saucers. Now for my revelations concerning the giant cigar-shaped Space Ships. These, my guides told me, do not come from Jokly, but from another unknown planet named Millokkom

According to my revelations, these Space Ships are wonderful machines. They run in size anywhere from a few hundred feet up to 1,000 feet in length, and look very much like huge flying submarines. The big ones resemble ocean liners inside, being luxuriously furnished with staterooms, salons, dining halls, observation galleries, recreation rooms, propulsion chambers, fuel tanks, engine rooms, navigation stations, a master control cabin up front, and many other features designed for the comfort and happiness of the passengers. The ships are operated by a form of energy unknown on Earth. It is "something like" atomic power, only "more so" my guides declared. Perhaps it is the Vril known to the Atlanteans. But whatever it is, it can run these huge, wingless monsters in an incredible manner.

## Marvellous Millokkom

In regard to Millokkom itself, my spirit friends assure me that it is one of the most marvellous planets in the cosmos. In size it is a little larger than the Earth, and is located a little farther away than the Moon. It is plainly visible from here, but because of peculiar atmospheric conditions and cosmic rays we do not realize it is a planet at all. Astronomers may smile at this statement, but they are the first to admit that they don't know *ALL* the facts about the Heavens; so, perhaps, there is such a planet, after all, unrecognized.

Very similar to our Earth, only infinitely more beautiful, Millokkom has oceans, rivers, lakes, snow-capped mountains, giant forests, rolling landscapes, and areas of indescribable scenic charm. Its cities are like ours, only more beautiful, cleaner, less congested, and less noisy. They have stunning residential districts, handsome private houses, imposing public buildings, ultra-modern factories, excellent schools and colleges, attractive theatres and concert halls, parks, hospitals, churches, and palaces of public assembly. There are railroad trains, which seem to run in grooves, as I understand it, motor cars operating by "condensed energy," luxurious vessels on the high seas, and smaller ships for local travel.

Politically, the government of Millokkom is about perfect. There is only one nation of people—literally One World—and it is governed by a Supreme Council of Wise Men. There is only one religion—a form of monotheism—based on profound teachings similar to the Spirit Doctrine that is found in our great faiths. The people are happy and intelligent, and have learned how to live philosophically, without fear or hate or worry. There is no crime or poverty on Millokkom, and no war. The people enjoy fine health and only have to go to the hospital in the event of some physical accident. There are animals and birds, some like our own, some exotic, but, oddly enough, there are no fishes or reptiles on the entire planet.

As I have previously mentioned, the citizens of Millokkom resemble us human beings to a marked degree, but with this basic occult difference: they belong to a different Life Wave. Also, their souls do not incarnate on any other planet; nor can these fine people mate with us sexually. Intellectually, they are far ahead of us and possess a degree of spiritual development found in few people on Earth. How I wish that I could meet some person from Millokkom! And, as a world traveller who has visited 94 countries on this planet, how I wish I could step into a Space Ship and visit Millokkom! That, for me, would be the Supreme Adventure...

# I Knew Then that They Were Space Beings

This curious account of a voyage in space was written by Arthur Henry Matthews, a native of England who was raised in the province of Quebec, where he lived on the secluded family farm at Lac Beauport outside Quebec City. Matthews explains in the full narrative that follows that his father was an electrical engineer who had worked with Lord Kelvin, and that as a youngster he had first met the eccentric but brilliant Serbo-American inventor Nikola Tesla.

Matthews further explains that before Tesla died in 1943, the inventor entrusted to Matthews' safekeeping the unpatented plans for certain radical new inventions, some of which he later perfected and constructed. Among these inventions are two that are mentioned in the narrative that follows: Tesla's Anti-War Machine, of which little is known, and the Tesla-Scope, an "interplanetary communications set."

The full title of Matthews' narrative is *The Wall of Light: Nikola Tesla and the Venusian Space Ship the X-12*. It was reproduced in a limited edition in California in 1973. Only part of the opening section of that work is reprinted here; the complete and fully illustrated work is approximately 70,000 words in length. It consists of Matthews' first-person account of his encounters with the Venusians, their numerous landings in their Space Ship the X-12, his visits to their ship, and his own voyage to the planet Mars and back. Of the latter he noted, "It reminded me of our beautiful Eastern Townships." The mission of the Venusians was to ensure that Tesla's inventions were not misused and to deliver a message of peace and hope for all mankind. As Matthews wrote at one point, "I expected wonders. I saw a miracle."

◆ ◆ ◆

In relating this account of the landings of a large spaceship on my property at Lac Beauport, of my strange experience in meeting with people who claimed they were from Venus and what I learned about life on their planet, I would like to emphasize that I consider myself of little importance in this story. If my name is known at all, it is due to my long friendship with Nikola Tesla and an intimate knowledge of his great work for mankind. Perhaps I may be excused if I say that it affords me a certain amount of amused satisfaction to realize that I am now probably the last living person who knew and loved Tesla, but in all humility, I am aware that it was only because Tesla left me some of his ideas to develop that I was thus able to meet these people from Venus who claimed Tesla as one of their own.

Due to the fact that my story covers several visits of the Venusian spaceship, I am, for space reasons, condensing its details into one account and will therefore leave out dates. It is sufficient to say that the first visit was in spring 1941, with continued landings about every two years until 1961, which, to date, included the last landing. These landings took place on my 100-acre property in the hollow of a large meadow formed by the sloping mountainside at the back and the rise of ground at the point.

It was on a spring morning in 1941 that I was standing near my workshop with my son Humphrey. We were discussing some matter relating to electrical waves when suddenly Humphrey looked up and exclaimed: "There's something wrong with the sun!" I looked to the east and gasped in astonishment. Exactly in the centre of the golden disc there was a round black spot about one-quarter the apparent diameter of the sun. It was too big to be a sunspot and, besides, was moving. As we watched, it crept slowly to the upper edge of the sun and in about ten minutes had left the solar disc, when it simply vanished from sight. We saw nothing more of it that day.

I went to bed early that night but could not sleep. An oppressive sense of something strange impending descended on me like a pall. Finally, I arose and dressed. I went outside and looked up at the sky, but all I could see were the stars sparkling in full brilliancy. I returned to the house and settled down to read—but not for long, for suddenly the alarm signal on the Tesla-Scope rang shrilly. I ran outside and at first saw nothing except the sparkling stars. Then I noticed something queer toward the mountain. It appeared to be darker than usual. It was, indeed, for some huge object seemed to cover most of the mountain! I began to walk toward it and as I came near to our barn, I was suddenly confronted by two persons.

Both men were nearly six feet tall, and in the brilliant starlight I could discern their bright blue eyes and golden hair, but what registered with me most was that these beings radiated an aura of perfect health and happiness. Immediately I sensed a feeling of goodwill emanating from them, which took away any fear I might have had at this sudden meeting. They were wearing grey coveralls, and somehow I knew then that they were space beings. I noted with interest that both were bare-headed, with no helmets or other apparatus, and yet they seemed to have no difficulty in breathing Earth air. I have since been asked if there were any physical differences from Earthmen about these space people, and I can only say that I saw none—and why should there be? Are we not all built the same, in the likeness of God?

Then one of them spoke to me in very good English, saying, "Good morning, Arthur Matthews. May we go with you into your workshop?" If this was a surprise, there was a greater one to follow, as he continued, "We are from Venus and we have come to see what you are doing with Tesla's inventions."

Completely taken aback, I could only blurt out, "How am I supposed to believe you are from Venus?"

The one who appeared to be the leader answered calmly, "When you see our ship, you will believe. But before we go, I will make a sketch of Tesla's Anti-War Machine. No one on Earth but you knows its secret. Will *that* convince you?"

I nodded and led them to my workshop. With a few deft strokes, he drew a sketch for me, which I could only accept as the truth. A brief inspection and explanation of the work I was doing on the Tesla devices followed. No comments were made, and I was left to assume they were satisfied with my efforts.

Then the two Venusians said they would take me to their spaceship. We walked toward the mountain, and soon I was staring wide-eyed at the gigantic proportions of the mother-ship X-12, hardly believing my senses, while my two companions chuckled at my bewilderment. The landed ship, which appeared to be made of grey metal (?), looked like two gargantuan saucers put together rim to rim. Circling these rims about twenty feet away from the main body of the craft was an unsupported band of material (later referred to as the "Guide Ring") which was not attached to the ship by any visible means and appeared to be held in place by some magnetic force. Penetrating the centre of the ship was a tubular shaft fifty feet in diameter and three hundred feet in height, the top and bottom ends of which protruded from the ringed saucers, which were seven hundred feet in diameter. The bottom end of this large tube rested on the ground, and I could see an opened doorway in which stood two of the crew, who greeted us with a hand salute.

My companions invited me in for an inspection tour of the great ship, and we stepped into an elevator, which I was told had no cables and was operated by willpower! We stopped off at the level which was devoted to the storage of some of the twenty-four small spacecraft this mother-ship carried, ground vehicles and other equipment. The second level comprised the living quarters of the crew, gardens, recreation area, study rooms and a meeting hall. Living quarters were compartments for single persons or "married" couples (for the crew was made up of both sexes), and these units comprised a small hallway, a large living room, bedroom, bathroom with toilet and storage locker. All rooms were carpeted with some form of pliant plastic and the walls were hung with beautiful paintings. I discovered the outer wall of the living room was in fact "see through," giving a full view of space outside. The outer door of each compartment led out on to a small flower-bedded garden. At this point, I commented on the lack of a kitchen in these units and was informed that Venusians never spoiled their food by cooking it. They grew their own produce abroad and ate it fresh.

We then came to the recreation area, which was covered with some form of simulated grass on which a number of the crew were playing a game somewhat like basketball. This gave me an opportunity to study these Venusians more closely, and I noted that they ranged from five feet six inches to six feet in height. They were blue-eyed, skin colouring a bronze suntan, and their hair ranged from golden blond to a reddish brown. They all appeared in glowing health and their eyes sparkled with a natural joie de vivre. Climbing to the third level, I found this was the horticultural section where all their food produce was grown and there were attractive gardens where the crew relaxed and ate their food. The fourth level was divided between storage of more of the small scout ships, heavy material, water supply, etc., and a number of workshops. I had noted that throughout the entire ship all floors were completely covered with some form of plastic material and that all the outer walls were of the same "see through" type. On each wall there was a circulate viewing screen, somewhat like television, showing a full view of outer space and the exact position of the X-12 in relation to other planets, and its directional trajectory in space, this changing picture being projected from the control tower to all parts of the ship. I was informed that built into these walls were "accumulators" for storing solar energy, which gave constant light and power to operate heating and air conditioning systems.

We then rose to the exposed top of the tubular shaft, which I was told was the control room. My Earthly mind had conjured up visions of all kinds of complex devices to operate this enormous spacecraft, but to my great surprise, there were no visible controls or equipment at all! In the centre of the room was a raised circular platform on which had been built a circular couch and seated with their backs to this and facing outward to the North, South, East and West, were four persons—two women and two men. I was informed that these four operators, chosen specially for their great mental powers, controlled and directed this giant ship! It all seemed completely unbelievable until across my doubting mind there flashed the biblical verse: "Faith can move mountains."

My leader-companion then took me to a lower level and introduced me to a lovely woman whom he described as his "life companion." She was indeed a most beautiful creature, with sapphire-blue eyes and golden-blond hair, and her face glowed with an inner spirituality delightful to behold. He stood beside her and said simply, "You may call us Frank and Frances, for we stand for Truth."

# The Car Started to Rise Up

Make of it what you will, a good many UFOs are spotted from moving vehicles, especially speeding automobiles at night. Strange sights are seen through windshields. Sometimes the car's ignition and electrical systems go on the blink.

The following letter was sent to me by Glenn Therens, who lives and works as a cook in Moose Jaw, Saskatchewan,. It was written on 14 June 1990 and sent in response to my request for "ghost stories," which appeared in the *Moose Jaw Times*. I wish I could deserve Mr. Therens' thanks. I have no idea what caused his moving automobile to tip to one side while he was speeding along a highway. The experience was a profoundly moving one, one that has been recalled in detail more than one-quarter century after it happened.

◆ ◆ ◆

There is nothing "ghostly" about what I'm going to write about, but it sure is mysterious.

It happened on July 6, 1964, at about 2:00 p.m., about four or five miles southeast of Weyburn, Saskatchewan, on Highway 39. It was very hot, 90 to 95°F, and there was absolutely no wind. I was with my wife and our two sons, five years and three years. At the time I was thirty years old and my wife twenty-eight. I was driving. My wife was beside me. The three-year-old was standing on the front seat between us. The five-year-old was in the back seat of our car.

Our car was a 1953 Pontiac in mint condition. It was kept in top-notch condition by my father, who was a garage operator. We were going home to Moose Jaw, after visiting my sister and her husband at Carlyle, Saskatchewan. I was driving approximately 60 mph, about four or five miles southeast of Weyburn, with no traffic ahead or behind me. I slowed down to about twenty-five or thirty miles per hour. Why? I don't know.

All of a sudden, very, very slowly, the right side (the passenger side) of the car started to rise up, and we were driving on the two left tires. The car continued its rise up until, even with my left arm bent at the elbow, I could have extended the palm of my hand and it would have rubbed against the pavement. The highway was in very good, very smooth condition.

The first person to speak was our older son, who was in the back seat. He asked, "Hey, what's going on?"

I spoke second, and yelled to my wife, "Grab hold of the kid," referring to the one standing between us, "he's gonna fall out of the window!"

I had my hands on the steering wheel all the time, but I was definitely not in control of the car. We travelled approximately one hundred yards in the proper lane, then the car started to right itself again, very, very slowly. Then we were driving on four wheels again.

I came to a stop and got out of the car. Still there was no traffic on the highway. I got back into the car and proceeded again. I was about to speak when my wife actually put into words what I was going to say, which was, "I don't think we should tell anyone about this. They'll think we're both crackin' up."

At the time neither of us drank alcohol—we couldn't afford it!

Some years later, on radio station CKRM in Regina, there was a man on a talk show who explained, or tried to explain, unexplained happenings. I tried to phone in, but the lines were busy.

I hope this will be of some use to you for your book. If you could enlighten me as to what may have caused this situation, I thank you.

All of this that I write is true, with God as my witness.

# Much of This Contact Is Personal

"Toronto Woman Has 'Space Contact'" was written by Joan Howard, and it originally appeared in the pages of *Saucers, Space & Science*. This mimeographed magazine was devoted to the subject of UFOs and was issued between 1958 and 1972 by the artist and UFO specialist Gene Duplantier in Willowdale, Ontario. Duplantier reprinted the account in his collection *Saucers, Space & Science Revisited*. The collection is undated—it probably dates from the 1970s—and no further information is available about Joan Howard.

◆ ◆ ◆

Prior to July 1968 I had no interest in or knowledge of UFOs, never read a book on them, and was unaware there were any books on them. Also, I do not read science fiction, I prefer Gothic mysteries. So my initial contact was a shock. It took me about three weeks to realize what had happened. Having always been "psychic," astral trips are not new to me, but this one was unlike any of them.

A barren terrain (seen many times since)—what appeared to be (and is) a military base... people in space suits (either thin atmosphere or no atmosphere) all busy around the place. I was introduced to one who appeared to be an officer of some kind... had a long conversation about ethics, politics, religion, etc. I became aware that my physical body back here was being worked over by some kind of ray... became physically awake and it was so. This ray centred in my head. I could even hear it. For several nights about the same time this ray came. The third night a voice came with it telling me not to fight it but to relax and learn how to use the power it brought. The next night both voice and vision came... my intellectual friend I met on the trip. He has been my contact since.

We are very close friends. He has shown me the beauty and wonder of the universe. Along with spacecraft, land vehicles, their uniforms, civilian clothes, gadgets, the insides of large spaceships with wall panels full of instruments, controls, dials, etc.

He also got me to study physics and astronomy so I would understand what he was talking about. He even tested me on this and still does sometimes.

One important rig, which I nicknamed the "Mind Machine," looks like a weird TV set. This electronic marvel can be used to contact, also "pick up" minds of both intelligent and primitive life forms. One of my contact's jobs is to use this rig to locate life in space. By this instrument he can tell what type of life is on a given planet. Also this rig can "process" (his word) minds and can produce "mind-pictures" (my words). These show what type of mental make-up or personality, etc., a life form has. I don't know how it works and don't pretend to know. These people have discovered how to manipulate thought waves. I could describe this more, but there are other things.

This rig was used on me till I was used to communicating with my contact by ordinary telepathy. Whatever he is doing while he is contacting me or just thinking about me unconsciously, I see him doing it. I see him working, writing and studying our languages. One time I saw him cut his finger while using tools. Another time I saw him washing his hair, which they wear quite long. He also sees me this way.

He puts on his radio or record player and lets me listen to their music. Some of it is beautiful. One piece is the most beautiful unearthly thing I ever heard. It is a sort of short symphony of a spaceship soaring into space and all the beauty of space. I have heard this several times and have asked him to play it for me. They also have a type of jazz all their own.

Although much of this contact is personal, not all of it is so pleasant. He tells me there are two groups in this world or part of the universe, something like the Commies and the Free World here. One group are cold-blooded fanatics with all the advantages of a superior science and technology to help them. They have no sympathetic regard for us or anyone else. The other group are the "good guys" and are the opposite. These two groups are not just one or two races, but are composed of individuals from all their races, as are our own groups.

He has shown me aerial photographs taken of North American cities. Both sides have the Mind Machine. The implications of this where planet Earth is concerned are obvious.

I believe they have a base in our solar system but I believe they originate elsewhere in our galaxy. Maybe outside our galaxy. They only tell me what they figure I ought to know.

My contact and his immediate associates appear to be a research team. At first they showed great interest in our flora and fauna, but they have other interests which I am not sure about. I think in general they are interested in all forms of life and what makes it tick.

I believe his people use telepaths and ESP-ers for special jobs, like his.

I have always heard many times their language, some words of which I have written down. Also I've seen their writing or printing. I have discovered both language and writing are closely related to the language and writing of ancient Mu. The writing is very similar to the hierarchical alphabet of Mu. I was led to this.

My contact has black hair; white-golden skin; long, slightly slanting eyes which sometimes look darker, sometimes lighter. Also their eyes can alter and send out light rays. On him it is very attractive. On his superior officer it is scary! A lady scientist at the research centre has brown hair, very slanting eyes. It is not always possible to tell the exact colour of their eyes. The slant is different to our own Oriental slant. Their eyes are bigger.

They are of average Earth height, 5'6" to 6'. My contact is about 5'8". I am 5'2 ½" and he is taller than me.

I am awake when he talks to me or shows me things. We talk any time of the day or night, but it is easier in the middle of the night when things are quiet. The visions, etc., I receive at night when I can close my eyes. Also sometimes in the daytime if I can lie down. I have also met him several times on astral trips since the first one. Once he came right to my apartment. He is a whiz on this type of stuff.

This has been a brief resume of events.

# Contact

Oscar Magocsi (1928–2002) was born in Hungary, came to Canada in 1957, and worked as an electronics technician. As a youngster he was interested in flying saucers (the term in the 1940s for what came to be called in the 1950s unidentified flying objects or UFOs). He claimed that he was contacted by alien beings in 1975, when he was taken aboard one of their flying saucers after it landed in Muskoka, Ontario. Then he was taken for a visit to the aliens' home planet "Argona" in the "Omm-Onn system, a member of the Psychean Federation Worlds."

Magocsi's account of his travels appeared in his breathlessly written, 146-page memoir titled *My Space Odyssey in UFOs* (1979). "Contact," the title of Chapter Three of that publication, is reproduced here.

What effect did the experience have on the contactee? A note attached to the publication explains it was all to the good: "Due to my experiences with the aliens and their effect on me, I became more spiritually oriented and psychically more aware, strongly life-affirming and as a result—better balanced, happier and luckier."

A discussion of Magocsi's contribution to contactee literature appears in my book *UFOs over Canada* (1991).

◆ ◆ ◆

That summer of '75 I arranged to take two weeks' vacation, starting with the end of July. I planned to spend most of that time at my Muskoka lot, in the hope of some revealing UFO encounters. Therefore, right after a friend's wedding, late Sunday afternoon, July 27, I was on my way, driving towards Huntsville.

I arrived at my lot by sunset, when most cottagers for the weekend only had already left for Toronto. There was enough time left before darkness to unload my camping gear and to gather enough firewood for the night vigil. I was quite determined to be up all night till the "wee" hours of the morning. Then I could still sleep until noon, and go to some nearby beach if the day became too hot. It was good to be back in nature after a long winter and with half summer already gone. Somehow I never got around to come up here since last fall, except for one short and uneventful trip in May.

It was already dark and the stars were shining brightly when I finally lit up my campfire. The night was dry, but not too warm. I had to wear my long-sleeved sweater as I sat on the stool by the fire, at the pile of wood, stacked within arm's reach. Mentally, I recalled the whole chain of strange events that led me up to this point, making me trust a stranger's word for some UFO experiences about to come. I still wondered about it. I hadn't seen Quentin, or Steve, since. I hadn't had any new dramatic encounters either, not even dreams or hunches. The last few months this whole UFO topic had faded into insignificance, as if it was unreal somehow.

Nevertheless, I still enjoyed sitting out by the fire, the same way I had done it many times before. Around 02:30 hours, though, I felt tiredness creeping up more and more on me. Since there were no UFOs about, not even a hint of a sensation, I decided to turn in for the night.

Next day, after sunset, I walked up to the ridge to my "eerie" twilight magic spot. Barely five minutes after I got there, a wave of excitement hit me all of a sudden. I just knew positively that I would have a UFO experience that night!

I am at a total loss to explain how this strong conviction came to me. One second I still felt pleasantly blank, the next second I knew "they" were on their way to transit into this dimension, and some time that night I'd be visited by a UFO. There wasn't even a pulsating glow in my mind, yet I knew they were coming and that there were only a few more hours left before actual show-up time.

I walked back slowly to my lot and lit the campfire. The vigil part ended, it was just a matter of some waiting.

It was shortly after midnight when I began to feel that the UFO already was very close. A few minutes later, I thought I saw a faint pulsating orange glow briefly. Whether I saw it in the sky or in my mind, I wasn't sure. But I was sure that this signal was directed at me, as a form of making me aware. A strange notion struck me: If this was their first deliberate signal, then how did I know hours earlier about their coming? Was it possible that I became more sensitive, no more passive telepathic subject any longer, but an activated mind "sniffing" way ahead? Or had my "eerie" twilight spot something to do with it, like triggering my knowing somehow? It was all very intriguing, especially with this new angle added to it.

I stopped feeding the campfire, and backed away from it to probe the vast expanse of the sky overhead. Soon enough I perceived the approach pattern of some blinking orange light on a zigzag course. It didn't behave like an aircraft, besides there was no engine noise. It kept disappearing, but kept converging on my hill. For a full two minutes it was blinked out of sight; then it got magically materialized out of nowhere, less than a few hundred feet away from me and close to the treetop level, glowing orange, a disc-like shape.

I got on top of my observation deck, well away from the slowly dying campfire. From this vantage point I had an unobstructed view across the valley. Also, I was fully engulfed by the darkness, which made me invisible to any observer farther than a few feet away. Then I raised both my arms and waved towards the motionless distant glowing of the disc.

The glow blinked twice, as if to acknowledge my signal of being aware of it. Although I half expected the blinking response, it still surprised me that the UFO could see me in the darkness from that distance.

Now the UFO started to pulsate in a slow manner, and I sensed that I was being probed to the core of my mind. This went on for about ten minutes, while the cycling pulsations nearly put me into a pleasant drowsiness of some hypnotic trance. To check if my conscious will was still functioning, I climbed down to the smouldering campfire momentarily, then climbed back on the platform. Well, it worked, but I don't know if it really proved anything.

Soon after my exercise, the disc stopped its pulsations, changed its colour into steady greenish and started moving in my general direction. Rising up higher, it swam slowly past me almost overhead with a faint purring sound, heading somewhere beyond the ridge towards "no man's land"! My eyes kept following it, trying to make out its detail. But all I could see was just a hazy glow of an oval shape that became circular when passing overhead. I couldn't detect its source of illumination: the whole disc was just one big blob of yellow-green luminous glow. Only the centre core of its underbelly, like a hole in a doughnut, pulsated with some blue light.

After the disc went out of sight beyond the ridge, I stayed another few minutes in the dark, in case it came back again. But somehow I knew it wouldn't, for it just must have landed in "no man's land," possibly waiting there for my move. Even though I became aware of a gentle pull in that direction as if telepathically induced, I was quite ready to go and see on my own, too.

I put the dying fire out, grabbed my flashlight and took off on foot for the logging road that led into "no man's land." The night was quiet, the few cottages this side of the turnoff were dark. No one seemed to be up. Other than me, perhaps no one even saw the UFO.

It took me a good minute's walk to reach the general area where the UFO might have landed. At a familiar turn of the logging road, I came up on a big clearing, close to my "power" magic spot.

And there it was! What a dramatic moment! Not more than about sixty feet from me, a real flying saucer was moving in the air just a few feet above the ground. I guessed its size for roughly thirty feet in diameter and ten feet in "thickness." It was bathed in a diffused, greenish-blush and soft-glowing luminosity that was radiating from its entire surface rather than coming from points of light. There were two porthole-like, dark oval spots resembling a pair of eyes. On its top there was a bubble-dome-like turret, on its underside there were some ball-like bulges that suggested a landing gear.

There I stood frozen in my tracks, by a clump of trees in the darkness. I was very much excited, but also very nervous with unknown fears. What a magnificently thrilling sight I beheld! This was the living proof of intelligent extraterrestrial life. For I had no doubt that this flying saucer was from outer space. Possibly even from another dimension, as Quentin claimed, but certainly not of Earthly origin.

At this moment, as if trying to prove the point, the saucer started to fade away without moving its position. Then "presto!" and it was gone with a peculiar sighing sound as if the air moved into its place. I shone my flashlight through the spot, but found nothing. The saucer went totally invisible...

Then, within a few moments, a very faint glow came from the same empty space, solidifying slowly back into the flying saucer again. It was very dramatic! After all, it was quite true about fading out of this dimension and fading back again.

This time the saucer gently lowered itself to the ground, into a real landed position. Then it stood there motionless, soundless—just like I stood farther away, frozen and breathless. No one came out of the saucer; it just sat there patiently, as if waiting for me. Somehow I knew that it actually was waiting for me, but I just could not make myself move. I was simply terrified to go near, that's all. Recalling a few speculations I read of sinister alien motives, my mind was working overtime. I guessed if the saucer wanted to, it could have attempted to draw me hypnotically towards itself. But there were no such indications; it seemed my move had to be made entirely of my own free will. For without my moving, there was no other way to learn more. It was as simple as that.

Finally, I decided to take the risk: With cold sweat breaking out all over me, I walked up to the saucer!

After some hesitation, I poked at its hull with my rubberized flashlight. The hull felt more like fibreglass than metal, yet emanating some heat like the hood of a car in hot summer. Next, I pressed my cigarette paper back to the hull for a second to guess at the surface temperature. My pack just got warmer, but did not get burned; yet I didn't feel like touching it with my bare hand.

I found the saucer's actual size to be about thirty-five feet in diameter, ten feet high from top to bottom, plus another two feet perhaps for the upper dome. I guessed its true colour for light grey. I walked around it a few times, looking for some door, or some indication of an opening. There were none. Equally set apart around the circumference, there were three oval-shaped portholes. I couldn't peek through them, for they were above my eye-level, as the saucer squatted on three ball-like protrusions that raised its bottom about three feet from the rocky ground. There would be no marks left by the landing gear on that rock; so far I didn't detect any burn marks, either. Yet there was the definite smell of ozone, as if some high-voltage coronal discharge was being produced by the saucer's hull. Maybe it was wise not to touch.

By now I was considerably calmer, although still on the jittery side. Satisfied with my close-up survey of the exterior, I backed away thirty feet or so, wondering about further developments—if any.

Less than a minute, there came the new development, and a rather dramatic one at that! A three-foot-long horizontal crack appeared and widened into a closed-mouth-like slot, well under the line of portholes and between two of them. Then the slot started to widen vertically, as if a gigantic mouth was opening up. Finally, it formed itself into a man-sized open doorway, while a short walk-up ramp got lowered from it to the ground. Soft yellow light spilled out from the interior, invitingly.

I nearly took to my feet in a momentary panic. Then I took a grip on myself, and decided on facing the aliens to come out of the saucer. Or else I'd never see one. This venture wasn't exactly for faint hearts, I thought. So I braced myself for my first alien encounter, and waited...

Finally, I realized that there would be no aliens coming out. There were no telepathic probings or hints coming, either. The saucer was just sitting there, blankly. Were the occupants incapacitated? Or were they some immobile life-form? Somebody had to be there inside; otherwise who did all the signalling, the telepathic probing earlier, not mentioning the piloting of the craft itself, the fade-out, the door-opening? I felt rather confused.

I edged up near the doorway for a peek inside. But this didn't give me a clue, for a partition behind the door prevented my looking into the interior. Obviously, I had to take another risk, and a tremendous risk this time: Since no one was coming out, I should go in and see for myself. Yet, only heaven knew what manner of alien monsters could be waiting in there! Besides, what about radiation, toxic air, or other harmful substances? Well, there was only one way to find out...

I summoned up my courage, and with a deep breath, I went up the ramp. Then I stepped onto the inner platform within the doorway, finding that there was no partition at all. It was only a curtain of yellow light, which had created the illusion of a wall from the ground at that angle. The square of the platform was illuminated, but the interior was shrouded in darkness. I tried my flashlight—it didn't work.

I hesitated for a moment, then took a couple of steps into the unlit area. My weight on the floor must have activated built-in sensors, for some blue-green glow sprang up all around me, illuminating most of the interior.

At first glance everything looked incomprehensibly alien. But I had no time to look more, for a subtle noise behind made me turn around fast. It was the doorway closing down. Sudden panic seized me; it was a wonder I didn't have a heart attack! Good heavens, I was captive. The closing crack sealed itself into one seamless wall, making me stare paralyzed at it.

Then I tried to calm down. Perhaps this was just another automatic piece of function—once the occupant was inside, the door just shut by itself. I stepped back on the platform and waited. Nothing. Meanwhile, I noticed one shaft of white light shooting down vertically from the ceiling, slightly to the left. I had a hunch this could be the door-opening activator. So I stuck my insulated rubber flashlight through the beam, and it did the trick—the door started to open up.

Just to make sure, I stepped out momentarily into the night, then back again, making the door close. I repeated the procedure to put my mind at ease. Then I started to look for some manual backup system for the door-opener, in case something went wrong with the light. I never trusted a fully automatic gadget, and felt safer if I found some manual override. Slightly to the right of where the door should have been, I found a fist-sized indentation in the wall. I poked my flashlight into it, which made the door open again. It had to be similar to a spring-loaded activator, which was the next best thing to a manual crank. I just wondered who or what made the door open in the first place, while I still had been outside, for I had the feeling that the saucer was devoid of any creatures.

Feeling much calmer now, I turned back to the interior for a close examination. My eyes were first attracted to a three-foot diameter globe hanging at eye-level. It was suspended in the saucer's centre, inside a transparent vertical tubing that connected the domed porthole in the ceiling to an identically shaped porthole in the floor.

The synthetic material of the floor was pearl-greyish and honeycomb patterned, as if a conglomeration of battery cells. Three curved sections of benches that resembled soapstone Eskimo sculptures were ringing the vertical tube. There was a circular railing of bone-like material that girdled the tube, convenient to grip if one was seated on the bench. Very handy in a turbulent flight for humanoids, or even for any creature with arm-like appendages. At least the saucer's interior walls were designed for transporting some manner of creatures. This seemed a reassuring thought, even if there was nobody home momentarily. Or maybe the occupants were just out on some business, liable to return soon; though somehow this line of thought did not make sense in view of the events that got me inside here.

All this left only one possibility—the saucer was a robot vehicle, an unmanned probe, or rather "manned" by some kind of a programmed computer—or remote-controlled by some unseen intelligence, perhaps through a built-in computerized system.

I found nothing, though, that would even vaguely resemble some computer system. Unless it was built in a completely alien manner, inconceivable to my earthly framework of possible technologies. There was no electronic gear or other gadgetry in sight. Therefore, it had to be a vastly different type of technology behind all this—if it was technology at all!

That thought gave me a shiver as I was scrutinizing the "suspended" huge ball in a vertical plastic tubing. Inside the globe itself, there were myriads of flickering lights in swirling patches of multi-coloured mists, as if some artist's conception to show a three-dimensional visual model of a supermind's functioning. Of which I had no doubt it was—either a living intelligence, or the strangest computer.

I tried to poke my flashlight through the plastic tubing-like shaft of light. I met a soft, but firm resistance of a flexible shield, which would yield only so far. Apparently, it was a force field that acted like a protective tubing. And inside it, perhaps the shaft of light was what held the globe suspended at my eye level. I noticed some very faint vertical "flow lines," or traces of energy flow taking place within the shaft. As I turned away, my left hand accidentally bumped into the force field. Much to my relief, there was no adverse effect, just a touch of silky but firm resistance.

I looked up to the gently domed ceiling—there was a wall-to-wall spiral that centred on the tubing like a gigantic heating element, made of shiny gold-looking material. Another energy device, I guessed, perhaps in conjunction with the vertical tube that centred on the globe. Or vice versa. Who knows?

I turned my attention to the circular wall. The blank space for the sealed doorway was flanked on both sides by huge, semi-curved bulges from floor to ceiling—perhaps some storage tanks or cabinets that I could see no doors for. Each bulge was followed by one porthole, with the third porthole being on the opposite wall section. They were equally spaced apart, slightly oval and about three feet in diameter. Then there were two towering "instrument" slabs jutting out from blank wall spaces—one to my left and one to my right, each flanked by a gigantic 6-x-4-foot screen with some sofa under them. And that brought my survey around the wall to its completion...

Matter of fact, that completed my first preliminary survey of the whole interior, for the time being. All of a sudden, I felt the exhaustion, caused by my nervous tension weighing down on me. I wondered if I should get into a much more detailed scrutiny, or just...

At that moment, the ceiling spiral glowed up to an intense orange hue, and started to pulsate slowly. Panic seized me again—I felt a drastic change to come in the "status quo," which I wasn't sure I wanted to face. Now, the shaft had energized, too—there was a strong downward flow of some currents taking place in it.

Maybe I'd better beat it, I thought, before this darned thing takes off with me, or brainwashes me, or disintegrates me, or who knows what.

Fear won over the spirit of adventure—in a hurry, I activated the door opener—and it worked! I scrambled down the ramp, retreating to the edge of the clearing like a frightened deer. Or rather like a dumb bunny—but I just couldn't help my reaction. I thought it would be wildly humorous if a hidden onlooker now took me for a scary alien out to eat him or something.

But there was nothing out there (or ran away and dropped dead since), except the darkness and the bush. I stopped and turned around.

The saucer glowed orange pulsatingly for a short while. Then it retracted the lamp and sealed its door. Now it changed its light into a steady greenish blue, and started to lift off the ground. It rose slowly up and up, to a few hundred feet. I wondered what could be its driving force. Some kind of anti-gravity device? For I did not detect flame exhaust, compressed air, not even sound except a faint whirring noise.

Now the saucer blinked twice and flew away rapidly into a rising arc, soon going out of sight.

It seemed that my encounter was over. Yet, I stood there for quite a while in the completely dark woods, filled with awe and wonder, relief and regret, pride over my bold adventure, but shame over my cowardly running away. And also, I felt terribly tired, drained.

Time to turn in, I thought. So I slowly walked back through the woods to my lot...

# A Giant Lizard with Wings

"So now with thanks also to Prince George radio station CJCI for its taped interview with one of the men (referred to as X) in the highway incident, and to Adrienne Radford for serving as a helpful contact person, we carry the story of these remarkable northern sightings, realizing there almost certainly will be more."

So wrote former Ottawa newspaper correspondent John Magor in *Canadian UFO Report*, Summer 1977, about this so-called highway incident. This is a reference to a specific sighting amid a series of sightings of UFOs reported in the summer of 1976 from the vicinity of Prince George, British Columbia.

Magor went on to reproduce the transcript of the station's interview with the truck driver who reported this strange encounter with an alien vehicle and its occupant. The experience even involves a loss of consciousness over a measurable period—a syndrome that has come to be known as "missing time."

The driver is identified as X. In a subsequent issue of *Canadian UFO Report*, Winter–Spring 1978, Magor, with permission, identified the informant as supermarket employee Kirk Alore. The episode occurred on Highway 16 between Prince George and Vanderhoof as Alore was en route to Fort St. James, early on the morning of July 5.

I am reproducing here, with slight editing, the transcript of the interview, followed by the substance of Magor's subsequent interview with Alore.

◆ ◆ ◆

X: About a mile before it happened I looked at my watch and it was about ten past four. I was coming on to this straight stretch, and I noticed this red light in the sky, and I noticed this car coming towards me. Our cars were about three hundred yards apart when this red light dropped right out of the sky and started coming towards me. In panic I swerved and almost immediately this light was right on me and lit up the interior of my truck. My motor went dead and my radio went dead and I passed out. About four-thirty a guy was shaking me and said, "Are you all right?" I said, "Yes." Then he said, "A strange thing happened. I woke up outside my car." "Then what am I doing here?" I was on the passenger side of my truck and our cars were no more than two feet apart and there were no skid marks. And he said he passed out, too, and his motor went all crazy and then died out.

Q: Could you describe the object you saw?

X: To me it looked like a giant lizard with wings, and it was a little over one and a half times the size of the road width.

Q: Did the object look foreign or like something we could build here on earth?

X: I don't think it was like anything we could build. That's how strange it looked and that's what scared me. It didn't look like anything I had seen before, except maybe the lizard part. That's about the only thing I could relate it to.

Q: Did it have wings?

X: Yes, it did. They looked like frog legs spread out, with that gap in them.

Q: Do you remember seeing engines?

X: I don't remember anything like that, but maybe on the back there was something. It was a round thing.

Q: What shape was the body?

X: It was oblong, and the outer surface reminded me of alligator skin. It was rough looking. On top there was a dome and that's where the light was coming from.

Q: Do you have a record of passing out?

X: No. I've never fainted before in my life.

Q: What sort of feeling did you have when you passed out in the car?

X: I felt as if there were a bunch of pins in me, and then I sort of went into nothing. The last thing I remember was my motor dying, my radio going funny and seeing this guy not more than a hundred yards away and heading straight for me. I was doing at least seventy miles per hour. I remember putting my foot on the brake, but there were no skid marks.

Q: Had you been drinking?

X: No, not a bit. I had even pulled over to the side of the road farther south and had two or three hours sleep, so I was wide awake and had the radio on full blast.

Q: Do you believe in UFOs?

X: I do now. I didn't before but I do now.

◆ ◆ ◆

I came up around a corner on the way from Prince George and noticed a red light about a mile away, to my right above some hydro towers. I just kept driving on and looking at it, and then I saw a car coming. He was about half a mile away. Then I noticed this red light move. I kept staring at it and it just sort of shot right over the top of the oncoming car.

I just stared at it in amazement. Then it shot towards me, when the oncoming car was about 300 yards away, and it was huge! It took up about two highway widths, and at that instant the red light lit up the interior of my cab and I got strange sensations, like my arms fell asleep and my legs fell asleep and they felt like pins and needles. Then I swerved and missed this thing because it was coming right towards me.

It all happened so fast I just don't remember anything after. I sort of blacked out, I guess. According to our watches it was 15 minutes later or so (making it about 4:30 a.m.) and this guy was opening my door and shaking me. He was asking if I was all right. I said, "Yes, I'm okay, I guess." But I was sort of sick at the moment and was aching all over. My arms and everything were sore. Our cars were about two feet apart.

He said, "A strange thing happened to me. I was outside my car when I came to." We could find no skid marks, and I was doing at least 70 miles an hour when I swerved into his lane.

We went to the hospital in Vanderhoof, both of us, and they checked us over and there was apparently just shock. That's all it was. I never did get the other guy's name.

*Asked for a description of the object, Kirk replied:*

It was oblong; the outer shell looked more or less like alligator skin. It had little protruding wings, except they were rounded. Underneath between the wings it had a circular thing, like an electric razor. You know, the discs? That's what it had underneath, one turning slowly inside the other, which was turning the other way. It had a dome on top with different coloured lights inside—green, red, yellow, blue, all like little dots. Then it had just one straight beam of red light when it shone the red light in my truck...

I could see everything in great detail.

# Strange, Screeching, Insectoid Noises

With the mail on 17 November 1992 came the memoir reproduced below.

It began with one sentence of explanation: "I was referred to you by UFO researcher Lorne Goldfader for the purpose of informing you of my own UFO experience through a 2–3 page short story."

I should explain that, at the time, Lorne Goldfader was a tireless researcher who served the UFO community as director of the UFO Research Institute of Canada (UFORIC), a Vancouver-based organization. Goldfader, who reported some anomalous experiences of his own, made UFORIC a clearing house for experiencers.

Melissa Steidman, a native of Brantford, Ontario, who was in her early twenties when she wrote this memoir, works as a security guard.

She is an experiencer, as her memoir demonstrates. I am not sure what to make of her record of sightings and soundings. There is an old theory that it is people that are haunted, not places. Today, when rational explanations are brought to the fore, all causes result in effects that can be seen and tape-recorded.

It is up to the reader to decide what to make of these strange experiences. I have reproduced the account in full with a minimum of copy editing.

◆ ◆ ◆

I had my first UFO experience in November 1988. At the time I was travelling with my mother from Hamilton to Brantford, Ontario, where I live. We were driving down Highway 99, when a strange configuration of three lights was suddenly seen to be hovering above the car. My mother and I got out of the car to get a closer look at the UFO.

It was huge. It was also triangle-shaped, a pyramidal configuration of three bright lights. It seemed to occupy about half the night sky, as it hovered there above the car for a few brief moments. Then it made a loud noise, rather like an engine. It accelerated away and disappeared into the night.

The next time I had a UFO "encounter" was in January 1989, when I was driving out to St. George to get some spring water from the artesian well that is located next to the Fire Department and the Township Community Hall. When you turn off Highway 99, and drive along the last mile of the road that leads into St. George, you encounter an intersecting country road that leads from the crossroads to the small hamlet of Harrisburg. There are forests and swamps on both sides of the Harrisburg Road, and this is where I saw an arrow-shaped UFO hovering above those swamps.

Its configuration was adorned with tiny bright lights that stood out starkly against the night sky. It looked like weird rows of Christmas lights. From it emanated a strange, high-pitched, insectoid noise that sounded electronically amplified. After hovering above the car for a few moments, the UFO disappeared into the swamps. I turned off the road to St. George and decided to drive directly into Harrisburg to see if I could follow the UFO and perhaps locate it. That's when I abruptly drove onto the shoulder of the road and slipped out of the car. Why did I do this?

I did this because I saw, hovering above the Sulphur Springs swamp, a huge, circular-shaped UFO. It began to move along the flight paths of airplanes headed in the direction of Toronto International Airport. At least it appeared to be headed in that direction. It seemed to have three levels—three levels of bright lights that were flashing on and off intermittently.

In April 1989, I had another UFO experience on the way to St. George. But this time the three-levelled UFO didn't simply disappear in the direction of Toronto International Airport. There was a UFO "flap" that night, or at least it seemed that way because bright lights that looked like suns were hovering above the Sulphur Springs swamp around St. George and Harrisburg. That's when I rolled down the car windows and heard those strange, screeching, insectoid noises coming from the swamp—*on all sides of the car!* Needless to say, I loaded up with spring water and got out of there as fast as possible!

One of the strangest of my UFO experiences involves a gargantuan black bird that looked like a giant bat. I saw it hovering over the swamps in May 1990 when I went out to St. George for the express purpose of tape-recording the high-pitched, screeching, insectoid noises.

I had just parked along the side of the road, and was tape-recording the eerie noises coming from the swamp, when I looked up. Suddenly I saw a large, black, bat-like shape, with a wingspan of approximately ten feet, hovering overhead, not far from where I was standing on the gravel shoulder of the road overlooking the swamps. It was flapping its huge wings very casually, and slowly its black outline was illuminated in the glow of the car's headlights. The black, bat-like form stood out against the murky darkness of the swamp for only a few moments.

Then it sped away out of the illumination of the car's headlights and abruptly disappeared into the night.

I never saw the "giant bat" again. But I did continue to see the huge, glowing orbs of light that hovered above the Sulphur Springs swamps every time I went out to St. George to fetch spring water.

These UFO encounters were not limited to the countryside. One night, as I was waiting in the parking lot of Lyndon Park Mall in Brantford, I saw a huge configuration of spectacularly bright lights, all arrow-shaped, hovering over the Agnew-Surpass shoe factory just across the street on Powerline Road. It was there, hovering for a few moments, before it accelerated away into the night.

I also saw several huge orbs of light hovering above my house one night in April 1989, shortly after the encounter with the high-pitched, insectoid noise. One of these UFOs even seemed to stop right above our house on 135 Sheridan Street, brightly glowing as if *homing in* on our house. The lights were like *spotlights*. My sister was standing outside, on the sidewalk, looking up at the UFOs that were hovering overhead, when one of the UFOs stopped, right in the middle of the sky, and shone its spotlight directly onto her, almost like a beacon.

What I have been describing are all real, "genuine," UFO encounters. I have family witnesses for some of them. I have sent audio recordings of the insectoid noises to UFO researcher Lorne Goldfader, and he, in fact, was the person who referred me to you, asking that I write a 2–3 page short story about my encounters. He also requested that I submit it to you as soon as possible. I hope that you will find my story "interesting" and thank you for your time.

# Part V
# ABDUCTIONS

*Perhaps there is a hopeful possibility here in the conquest*
*of outer space. Interplanetary activity may well give us*
*planetary peace. Once we discover Martian space ships*
*hovering over earth's air-space, we will all come together.*
*"How dare they threaten us like this!" we shall shout, as*
*one, at a really United Nations!*
—Lester B. Pearson, diplomat, Nobel Peace Prize Lecture,
Oslo, Norway, 11 December 1957; *The Four Faces of*
*Peace and the International Outlook* (1964) edited by
Sherleigh G. Pierson.

An abductee is a person who claims that he or she has been kidnapped
and taken by force aboard a UFO and psychologically, physically, and
sexually abused by alien beings. By this definition very few Canadians
could claim to be abductees, but there are a fair number who feel that
they have, without their conscious consent, been singled out, targeted,
marked, or otherwise specifically used and misused by alien beings for
obscure purposes of their own. Budd Hopkins, David M. Jacobs, and
John Mack have written extensively about "the alien abduction scenario"—Hopkins as investigator and counselor, Jacobs as social
historian, and Mack as psychiatrist.

Also to consider are the important findings of Thomas E. Bullard,
the folklorist, who wrote in his book *UFO Abductions: The Measure of
a Mystery* (1987): "If abductions are literally true, they are the greatest
story of all time." He then added, "If they are subjective, they offer a
seldom-equalled opportunity to gain insight into human mental func-
tions, the interaction of belief with experience, and the social
transmission of ideas."

This chapter on "the alien abduction scenario," offers the reader some accounts of maltreatment by alien beings, who are generally sensed or seen to be cold and uncaring, but also some accounts that present superior beings who are sometimes obscurely empathetic and understanding.

# A Creature Sort
# of Whitish
# in Colour

Do children experience the mysterious? Are the memories of childhood as recalled in adulthood the material of alien encounters?

This account of alien visitation comes in the form of a letter addressed to Bonnie Wheeler, who for a good many years was the prime mover of the Cambridge UFO Research Group, one of the few Canadian UFO groups that undertook to research and release its findings in its own quarterly bulletins, which Wheeler edited.

The letter was written by C.B., a woman who at the time was living somewhere in the Maritimes. As a child she lived in Quebec, where she had an unusual encounter. She wrote about it in this letter addressed to Wheeler. The letter is dated 4 September 1992.

The contents of the letter are reproduced here with the kind permission of C.B., who wishes to remain anonymous, and with thanks to Wheeler, who first drew the letter to my attention and then arranged for me to communicate with C.B.

It is a psychological fact that children sometimes fantasize about "imaginary playmates." Fantasy may be a way of dismissing this lucid recollection; yet, if it is a fantasy, it is an incredibly detailed one.

◆ ◆ ◆

Cambridge UFO Research Group
170 Strathcona Street
Cambridge, Ontario
N3C 1R4

September 04, 1992

Attention: Bonnie Wheeler

Dear Bonnie:

I must state before I commence that I am indeed extremely apprehensive and nervous about this letter but, at the same time, very compelled to send this information to you.

As I stated to you on the phone, I am 32 years old. The events that I am about to recount happened to me at the ages of 8, 9, or 10 in the years 1968, 1969, or 1970 respectively.

During the period from 1965 to Sept. 1970, I lived in Lachine, Quebec. Across the street I played with a girl two years older than myself whose name was J. We became great friends. Both of J.'s parents worked. She had 3 much older siblings... K. (a boy), H. (a girl), and D. (a boy). Her older brother K., along with the help of his dad, built a cottage on Lac Lebeau some time prior to my moving to Lachine.

E. and M. (J.'s parents) used to invite me to the cottage almost every weekend in the summer. I was a playmate for J. I enjoyed going there very much and looked forward to the weekends. As young girls, our favourite pastimes were swimming, canoeing, boating, water skiing, and swinging on the one swing overlooking the water. To get to the cottage, we had to cross by the boat that belonged to J.'s Dad. The cottage, to my recollection, was partly built on rocks. It was red and white in colour, with miles and miles of wooded area behind it. At that time there were not very many cottages on the lake, and they were sparsely placed. I recall only 3 bedrooms in the cottage. J. and I slept in bunk beds. Her parents had a double bed in the same room. Her older sister and K., one of her brothers, were married and usually occupied the other rooms.

One particular night I woke up to find myself floating out the bedroom cottage window. (I cannot remember if I was sleeping on the lower or upper bunk that particular evening... J. and I usually took turns.) I was very astonished. In particular, I thought, "Wow, what a neat dream I am having!" My head was turned to the left side. I remember turning it to the right. To my horror and utter amazement, I remember seeing a creature sort of whitish in colour with big, big black eyes. I was initially scared, and even more so when I slowly floated down toward this creature, facing him eye to eye. I believe at this particular time I fell unconscious. The next thing I can consciously recall is that I had a terrible pain in my right ear. So intense was this pain that it caused me to have an excruciating, pounding headache. I felt like my head was going to burst open. I begged God to stop it, but then I thought that this was silly, God would not hurt me. The pain did stop, and I thought, "Oh, thank you." To my surprise, a voice replied, "That was nice." (I will state here that the particular conversation to follow was done through thoughts only. I did not speak out loud, or at least I don't believe I did.) I do not recall the sequence of the conversation, and I cannot even be sure of the exactness of this conversation.

"What was nice? You mean... saying 'thank you'?"

"Yes."

"My parents always taught me to be polite."

"Are you God?"

"No."

"Then you must be Jesus?"

"No. I can see you are disappointed that I am not these particular people. I am from another planet, far, far away from here, past the Milky Way.

"Another planet... oh? What is your name?"

I recall him mentioning his name several times to me, but I could not grasp how to pronounce it. I think it was rather long.

"You will find it hard to pronounce. We do not have an alphabet like you."

I believe he was referring to our phonetic alphabet.

"May I see what you look like? Can I open my eyes?"

"You would only think I am ugly. I would scare you and I do not want you to be scared."

"Then what do you look like?"

"I am rather thin, no hair on my head, pale in colour, very white, large black eyes.

"No hair, pale in colour. You'd better sit out in the sun and get a suntan. How come you have no hair?"

"We are born with no hair. We cannot go out in the sun. It is very bad for our body type. You should not stay in the sun very long either."

"Oh, but I love the sun and suntanning. It is good for the body. I love the water too. You should not say you are ugly... it's not what you look like that counts but what is in your heart."

Then I sensed another presence in the room. This "voice" seemed to turn away from me, as though he was communicating with someone else. I heard no conversation.

"Who is with you? Is there someone else here?"

"Yes. My friend, who would be considered a doctor on your planet, and I am a scientist. We are, however, much more advanced than your doctors or scientists. Your heart is only an organ. It is not what is in your heart but your head that makes you feel."

I became confused, as this was not what we were taught as children and adults. I changed the subject.

"I do not need a doctor, I am not sick."

"The doctor is examining you."

I remember this conversation continuing. I can recall that he mentioned that I was healthy, both externally and internally, except for one internal part of me that was not correctly placed, but that they would fix it when the time came. (I do not want to mention what I believe they may have fixed.)

I recall him expressing his desire to become very close to me, as close as I was with J. I was edgy and nervous about this and informed him that he could not become as close as J. was with me. He stated the reason why he wanted to become close to me. (I do not wish and cannot now bring myself to recount this reason to you at this point in time.)

He informed me that he had been watching me from the woods that particular day. Maybe it was in the afternoon; it had been a sunny day. (I become confused here. I knew that the sun bothered their skin, because he told me so.) He was fascinated by the ease in which I swam on top of the water, and in particular how I dove underwater and popped up in different locations. It amused him too.

Then I recalled diving under the water and surfacing. I was scaring J., who was lying on a flotation device. I was just having some fun with J., who would laugh and scream with delight every time we played this game.

"Can you swim?"

"No."

"Then I will teach you. I can swim very well."

"I would love to learn how, but we cannot go in water."

"How sad. That is too bad."

"I will be content just to watch you."

I recall him wanting to know what the water felt like on my skin. However, I do not recall having the words or the intelligence to really explain how water feels on the skin. I might have mentioned that the sensation was "so beautiful."

I know at one point that I informed him that I was left-handed and that the majority of people were right-handed. I asked him which hand he used. He stated that they can use both hands equally, that one hand is not better than the other, and that their brains are not divided like ours. I sensed that he meant there was no division.

I recall that he inquired if I ever took walks in the woods. I replied no because I was afraid of bears. They would eat me. I think he asked what bears are, though I am not sure about this. He said that he hadn't seen any bears and that it was beautiful in the woods. He asked if it would be all right if he came and got me from time to time to take me to his home in the woods. (He informed me that his home was not like ours, that it moved and had long rectangular windows to see out of.) I "thought" sure, since he promised me that no bears would hurt me.

I know he liked our woods and thought they were beautiful. I gathered that their planet must be somewhat barren. At this point I believe he took my earring from my right ear as a souvenir. I have pierced ears. He then told me to go back to sleep, at which time I informed him that I did not want to go back to sleep. He insisted that I go back to sleep, and with much reluctance I did.

I know I woke up again, looking at that window, wondering what had happened to me and whether or not it had been a dream. That morning I told M. (I am using his first name, but as a child I used Mr.) about my experience, about floating out the window, seeing the creature with the black eyes, etc. He then laughed and laughed. I became very angry. I don't recall ever being angry with him before. He knew I was angry and inquired about my dream. I said, "You will only laugh. Why do you want to know any more?" He stated that he wanted to know more because he had had a similar dream, except that there were bright lights and that every time he had this dream he felt sick. He inquired if there were any bright lights in my dream. I told him I did not remember bright lights. He told me it felt like he was on a table with bright lights and could see some figures but not their eyes. He could not see the figures clearly.

I told him that his dream was not the same as mine. (I was a child of 9 or 10 at the time. I did not know what UFOs were; I had no idea that there could possibly be life on other planets. I cannot recall if I had ever heard about flying saucers.)

M. expressed the desire to know more. He asked me to tell him if I ever had any more dreams with creatures in them. I believe there may have been another dream, though I know I never mentioned it to him or to anyone else.

Some weeks later, M. expressed the desire to go walking in the woods. So E., M., J., and I went. (I do not recall liking the idea very much, being nervous about bears that might eat me.) We walked for some time. I would look up through the trees, quite fascinated by the sun's rays as they were reflected by the leaves and the ground.

Eventually we came upon a rather large, burnt area. To my recollection, the area was circular (disk-like) in form. Outside the circular pattern, none of the other trees had been burnt. There was no debris, no signs of trees that were burnt in this particular patch. It was just scorched black. M. became very excited about what he saw, and started discussing this particular burnt patch with his wife. J. went down into the burnt area. M., seeing his daughter in the area, screamed at her to get out of there and stay away from there. I didn't understand why he became so upset with her.

There is one more event that I must mention that also frightened me. One afternoon I was swinging on the swing overlooking the water. I stopped the swing to look at the ground. I believe I was singing or day-dreaming. I looked up into the woods and saw a form. It was quite thin. I was not sure about its size, but it seemed to be wearing a dark blue suit that covered its head and went all the way down to its feet. Upon realizing that I had noticed him, this thing quickly hid behind a tree. I stared into the woods just waiting for it to reappear. It did not. I then called out, "Hello." No response. "Hello." No response. "I saw you." No response. I then became frightened. My thoughts were that this thing was going to steal me.

At that time no one else was outside. I ran inside the cottage. E. inquired, "Who were you talking to?" I explained to her what I thought I had seen. I believe she doubted me. M. asked me again to describe what I had seen. I explained again. He asked me if the mask looked like a stocking. I said no, it was like a suit that covered his whole body. They then told me not to go outside.

Later I did go onto the balcony. E. asked M. to check before I could venture down to the swing again. (The swing was not far from the cottage.) I told M. which tree I believed I saw this particular form near. He looked behind it. There was nothing there. He told me everything was okay. I was still scared. M., upon realizing this, called out into the woods, "You see this little girl. If you touch her I will come after you and if I catch you I will kill you! Do you hear me? I will kill you!"

I was very upset by his tone and turned to M. and asked, "You will kill him?"

"I'll kill him," was his response.

This is all I can remember. If it is truly only a dream, then it is the most unusual dream that I have ever had. In fact, I never remembered a dream in so much detail. This is the only one. I have no explanation, but I remembered this event for some time after, then forgot it for a long period of time. I know it is quite unusual for someone to remember this much after, say, 23 years. I have no explanation to offer you as to why I remember this much. I can understand it if you find these events unbelievable.

These events were very real to me, and I have had great difficulty just passing them off as an extraordinary, unusual nightmare. Their reality is what I think compelled me to recount these events to you. In some way doing so makes me feel better.

Sincerely,
C.B.

# Missing Time

The words "missing time" are identified with Budd Hopkins, New York painter and "abductionist." He argues in his books about "the abduction scenario" that the inability of people who claim they were abducted by alien beings to account for the passage of time that corresponds to the period of their abduction is a good indication of the reality of the phenomenon.

Hopkins was not the first person to note this feature of alleged abductions. Canadian community college teacher David Haisell wrote what is probably the earliest book on the subject of "missing time." He called it *The Missing Seven Hours* (1978), and in it he discussed the case of a businessman who suffered just such a "time loss" in November 1973 in the vicinity of Jackson's Point, Ontario.

Here is another early case.

I am grateful to Barbara Neyedly for publishing this article in her community paper, *Toronto's Midtown Voice*. It was contributed by a reader, Pat Connor, and it appeared in the October 1991 issue.

◆ ◆ ◆

*Starry, Scary Night*

The sobering reality of it all captivated our minds with a jolt early that morning in August 1976. We were not going to be alone during our overnight adventure up north. And there was nothing on this Earth that was going to change this fact.

I was on a twenty-four hour leave from waterfront duties. My friend, whom I'll call Salty, and I loaded up the Blue Bomber with provisions and maps and headed north from Stouffville, Ontario. We made no exact plans as to where precisely we were going. The sun was setting as we drove off the camp road onto the main highway. Our minds were overflowing with excitement and anticipation as we drove into the northern horizon, constantly remarking to each other about the wisdom of such an unplanned adventure, but we drew no conclusions.

The short first leg of the trip ended in Uxbridge and dinner at a small country inn. It was about 10:00 p.m. when we hit the road again, with Salty acting as navigator, using the North Star to guide us. As we drove, our senses were continuously treated to the beauty of an unfolding carpet of the stars and the dark forests, still green to the eye despite the night.

There's something inexplicable about driving through the night on unlit highways with starry clear skies reigning overhead, headlights barely blotting out the darkness. Before the second leg of the drive ended, we concluded that it was uncharacteristic of us to set out on such a bold and risky drive into unfamiliar territory. Undaunted, we kept driving, knowing only that we were headed north. And that, we explained, we seemed to feel compelled to keep going.

We arrived in Fenelon Falls around 11:00 p.m. and promptly sought out a local tavern called the Skipper's Den. The friendly waiter sat us at a table beside a wall decorated by an antique porthole. We ordered drinks and chatted with the waiter, who asked us where we were from and where we were headed. We explained that we were on twenty-four-hour leave from a waterfront in the Stouffville area. However, we couldn't tell him our destination. The three of us were humorously mystified by this.

We left the Skipper's Den, then headed back to the car. After driving around Fenelon for a brief period, we headed into the northern horizon once again. About five miles north of Fenelon, Salty requested that I stop so she could answer nature's call. As she returned to the car, she asked, "Do you see that?" She explained that when we stopped she thought she saw a light a few miles behind us. She saw it suddenly rising into the sky and hovering over a nearby treeline.

I slowed down and observed the light. It was moving slowly, and as we drove, the road curved to the east. It became parallel with the treeline and we lost track of whatever it was. I then noticed in the rearview mirror that there was what I thought was another car. I signalled for it to pass. Then, suddenly, the entire car became engulfed in a brightness that flooded the road with light in front of us as well as behind us. We increased our speed dramatically, but the object above us sped along with us.

Then it was gone in a flash. Or so we thought. It reappeared above the treeline and was still keeping pace with us. The Blue Bomber was still co-operating at over one hundred miles per hour. We concluded that the object showed intent and that our lives were in danger. Salty took notes. I can't say precisely how long this segment of the experience lasted, but it was at least ten minutes in length. We passed one other car during this period. We saw it enter the highway at high speed from a dirt road, leaving a cloud of dust in its wake.

The light disappeared momentarily at a bend in the road. But once we rounded the curve, it was sitting about two hundred feet above the road. Then it shot straight up. I stopped the car to catch my breath. It was at this point that we could hear farm animals and birds. Perhaps they too were sensing what had happened.

Salty suddenly began to demand that I start driving again. She pointed to a shadow-like distortion in the sky, close to where we were parked. She said that it was still with us. Then the elusive object reappeared, this time noticeably dimmer, then brighter, until orange rings of light appeared at its base. Then they too brightened, and together the two colours of light began to pulsate, slowly at first, then faster and faster like a strobe of light, illuminating approximately an acre of the treeline and adjacent fields.

Salty's words finally got through to me, and I began to drive frantically while our visitor kept us company, moving with us, sometimes ahead of us, at times beside us above the trees, until it left us a few miles shy of Kinmount.

At Kinmount, we begged our way into a bake shop, where the female proprietor was preparing goods for the next day. She listened to our account and advised us to promptly inform the OPP (the Ontario

Provincial Police) using her phone. Afterwards, she soothed us with cakes and coffee and words of how she had gotten accustomed to lending her phone to strangers on recent nights—and on other nights like these over the last years. As we left, Salty glanced at the wall clock and screamed, "Look at the time!"

It was nearly 3:00 a.m. It couldn't have taken us all that time to make the short drive from Fenelon to Kinmount. After all, we had only stopped twice, and each time momentarily. We were also driving excessively fast for much of the distance. We had left Fenelon about midnight. The distance between the two towns is less than forty miles. It should not already have been 3:00 a.m.!

Our watches had to be wrong. As we started to compare their time with the time on the shop clock, the baker told us not to bother, adding, in her kind and quiet way, "Your watches are working just fine."

# Alien Abduction

UFOlogy entered a new and dramatic phase in the 1980s when it was revealed to the public that there was a motive for and a method behind the UFO experience: Apparently alien beings were intent on abducting men and women at will and subjecting them to bizarre examinations and procedures. This was the burden of books written by investigators like Budd Hopkins, Whitley Strieber, David M. Jacobs, and John Mack, which offered first-person accounts and arguments that everything could be explained by the knowledge that behind the seemingly random sightings of alien craft and contacts and abductions with alien beings was the production of "a new race." There were to be hybrid creatures, half-human, half-alien... monsters if ever they existed.

Sceptics like Philip J. Klass would have none of it. In his analysis *UFO Abductions: A Dangerous Game* (1989), Klass argued that the hypothesis was wrong and that there was no credible evidence that any of it had occurred. He noted that not one of the self-styled abductees bothered to report his or her "kidnapping" to the FBI, so he offered the sum of $10,000 as a reward to any victim of an abduction, "providing the alleged abduction is reported to the Federal Bureau of Investigation and FBI investigation confirms that the kidnapping really occurred." Klass attached the following warning to his offer: "Anyone who knowingly reports a spurious kidnapping to the FBI is vulnerable to a $10,000 fine and up to five years in prison." To date Klass's reward has gone unclaimed.

In *UFO Abductions*, Klass described the appearance of two women who identified themselves as abductees on the *Oprah Winfrey Show* on 22 May 1987. One of the women was Constance Morgan, an aspiring New York actress; the other was Dorothy Wallis, a middle-aged woman from St. Catharines, Ontario. Ms. Wallis was identified as one of the people who sought out Budd Hopkins for help and who subsequently made an appearance with Roy Bonisteel on CBC-TV's *Man Alive*. Ms. Wallis described a series of three abductions and the presence of a mysterious "implant" in her nostril. There was a third guest on the show that day, and that was Klass himself. He represented the sceptical point of view. Here, in dialogue form, is the substance of the remarks made on that occasion by the Canadian abductee.

◆ ◆ ◆

Winfrey asked Wallis if she had a number of alien abduction experiences or just one.

Wallis: "Yes—I've had a number of experiences. My first was when I was eight years old. I woke up about 11:00 p.m. with this compulsion to go down to a nearby field... When I went out of the house, the clock said 11:00. So I went down, and in this field was a very bright light, obviously shining out of a doorway. And there was this huge craft behind it—I would guess 30 feet across—and there was this little being in the doorway—very much as she [Constance Morgan] described it. Three-and-a-half to four feet tall, with huge, compelling eyes, and he communicated that he wanted me to come in."

Winfrey: "How did he communicate that, and how do you know it was a 'he'?"

Wallis: "I don't know. I had a feeling of a man."

Winfrey asked if the alien's skin was black.

Wallis: "I would call it more like a tannish grey... The door closed behind me, and he asked me—there were two other beings, maybe three inches taller—and they wanted me to get up on the table... They asked me to get up on this table."

Winfrey: "How did they ask you?"

Wallis: "When I argued, they just put their hands on my arms and I was flat on my back on the table. I was absolutely unable to move. I could move my head, but the rest of my body was just paralyzed. They proceeded to take this scraping off the arm."

Wallis reported that the aliens inserted an instrument "with a 2 cm. metallic burr up into the nostril. And they just sort of generally examined me all over."

Winfrey asked about subsequent abductions.

Wallis replied that the second had occurred when she was fifteen. She and her brother were returning home from school at about 2:30 in the afternoon when they saw a flying saucer, about half a mile from where the earlier incident allegedly had occurred. She described this UFO as having "a slightly different shape from the first one. And there was one being on the outside who was wearing a sort of coverall... and he was digging away on the other side."

Wallis continued: "The same fellow who met me at the door the first time was at the door again and he told me I would have to wait until the other one had finished what he was doing, because he could not breathe our air and that's why he was wearing a hood..."

Wallis said the aliens "examined me again… They checked the thing in the nostril."

Winfrey asked if she could feel the "thing" that had been implanted there seven years earlier.

Wallis: "No, I could not. They inserted a long—it looked like a knitting needle—a long probe inside the navel… rather painful. And he told me they were taking ova—I was fifteen.… They said they were going to see if they could create a hybrid. *And that really upset me!*"

Winfrey asked if she had ever seen her offspring or pictures of her offspring.

Wallis: "It horrifies me. I've had dreams where I'm holding a malformed child."

Winfrey asked how she knew it was not simply a dream.

Wallis: "Well, if you're using five senses, you're usually awake. And I could hear. I could see. I could feel. I could smell, and whatever the other one is."

Winfrey added the fifth sense, taste.

Wallis: "They gave me a kind of blue thick stuff to drink at one point. When I left the craft when I was eight, he told me I couldn't remember and my thought was, 'I will if I damn well want to.' I have two-thirds recall from that strong effort."

Winfrey asked if she had told anyone about her UFO abductions as a child.

Wallis: "No. My father was of a religious persuasion. My experience had a lot of demons in it, so I wasn't about to put myself in that."

Winfrey asked what such an experience "does to your life." "If you know it's not a dream, do you spend the rest of your days wondering if they're coming back, or why you were chosen?"

Wallis: "Yes, you always have a sense that—they did say they would be back, that there would be things that I would be expected to do."

Winfrey asked if the aliens had told Wallis why they had come.

Wallis: "Well, they wanted the ova."

Wallis went on to say that under hypnosis she recalled that the aliens had shown her a sort of "movie" that gave her a "horrendous feeling of cataclysms on the earth, with people dying all over the place... Under hypnosis I hardly looked at it. It was horrifying to me."

And on that note the interview ended.

# Incident at Onion Lake

This account is quite disturbing. It was sent to me in 1990 in response to my request, carried by *The Thunder Bay Chronicle-Journal* and other weekly papers across the country, for first-person accounts of "extraordinary experiences." Its author, whom I have identified as W.A., is a resident of Thunder Bay, Ontario. It is not pleasant reading.

◆ ◆ ◆

In 1966, June 30th, my husband, aged 55, my son, aged 13, and I myself, aged 45, went fishing 20 miles from home at Onion Lake—a very remote lake with a gravel pit which is kind of hard to get to because of a poor road. We had a reliable truck, a half-ton, with a camper on back—a 1940 truck. My son was smart, an excellent student, with a winning personality—high IQ and a perfect person.

The sky was clear as we started out at 11:00 p.m., hoping to sleep in the camper and then spend the morning fishing. The sky was clear all the way. We arrived at the spot and we decided to spend the night in the gravel pit. No one else was there—we had the whole lake to ourselves. We were just about to climb into the back camper when we were engulfed in a total, complete darkness and stillness. Not a tree rustled— nothing except a grinding noise that was intermittent. I was scared stiff—I had never had such an experience. There was a strange smell like that of carborundum rubbing on steel—I had never smelled that before or since. Then all of a sudden my son completely disappeared— no sound of him walking away. I called and called and tried to look, and my husband did the same, but everything was so black—couldn't even see any sky at all—just like we were in a bowl of blackness. It seemed like years but I guess it was about 15 minutes—all of a sudden my son appeared as if out of nowhere again—very agitated. He said he had seen a plane, saucer-shaped with red and blue lights, and went over toward it, and doesn't remember anything else. We tried to start the truck and there was no spark—the first time the battery was ever dead in all the ten years we had owned it and there was no reason for it to be dead, because we didn't have a radio, heater or lights on.

But my son was never the same—he had lost his mind!

He has been in a mental hospital ever since and is still there—so ill that even with the mass exodus of patients from mental hospitals during the last year he has to remain. He has a round mark on his left leg near his ankle, about the size of a dime, like a vaccination mark, which came that night and the scar is still there.

My son had all the great potential of being prime minister or some- one great because he was well read, very obedient, very intelligent. Now he's a complete vegetable, unable to speak or hear. My sorrow has been great, as people blame me—I won't go near Onion Lake again.

I feel that you will tell me if you know of anyone else who has had similar sad experiences. I've cried and cried for 23 years. My son is now 36 years old. His whole life is ruined, and mine and my husband's also. I can't tell this story to anyone but you and it's so true. What an expensive fishing trip.

# Alvena's Account

One case of extraterrestrial abduction has come before the British Columbia branch of the Human Rights Commission. This is the case of Alvena Scott, whose own account appears below. Scott's story was initially investigated by Lorne Goldfader, the active founder and director of the Vancouver-based UFO Research Institute of Canada. Through UFORIC, Goldfader has championed the causes of a number of men and women who have, hesitantly at first, boldly later on, come forward with astonishing recollections. These recollections concern contact with extraterrestrial intelligences, and in some instances with abduction by such beings.

Scott's case is one of these. Her social problems began when she "went public." Her abduction story was told by journalist Barbara Tandory in the 27 May 1991 issue of *British Columbia Report*, and this brought it before a wide reading public. Tandory contributed a follow-up story in the issue of 21 October 1991.

What led Scott to the Human Rights Commission was the desire for redress for the loss of her job as a receptionist with one of the country's chartered banks. She maintained that she was "let go" because she "went public" with her story. This is probably the first time the Commission in any province had been asked to investigate a case with a claim that involved extraterrestrial beings in any way!

Through the good offices of Goldfader, I was able to reach Alvena Scott. She kindly agreed to prepare a short written account of her early experiences. The account appears here as she wrote it. In an accompanying letter, dated 15 January 1992, Scott added the following note: "I have only one request, and that is when the following goes public—if anyone approaches you about me, please refer them to Lorne Goldfader first. As we discussed, I'm seeking to help others, and I'm not looking for publicity."

◆ ◆ ◆

In June 1975 I had major kidney surgery on the left side to remove a kidney stone and part of the left kidney. The stone was quite large (the size of the thumbnail) and I couldn't pass it. It caused a lot of damage inside the kidney.

I nearly died from the surgery. Thereby began the first change in me that I'm aware of. I developed psychic abilities, which are quite accurate, and a form of highly developed intuition. In the beginning both powers were quite frightening.

The pain and bleeding of the left kidney continued for the next ten years. Its pain was unbearable at times because of the blackouts and extreme weakness I endured. The right kidney began to go sympathetic. My kidney specialist said (and the words just rolled off his tongue), "The total removal of the left kidney would stop the problem." Easy for him to say! What I said to myself was: "This is my kidney and I'm keeping it for as long as I can!"

During this time period, I began meditating and praying (if you like) for help to remove the pain or for healing of some sort. It became a daily ritual.

I had my answer in the spring of 1985. I can remember it *now* like it happened yesterday.

I was sleeping (I'm not sure how long) and suddenly there was a bright light in my eyes. I awoke and saw three figures in my bedroom. There were two males and one female. They were dressed in white—like a medical team. The female figure communicated by telepathy. "We came in answer to your call."

I was not frightened and not in fear for my life. I knew the beings would be able to help me and that I'd be okay.

The beings told me to lie on my right side. I was told when to take a breath in and to hold it. I was told when to let out a breath and not breathe in. Then they worked on my left kidney area.

When I awoke the next morning, I had no recall of what had

happened. At the time I had no explanation for why there was dried blood on my skin, nightgown, and sheets. For whatever reason, I just let it go. I have a mark on my left side that's inexplicable.

I have no more pain or bleeding from the left kidney. I can stand up straight and I can take a full breath whenever I breathe deeply. And when I'm not lazy, I can exercise with ease.

Thus began the second change in me that I'm aware of.

I have developed a more cosmic understanding of life around me. I have a profound understanding of health care (in a symbolic way), which has never been studied.

For example: The female being telepathically said she was glad I didn't agree to the removal of my kidney. She also added: "Your species is interesting—you 'mess up' where transplants are concerned. We realize doctors are not meaning to. They are trying to help others with damaged bodies, but instead of seeking a way to remove the trauma, they only add to it. Whenever transplants are done on organs like kidneys, hearts, livers, etc., from others—it's like mixing apples and oranges and it creates a mess. The body energies become confused and from an energy point of view, this is what happens when a rejection takes place. If you are an upbeat, happy type of person and you receive an organ from someone who is depressed and angry, there is an almost immediate rejection. If doctors would match the body energy, as well, they would have accomplished something that *will* work."

The instant the female shared this and other information with me, I understood. It really made sense to me!

Late spring of 1986, there was, once again, a being in my bedroom. There was a male speaking to me. He was a hybrid creature, seven feet tall. Telepathically he spoke: "Thank you for being the donor. I wanted to thank you for in part giving me life."

I was shocked and frightened at this, and I really didn't understand what he was saying. He explained, through telepathy and through "picture thought," what had happened to me with the three beings and that they had removed ova or eggs from my body.

Crazy as it sounds, I suddenly understood all this and recalled that the beings were concerned that I didn't have any children and they felt my gentle qualities and abilities were not being passed on. They had sympathy about my kidney problem being so bad and how it had affected my life-force energies. In effect, I was dying on my feet, and doing so slowly.

At this point in time, I'd rather not go into details of my UFO experiences in 1990. It concerns the "Greys" and is too painful to mention right now.

When I met Lorne Goldfader a few years ago, he asked me to come forward with my story. It took a lot of convincing on his part for me to do so. He felt I would be able to assist others to better understand what they had been through and, most importantly, that they are not alone.

An article came out in *B.C. Report* magazine re my UFO experiences. Because of it I was pressured to leave my job. I have approached the Human Rights Commission about this and everything is being looked into. It is an ongoing process, so nothing is finalized yet.

I feel I am now into the third stage of this process. I do not have any anger towards my antagonist in the workplace. I can understand the point of where she is coming from. A more universal understanding of life, if you will.

I'm not sure if this is the first case of its kind being looked into in Canada. But if I win my case, maybe it will be an example for others.

I'm slowly remembering more of what I have experienced and learned from the beings. I am sharing with others in lectures and will share in book form at some point.

I get triggers every now and then, and it flows forward.

Thank you for your time and for listening.

# Alien Imprint

"Alien Imprint" may well be the first poem to be written about the specific subject of alien abduction. The verse—twenty-lines, five-stanzas, regularly rhymed—was composed during the summer of 1992 by Lorne Goldfader. Goldfader is the prime mover of the UFO Research Institute of Canada, a Vancouver-based group that collects and considers reports of sightings, contacts, and abductions.

Goldfader was the subject of a bizarre series of events that culminated in the appearance on his body of UBMs, his term for Unidentified Body Markings. He coined the term in August 1992 to indicate unusual diagrams, symbols, or marks found on the surface skin of abductees. Another term for UBMs might be "dermaglyphs," modelled on "agriglyphs" (better known as crop circles).

Goldfader composed this poem about the experience. In the verse, Estera is the female alien who is in some way connected with the "implant," the anomalous material introduced subcutaneously into his body by alien technology. *Estera*, Hebrew for *star*, is another form of the word *Easter*. *Ra* is Egyptian for *sun*. Jungians may see Estera as Goldfader's *anima* figure; folklorists might describe Estera as the succubus, or the Old Hag, the terror of the night who paralyzes sound sleepers. Whoever or whatever may be the nature of Estera, the sense of presence inspired "Alien Imprint" and continues to haunt Goldfader.

◆ ◆ ◆

*Alien Imprint*

I have been touched by the light of a friend
Who knows every thought from beginning to end.
The purpose of my life on a screen in a room
Unfolds like a scroll inside a cocoon.

The planet below me shivers in cold
Like a ball of clay shaped from a mold.
No life on its surface, no children to play,
No parks or streams, no night or day.

The symbols and warnings in fields were ignored,
The signs in the sky were heeded no more.
An abductee's cries were scorned and mocked
And the Earth begun to quiver and rock.

The scene then shifted to a planet of peace.
No anger existed, all hostilities ceased.
The animals roamed without fear of men
And all species of humans were together again.

The choice is yours, Estera thought,
And into my mind the impression was wrought.
I was lifted back into my room
And left with the choice of survival or doom.

# Alien Perspective

"Belief is the bridge between where we are and where we wish to be."
I like that quotation and feel it defines the essential nature of belief.
Someone told me it originated with Norman Head, a Torontonian who
has experienced alien encounters.

I met Norman Head at the Metropolitan Toronto Reference Library
in 1992. We were attending a seminar that featured UFO abductee
Betty Stewart. We talked briefly about contactees and abductees. Some

months later he kindly sent me a personal letter, along with a chapter from his memoir (titled, curiously, *The Mole Experiment*).

Both the letter and the memoir are interesting in a variety of ways, so I am reproducing both of them here.

◆ ◆ ◆

Dec. 29/92

Dear Mr. Colombo:

I am quite happy to have you use whatever you wish from my material. I will be happy to rewrite a passage specifically for you if you wish, or you are free to use the one you chose as long as that will still permit me to use it at a later date. My main concern here is to facilitate the release of pertinent information.

I am much more comfortable writing magazine-length articles than the type of ms you have read. The quote you have asked to reproduce if my memory serves me well may already have appeared in a couple of places. Back when I was a Quaker I was published at least seven or eight times by their various journals and newsletters. It would have been years ago, and I doubt anyone but me would remember now. In fact I'm not even sure that that line ever made it into print.

Biography: I'm a 44-year-old high-school teacher. I have a lifelong interest in things of a spiritual nature and am a participant in whatever athletic endeavour I can get into. I currently teach photography and drafting. I also enjoy canoeing, camping and travelling.

My memory of past events has come a lot more clear in the past little while. My current focus seems to me on past-life information as it pertains to this life, perhaps not as much of interest, especially since it is not directly related to UFO experiences, or at least more likely to be written off as an overactive imagination. I have memories of being a fighter pilot, flying UFOs. When I finally got through the last block in my "abduction experience," it turned out that I knew many of the persons who abducted me on a first-name basis, including the person I called Ali in the book. I, at one point, wrote out a dialogue that was more like a B-movie script than a personal account of someone who is supposed to be terrified. Over the course of the summer it was suggested that I might like my old ship back once I get off this planet. I don't know if that counts as something to live for (more like something to die for).

I was part of a sort of intergalactic hit team. They attack and destroy errant civilizations which through abuse of space travel or nuclear power threaten other civilizations and dimensions. (Our current situation here may in fact become one of those situations. My reason for being here is to give me an understanding of the group psychopathology that leads to such a situation, in hopes of curing some pacifist tendencies I was developing.) I have joined this team in the past from at least eight or nine different places and races. I would have done the same from this planet except that you can't get there from here. I also have a much greater understanding of the nature and propulsion systems, armaments and offensive capabilities of these craft. So much so that I do not wish to make it known to anyone how much or little I know. Not that it would do them any good. The way these machines work is not at all like driving a car. Most people would not be safe attempting to fly one. One errant thought at the wrong time can mean the loss of a craft and crew. It's not for the faint of heart.

In fact, it is possible that I will be back in space before the end of this lifetime. They are keeping me current. The drawback for them is that people here have such a short lifespan. A good pilot from most star systems can fly 300 years after 10–15 years of training. I would have to remember everything. That is next to impossible (even though I haven't been gone long). And I'd only be of any use to them for another 10–15 years anyway. Hardly worth the effort. Besides, technically it's not allowed, and they've never bent that rule before. They'd always have to worry that some of the suicidal tendencies of the population of this planet may have rubbed off on me. On the positive side, it would be good for me to get back into action. Life here is incredibly slow-paced. I really feel like I've been banished to the far end of the galaxy. (Which is not far from the truth by the way.) It would be good therapy just to go along on a couple missions as an observer (especially if they come here)...I can always dream. It's more likely that they'll just continue to visit, keep me informed about current concerns and missions (believe me this little planet is a mild annoyance that won't mean more than the blink of an eye if action is necessary), not to mention the important stuff, like who's sleeping with whom. In some ways they are not so different from us. God, I miss them sometimes.

I will be happy to share whatever I can of the basic stuff with whomever wishes to know about it, but it would appear right now that the new stuff that is coming to me is information I cannot share with any of the general population of this planet. The information coming to me now would probably be misinterpreted in the worst possible way even if it was to be believed.

At present it appears that in terms of information I may wish to reveal that what you've read is about it. No sequel.

So good luck in the future, especially with your personal accounts book. I am myself indebted to this type of book in my own awakening, and can only hope to return this favour. At this point I still feel like I have a few cobwebs. This is what recovering from amnesia must be like.

Yours in peace,
Norman Head


*The Mole Experiment*

*Chapter 2: How I Became Aware of My Contact with Aliens*

After fifteen years of life together, my wife came home one day and announced it was time to end our marriage. Over the next three months, as I began to adjust to my new living situation, I began to become aware of my contact with non–*Homo sapiens* humans. I read *The Interrupted Journey* by John G. Fuller. I began to explore my own memories.

That was over four years ago. But I remember reasonably clearly how it happened. I remember reading a passage in the book where a visitor requests an abductee to have intercourse with him. At that point my mind flashed, and suddenly I was seeing the inside of the spacecraft, just as described in the book. Only I saw details that aren't in the text. Having worked as a cabinet-maker, I am particularly drawn to the interior features. Counters, drawers, etc., hardware, so much so that though I am aware that I had a sexual experience with a person in this place, I can't remember what she looked like. But the interior of the room I was in, that is my first hint that I had been in a same or similar place. When I first saw the cover of *Communion* I became sexually aroused. This was my first clue as to what she might have looked like.

During this time I came into telepathic contact with a being I refer to as Ali (short for alien) because I cannot pronounce her name as she would say it. She told me it is she who was my mate. She told me that I have two children from this encounter. One conceived at the time I was aboard the space craft and one conceived through artificial insemination a few years later. I find this mildly amusing because I always told my first wife that I had a wife and two kids before we were married. I said it all the time. It was a standing joke. One day she asked me why I thought it was funny and I couldn't answer. I wanted to say, "Because it's true," but I couldn't at that time remember.

Later in a dream I had a vision of a friend of mine who lives in the Rocky Mountains. Her name is Mary. In the vision I saw her as a solitary figure, sort of floating in space. She was dressed in green, the colour of healing. She asked me when I was coming and suggested that I come soon. After this vision, which left me wide awake at 4:30 in the morning, Ali suggested that if I would visit Mary she would arrange to let me meet my half-alien children. So I wrote to this person, who was a childhood friend, and whom I had not seen or contacted in over eighty years, and arranged for a visit.

I had a very good visit, which turned out to be beneficial to both of us. At one point I went to the garden to get some carrots for dinner. On the way back, as promised, I heard a repetitive electronic beep from up the mountainside. I started towards it, carrots and all, and got about two steps. My stomach knotted, and an image came back to me of myself being carried on some kind of stretcher by little blue men, and I became intensely frightened. I called via telepathy, "Ali, I don't want to see any little blue men." The answer I got was that there were some present. I responded that I wasn't ready for that. And I immediately felt sympathy and understanding being directed at me. It was almost as though they knew I would not be able to come. They just wanted to help me unlock the memories. The way they work, it almost seems to come from inside. Later I told my son (who has memories of a "dream" about a little blue doctor with a light wand) about this incident. I suggested he might like to go out and look around with me. He suggested that I might be nuts and we spent the rest of the evening indoors.

At times I suspected that they have affected my relationships with others. One of the last times I was together with my first wife, I felt myself accelerate in vibration. And it was like seeing her for the first time. She was by now hopelessly in love with another man and had not been eating properly for about two weeks because of the tension of the situation. I noticed that I could see all her ribs and that her breasts were smaller than usual. I commented on her small breast size. This had an immediate effect on her that I had not intended. (Make note, all males: Never tell your wife her breasts are small.) I felt after as if I had been manipulated, that someone else had spoken through me. So after establishing contact with Ali, I asked her about it. Her response to this situation is as follows:

"You were caught in an unacceptable situation. Your ex-wife craves what she considers to be a 'normal' situation. As you were becoming more and more aware of us, she was becoming more and more determined to escape from you. There were other incidents where we altered your thinking to the point where you said things that were more honest than you could have been on your own. They were not things that helped you, but things that clarified the situation for her. So in essence, while nothing had changed for you, you were expressing your deeper self. And that clarified for her some of the things she really disliked about you. We did not cause the breakup of your marriage, but we saw it coming before you did and moved to ensure that it happened quickly, completely and to the mutual benefit of both parties."

It is possible for me to allow this type of thinking to happen because I sometimes intuitively understand the interconnectedness of all things. Science is into specialization. I am more into general consciousness. Science claims that my consciousness is a function of my physical body. I claim that my consciousness is a function of all consciousness. A tree cannot speak for itself, but sometimes I can express in human terms what it would like to convey. Consciousness is everywhere and in everything. To hold a conversation with Ali all I need to do is to hold her image, her vibration, in my consciousness. We interact vibrationally and I then try to express as best I can what she says. But there is another catch, there has to be a real need. I cannot call up like talking on the phone, just to find out more about her. I already know everything I need to know about her. And if I don't know more, it is because I don't need to.

I have been promised that at some point in my life I will live in a mountainous area, or at least have a summer home there. In this mutually acceptable environment she will be able to visit with me in flesh. But there is much water to go under the bridge before that time. That doesn't mean she isn't a part of my life. For many of us the most important parts of our life are never seen or heard. Monks, mystics, hermits and saints, the most important aspects of their lives are unseen and un-detectable. To understand the visitors you must become saints. (I love making pronouncements like this. The trouble is, they need so much clarification. This one must be left for later.)

# Other Weird Experiences

A couple of weeks after I talked about UFOs with Bill Carroll on Q-107's popular *Barometer* phone-in show, I received a late-night call from Larry Drummond. (The name is a pseudonym.) Larry proceeded to relate in a moving manner an account of the weird experiences that have happened to him over the years. I encouraged him to write an account of these and send it to me. As it happened, he had already written down some of his UFO-related experiences. Anyway, he sent me this account of his unusual experiences. I received it on 4 December 1991.

Here is Larry's letter in a minimally edited form. There are references in it to Budd Hopkins and Whitley Strieber. Hopkins is the New York–based author of *Missing Time* (1981) and the founder of the Intruders Foundation. Strieber is the noted horror-story author who shot to fame with his best-selling memoir *Communion: A True Story* (1989).

◆ ◆ ◆

Dear Mr. Colombo:

I'm the person who phoned you a week ago. My name is Lloyd, and I live in downtown Toronto. I'm 42 years old right now.

I'll start my story in the middle because this is the beginning of my belief that I may possibly be involved with UFOs and even abductions.

As I explained, I wrote a letter to Bud Hopkins that was not answered, and I still have the rough draft. I'm glad I kept it because I hadn't read it since it was written, and there are a lot of details about this incident that I'd forgotten about.

So here it is.

The date was Friday, July 7, '89. It happened at a campground near Alliston, Ont. It is very close to Bond Head, if that rings a bell.

Anyway, we were up there (my wife and I), with my son and his wife, and my wife's sister and her husband. We had had a campfire that broke up at approx. 1:00 a.m. It had been very hot, so my wife and I went for a drive with my son and his wife. The others went to bed. We returned at 2:31 a.m. I know this because my son asked the time as he dropped us off.

We then went inside, and my son went across the river to his trailer. My wife and I talked for approx. 20 minutes. We then decided to go to bed. We went outside to go to the bathroom. We had just moved to a different lot and had not hooked up the toilet yet. So it was outdoors.

Anyway, I stopped out the door to the edge of the deck with my wife behind me. Instantly my wife was beside me, saying, "Look at that light."

Now this was really strange because she had followed me out and gone to the opposite end of the trailer. She didn't even have time to walk back to my position, yet here she was beside me.

I asked her if she had already gone to the bathroom and she said, "Yes, yes. Look at that light. It's moving."

I looked up and saw nothing. She kept saying it was moving, and then she said it had a halo. Then she said it stopped for a short time and then continued on. The time lapse was about two minutes before disappearing. I saw nothing during this time, and none of the stars had a halo. It was a very clear night.

We watched the sky for a few minutes and went back inside.

I've read a million books on the subject of UFOs, so I asked my wife some questions. I've got this all written down, but I'll shorten it to what she saw and felt. Here are her replies:

—She doesn't know why she looked up.
—It went in a straight line.
—It had a halo and was white like the stars.

—It had no coloured lights.
—It definitely stopped.

Now, I looked at the clock. 4:35 a.m. No way had we been back for two hours. It hit me hard, to say the least. We were having a "missing time" episode. I asked my wife more questions. Again her replies:

—We've been back less than one hour.
—She didn't see it on the ground.
—It didn't go from big to small (as in taking off from a short distance).
—She just saw it up in the sky.
—It was bigger than a star while moving, but the same size as a star while stopped.
—It moved very fast.

Her answer to the next question knocked me out.I asked her what she thought about it.

She said, "It was beautiful, really beautiful. I wish it would come back. It was really neat."

On a clear night my son and I watch for satellites and usually see four or five. I pointed one out to my wife weeks later, and she said the UFO moved a great deal faster. She asked me if they ever stop, and that sort of put a lid on it.

The next day my son asked me a question, and it was a beauty. Did I hear the noises last night? What noises? Apparently all the dogs in the park were barking, and the cows in the field next to us were making noises like they were being chased. We didn't hear anything. He looked out the window but not one faced us. He said all this started about 20 minutes after dropping us off. I asked my sister-in-law if they had heard any disturbances, and they had but they didn't know what time they occurred. Nobody remembered how long the noise lasted. We had three dogs within 100 feet of us and the cows are within 200 yards of our trailer. We heard nothing.

The next day I had stomach cramps and felt like I had the flu. My wife was full of energy. I've had these symptoms since and can relate them to at least one strange incident. I woke up feeling this way one morning, and while we were driving to work, my wife told me she was lying in bed and something touched her right in the middle of her forehead and put her to sleep. I don't remember anything happening.

I also had my first migraine aura on the Monday following the trailer thing.

The scariest thing that ever happened to me was in the early '80s. I woke up in the middle of the night and saw three beings standing beside my bed. I was fully awake but didn't believe my eyes and put my head back in the pillow. I knew I wasn't seeing things and looked up again. They were still there. I buried my head in the pillow in terror. I then got an electric shock from the base of my spine to the top of my head and I guess I blacked out. I remember nothing after this.

Back in the '70s, we lived in the house at 664 Woodbine Ave., attached to the house at 666 Woodbine. I just thought I'd mention that, since someone brought it to my attention years later. Anyway, we had the top floor and my brother-in-law and his wife lived downstairs. We used to get very loud pounding noises at the foot of the bed almost every night. Nobody downstairs ever heard this.

One night some friends stayed over downstairs. I asked them what they heard the night before. The girl said she heard little feet running back and forth all night. She thought it was mice. We had none. This ties in for me because I read this same statement in W. Strieber's book.

Also in Budd Hopkins' book I read about scars. I didn't look for any for a long time because I didn't think I had any that I didn't know about. But when I did look, there was one on my hip. It looks like a vaccination mark but isn't.

Late this summer my wife and I were sitting on our balcony on the 11th floor. I turned around opposite to the way I was facing and saw what I thought was a plane with its landing lights on (two of them). (My wife saw only one white light and it was not flashing.) It looked stationary. Suddenly the two white lights started flashing alternately like those on a school bus do. I don't know why, but I started saying, "Come here, come here." And it did come closer. Then it left, moving north at a slow speed. Those lights always faced me, so if it was a plane it was moving sideways. Later my wife said it had come from the north, which is the way it retreated. It was noiseless. This is not the first odd-ball thing to cruise over our building.

I'll relate some of my UFO dreams to you. They seem to be the only kind I remember. The first one is really strange. Not the dream but what I did after. It's also the first of them.

I was dreaming of formations of UFOs (lights), hundreds of them. All kinds of formations. I woke up scared, with my heart pounding. I sat up on the edge of the bed and said to myself, "What am I scared of? I see UFOs all the time." Then I went back to sleep. This occurred in the early '80s, but I certainly did not see them all the time.

The next one I remember was with me standing on my balcony naked watching a saucer cruising down my street about four floors below me. It had coloured lights around it and beams of white light shining down to the ground.

Another dream was hiding from a helicopter that was landing in my brother-in-law's backyard up north. I was with two or three other people and we knew it was no heli.

I've had two other dreams while at that house up north. One was that lots of little people were running around the house trying to steal my wallet. Another was sitting on the front porch watching a beautiful neon butterfly flutter around. Suddenly it swooped down over my head and I ran screaming into the house yelling, "They're here." In yet another one, saucers were flashing lights onto clouds and spelling words, but I don't remember what they said.

When I was a kid, I had two recurring dreams that may be related. In one, I was trying to run away from something that scared me. But I was hampered by some kind of unseen force. Just like trying to run in a swimming pool. I always woke up soon after it started. I never knew what I was running from.

The second one involved me running along a wood fence. As I was running, a loud noise on the other side was following me. The noise was not on the ground but above me, and it really scared me. The problem here was that as I started running, the fence was very high. The farther I ran, the shorter the fence got. I knew that if I kept running, the fence would become so short that I would be exposed to whatever was on the other side. This was the last thing I wanted to happen, but, I couldn't stop. I always woke up in a panic before that happened.

I could probably come up with some more things, but this should do for now. I've had other weird experiences but do not connect them with UFOs.

The UFO that passed over my building with its lights flashing made me wonder how many people could see this. Was it meant for many or just for me? Seems like a lot of work to go through this display for just one person.

I think that's about it for now. Please excuse the poor grammar and horrible spelling, but I'm no writer. Thank you for your time and concern. And thank you for letting me get this off my chest to someone in the know who actually talks back.

You asked me for a pseudonym and I'll give you one. Please do not print or discuss my real name or other personal info such as phone no. or address with anyone. The rest of it is all yours to do with as you wish.

I figure the more info put out there the better chance we have of understanding it. Maybe even the answer.

Thank you very much,

Larry Drummond

# My Personal Search

Stephanie Smith is the pen name of a sensitive young woman who lives in Toronto. At my request she typed out from her journal accounts of two highly unusual and possibly related experiences. The experiences occurred in the year 1989, and they led her to the conclusion that for no known reason she had been singled out by an alien intelligence and that she was chosen to be the victim of an intrusion or an abduction of some sort. These two accounts are reproduced from the letter that she sent to me on 21 October 1990.

◆ ◆ ◆

There are two separate accounts that I have decided to submit to you. I will leave it up to you to decide which one (or both) you would like to use. Both of these experiences were very powerful and forced me to re-evaluate my beliefs.

The first experience occurred in Arizona last year. I went to Arizona for four weeks with three other women. We camped the entire time, and all of us had some very powerful experiences.

The second experience occurred in Toronto while I was at home. Of all the experiences I have had, this one was the most profound. It started me on my personal search into the UFO experience.

1.

I spent the month of August 1989 camping and hiking through Colorado, Arizona, and New Mexico with three other women. On August 16th, Trudy (not her real name) and I decided to hike into Boynton Canyon. Sally and Cathy (not their real names) were tired from all the hiking we had been doing and had decided to remain at our campsite to relax.

Trudy and I left early in the day with the intent of returning before the heat of the day. Armed with canteens of water and various energy foods, we started our trek into the canyon. It was a beautiful day—hot and sunny. We felt compelled to continue hiking deeper and deeper into the canyon. We ended up walking for a couple of hours and climbing way up the canyon wall.

It was beautiful. There was no one else around, yet both of us had this feeling of expectancy. We mentioned to each other that there seemed to be something for us to see or do before we began our trek back to the campsite. Finally we found a spot to sit. Quietly we sat and enjoyed the feeling of being alone in nature—silent and peaceful. We were hot and tired after our hike, and we were engrossed in our own thoughts.

It was about 12:30 p.m. I was sitting on a rocky ledge jutting out from the canyon wall. All of a sudden I got this sensation of flying over the cliffs. I could actually feel the sensation in my stomach, as if I were on a roller-coaster ride at a fair. I placed my hands and feet firmly on the rocks to ground myself.

We continued to sit there, Trudy and I, when all of a sudden I saw this large, round spaceship coming into the canyon right in front of us. I turned to look at Trudy, as she turned to look at me. Neither of us said a word. I didn't say anything to her, as I thought I must been imagining this—it couldn't be real. (Later she confessed to me that she was thinking the same thing.)

I turned back to look and it was still there. It slowly came down in front of us. The UFO continued down into the canyon and then must have landed. From our spot halfway up the canyon wall, we lost sight of it as it landed. We could, however, still see the light that was emitting from it.

As this was happening, the temperature around us felt as if it had dropped about ten degrees. The day was hot, in the nineties, yet when the UFO was landing, there was a slight breeze, and the air felt quite cool. I kept looking at the light and thinking it would disappear at any moment. I had a queasy feeling in the pit of my stomach and my heart was pounding.

Finally, I turned to Trudy and asked her if she could see the UFO. She turned to me and showed me a sketch of it that she had drawn in her journal. (Throughout this whole trip we all kept journals.) The UFO was round and very large. It had flashing lights all around it and it emitted an eerie glow.

At 1:30 p.m., it was still there, in the canyon below. I had two exposures left in my camera. I took pictures from the ledge where we were sitting—pictures of the soft glow around the UFO. I did not expect these pictures to turn out. By 1:45 p.m., we finally accepted the reality of what we were seeing. I kept looking, expecting it to be gone—as if I had never seen it to begin with. I can't describe the things that went through my head during that hour of watching.

Trudy wanted to hike down into the canyon where they had landed. However, it would have taken at least one hour to get down, so we decided against it. Anyway, I did not have a good feeling about hiking down there. When we left, the UFO was still there.

I've always believed that we are not the only life forms in this vast universe. However, even though I hold this belief, I was still not prepared for the actual experience of seeing a UFO.

(Note: The pictures turned out—I have them at home.)


2.


This encounter happened to me on the eve of November 3, 1989.

The only thing that sticks out in my mind before going to bed is that I double-checked the doors and windows of my apartment. I had an eerie feeling, and I remember thinking that it was silly to feel this way.

I could not sleep and tossed and turned for the first part of the night. Finally I decided to get up and read. I read for a while, watched TV, and read some more. About 2:00 a.m., I put my book down to see once again if I could fall asleep.

I had hardly put down my book when I felt a wave of energy starting in my feet and moving slowly up my legs. It felt very heavy and I thought to myself that it felt like anaesthesia or maybe some kind of paralysis. This feeling continued up my legs and up my body. As it passed a certain region, I could no longer move.

I felt as if I was beginning to slip into unconsciousness and I became terrified. I felt as if I was losing control and I became groggy. I closed my eyes—feeling as if I was being drugged. At this point I could not move or feel my body from the neck down. The feeling moved into my head, and I began to slip into nothingness. I fought this feeling—fought to stay alert. It is difficult to explain. I kept trying to feel my body and to keep my thoughts clear. It was becoming more and more difficult even to think at all.

I opened my eyes and I found I was looking directly into flashing, pulsating lights above me. Some of these lights were pulsating at different speeds. They seemed so close to me that I felt as though I could reach up and touch them, had I been able to move my body. I thought of a tractor beam. I tried to speak—to call for help. I was paralyzed. I kept fighting for control of my senses.

I saw these beings leaning over me and looking at me. The lights above were highlighting them, and they looked like light themselves. They had huge, dark eyes and they seemed to be quite thin. I closed my eyes again and continued to fight for control of my thoughts. Mentally, with great discipline, I forced the thought, "I am in control," over and over again.

In the background I heard a voice say, "She came out too early... this one is a strong one..." I continued to concentrate all my efforts on the one single thought: "I am in control." At first the words were very difficult to think. The full sentence came slowly, word by word. At the time it felt like hours were passing, but I'm sure it was only seconds. I don't remember how many times I repeated that sentence, but I could feel myself regaining control.

The next thing I remember is my body hitting the bed as if being dropped from above. I bounced in my bed, jarring my body. I opened my eyes and saw the familiar room around me. I was panting and wheezing, my body was tingling, and my mouth was extremely dry.

There was and is no question in my mind—this was not a dream. The terror that was felt was like no other terror that I had ever before experienced in my life.

It was a deep, deep feeling of fear, yet I do not feel these beings are out to do us any harm. Anyway, the experience made a profound difference in my life.

In the process of writing out these incidents from the entries in my journal, I experienced many emotions and thoughts that I have hidden away. I feel I have come to terms with more of my experiences than I did before, when these encounters were new to me. As well, I feel I have a better understanding of some other events in my life.

I want to thank you for giving me the incentive to dig back and face it all.

# UFO Mind Transplant

Winifred G. Barton attracted newspaper headlines in the 1960s and 1970s when she travelled across the country conducting metaphysical workshops and collecting accounts of paranormal events and experiences. She edited a collection of these "extraordinary experiences" called *Psychic Phenomena in Canada* (1967). The appearance of her book predated the well-heralded advent of the so-called New Age; newspaper editors had not yet turned their editorial attention to mystical, spiritual, and metaphysical adventures.

Mrs. Barton dropped out of the headlines, and many people assumed she had left for greener pastures or gone beyond the veil or passed into the great beyond or entered into a nunnery of some sort or other. But the writer Michael Poulton discovered her—through a classified advertisement in the "National Personals" of *The Globe and Mail*!

It turns out that what happened to Mrs. Barton is much more exciting than any of the statements above. It seems that she had a "close encounter" with alien intelligences and that she was abducted by alien beings and taken aboard one of their star ships. As she explained in a letter to the present editor, dated 25 April 1991: "I was abducted on September 26, 1973, and was taken "through the mirror." The next 17 years were spent in getting an intensive education. I was caught between dimensions, locked into a scenario over which I had no control. My psyche alternated between experiencing the heights of heaven and the depths of hell. It was like dying. Only now that I am fully "processed" as Biological Mutant can I come back to tell about it."

At one time Mrs. Barton ran the Institute of Applied Metaphysics (I AM). Generally addressed as Dr. Barton, she currently lives near Frankford, Ontario, where she serves as public-relations officer for the Golden Triangle UFO Club for Ontario.

◆ ◆ ◆

*I Had a Mind Transplant on a UFO*

Against my will, and without any anaesthetic, I had a mind reversal on a UFO. It happened during and in the period following an abduction on the evening of September 26, 1973, at the Lester B. Pearson Peace Park, at Actinolite, Ontario.

It had been a glorious autumn day. I was with a group of friends who had gathered from many parts of Canada and the U.S.A. to enjoy the end of the summer season. We were using the old Madoc Art School, which sits at the foot of the hill next to the Peace Park.

The Peace Pagoda was a favourite place for our evening meetings, but on this particular night a sudden heavy mist seemed to envelop the area. The mist did not seem like a normal mist; it seemed to have a silvery glow as if there was a light behind it. I went to investigate, and as I walked up the hill, pieces of the mist seemed to break away from the mass and coagulate into the forms of beings.

Nothing touched me, but I felt a powerful magnetic attraction to continue towards the central glow. As I got closer I saw in it the outline of a Starship. I could hear some of my friends calling out to one another as they too were drawn towards the celestial car.

My will to resist was completely paralyzed. The hatch was down and I went into the foyer, where I vaguely saw some of my friends being led to different rooms or parts of the ship. I was taken to a large circular room—a translucent aqua colour—with two transparent doors set approximately opposite each other. Through these I could see that there was an outer walkway which seemed to go right around the room. I could see a woman sitting at a communications desk through one of these windows.

In the beginning I was alone in the room. I felt no sense of fear, only curiosity. There was a large circular, lazy-Susan-type table in the centre of the room with chairs around it. I sat on one of these. There was a bowl of fruit—small berry-type fruit on the table. I was tempted to eat some but decided it was best not to.

A man came into the room from the opposite door to where the woman was sitting. (I guessed she was keeping an eye on me through the door.) The man barely glanced in my direction but walked straight across the room to what seemed like a circular shower stall, where he dropped off his dirty overalls and stepped into the stall, which lit up. He emerged a few moments later and put on clean clothes.

Books I have written clearly record how since infancy I was trained in telepathic communication. So though no words were spoken, I had no difficulty in communicating with this Space Being. He offered some of the fruit. This time I took it and ate. It was like mango.

I could sense this man was trying to override my free will. At first I firmly resisted. Then they changed my electromagnetic circuit from

Alternating to Direct Current. I emerged as a circuit in a *Gigantic Robot* known as "Hal." I was wide awake but completely paralyzed during the proceedings. There were about thirty other persons besides me.

Now everything looked transparent. Form and finity was meaningless. It was as if my bony skull was replaced and my head put into a glass bubble. As a circuit in this *Giant Robot* I was powerless to escape over a fifteen-year period. If I struggled they prodded my neurons here and there with electrical sticks...

When I returned, just before noon on the morning of September 27th, 1973, I was no longer "Winifred." I was "Sasoleah," a citizen of Sumeria who had reincarnated in the 20th century through my physical instrument.

The same thing had happened to at least twenty of the other abductees. All had undergone some sort of a transmutation technique and mind transplant. All were trapped in the world of Robotics. Each had been given a silent mission. Each brain had been joined to an ancient personality. Each one was under total mind control and forced to keep the intruding ancient soul a secret.

Over the next decade the abductees got to talking about their "inductees" and how we found that "aliens" were actually ancient peoples who had completed a Universal cycle and were coming back to claim the modern world. They had left overwhelming mounds of evidence to prove this point... "That the sower and the reaper may rejoice together in the New Heaven and the New Earth on the completion of the life cycle Genesis I—from chaos to cosmos via Robotics."

One of my fellow abductees was a man from Ottawa named Marcel Lafleur, whom I had known for some years. After the operation we watched the whole scenery around us being torn down like a ragged canvas. The colours behind the canvas were brilliant. We understood that it is only the light energy of the real world shining through the web of matter that makes the holograph on our mirror world of the illusion tick.

Lafleur drove me home. We were both in a state approaching incoherence. He drove into the driveway of my home at 3045 Otterson

Drive, in Ottawa, but I did not recognize the house. When I got in the house, I felt exactly like a stranger walking in for the first time. I could feel Sasoleah tapping Winifred's computer to find her way around. Sa was in total domination at this time.

About now I realized something else. "I" was neither of these two. I was an observer watching two actors using my mind. I watched them interacting, arguing points of logic, as they began to make a harmonic convergence in my mind. I understood the principle of the left- and right-hand sides of the brain being kept in perfect balance. One living in the finite now, the other accessing infinity. One bent on "rendering unto Caesar that which is Caesar's," the other committed to "and to God that which is God's."

But I am neither... *I AM*... My Divine Will is the Umpire between the two. I have watched Sasoleah writing "*I Am, The Book of Life*, using Winifred's professional skills. I look in one direction and see that Winifred has been held like a bond slave to serve the cause of Sasoleah and the Space People for eighteen years. In return, Winifred has been in an advanced interdimensional classroom wherein she received the full and complete knowledge of the Gods.

Winifred mostly ruled the daytime consciousness (Hadit). Sasoleah could flit all over the Universe at will and usually took over when the sun went down (Nuit). Sasoleah could work miracles with ease. For example, some fellow abductees took us on a fully paid, two-week trip to Egypt to celebrate the Equinox of the Gods. I knew nothing whatsoever about these people, nor they of me. That's what their instructions were and that's what they did. That's how the "COSMIC WAY COMMUNITY" operates. It's called spiritual humility.

Today the three of us are one. The actor and the observer function as an integrated unit. In physics this reads $( + 1 ) + ( - 1 ) = 0$ or $E = mc^3$— all of which is detailed with extensive diagrams in the *Cosmic Cube*.

Today, if I speak a word that is not the Triple Truth, I feel a tremendous weight on my heart and mind. I get rewarded with an inrush of light energy when I please "The Master's Will."

On the lowest end of the dimensional scale in some ways I am no more than a meticulously accurate translation device though my human emotions are still locked deep inside me. There are many more of us who have been stripped of our flesh-and-blood kinship connections and locked into the ETI system of the "Mighty Ones" which makes us "Walk-ins" or "Superbeings." It means we have 20/20 vision of the reality both above and below the abyss.

Earth Governments have maintained silence about this matter, though they knew full well what was going on. They agreed to let us be used in a potentially diabolical experiment in return for hi-tech data. However, the "Time Bomb" is about to explode and the story is due to climax in a wonderful state of Millennium for the whole Earth Starship as She slips out of the time warp to regain her rightful place in the Cosmic Fleet.

Yes, there is a Cosmic Conspiracy—yes, there has been a deliberate conspiracy of silence on the part of global governments everywhere. Yes, there is a flip to Millennium. Yes, there is a Cosmic Changeover for the whole earth system. Yes, the ultimate outcome is GOOD!

# Joyce's Story

The author of this memoir is Joyce Aldrich-Halfin, who is a singer-songwriter and lives in Toronto. She responded to my invitation to prepare a first-person account of her experiences as an abductee for my book *UFOs over Canada,* which appeared in 1991. In this account, which was written the first week of December 1990, when she lived in Bradford, Ontario, Halfin refers in passing to two important people. The first is a Toronto family physician and psychotherapist with an interest in the abduction scenario, with respect to understanding patients who present symptoms of distress that may or may not be connected with the UFO phenomenon and alien abduction. At the time of writing he was a director of the Intruders Foundation established by Budd Hopkins in New York City. The second person mentioned is Betty Stewart, a friend and neighbour, who appeared on radio and television, notably on CBC-TV's *Man Alive*, to recount her own experiences as an abductee.

◆ ◆ ◆

I came to the doctor through a dear friend of mine, Betty Stewart, who is a UFOlogist and contactee herself. She directed me to the safety of his office after I had a traumatic encounter with—no, not aliens—but with a local UFO research group masquerading as a support group. Members of this group were obviously looking for the "smoking gun," and after my experience with them, I wanted to shoot them with it.

They left me feeling two inches high, causing me to doubt everything I believed in, including my psychic abilities. Needless to say, my self-esteem was badly shaken. To add insult to injury, a reliable source told me the support group had called me a "flake" and a "psychiatric case" because I dressed colourfully, had a fixation on anything Egyptian, which was evident in some of my artwork, and had fifteen years of psychotherapy behind me. (This "support group" was made up of three psychics who chase down UFO sightings. Nothing like being called a "flake" by your peers!)

They hadn't discounted my stories of alien contact, but had I been an average housewife, perhaps I would have been taken more seriously and been offered some real help. Fortunately, the doctor was able to assure me that I wasn't crazy or living on the edge of the lunatic fringe and that what I had experienced was real. Whew!

My first experience occurred at the age of six. We lived on Eastern Drive in a suburb of Ottawa called Alta Vista, right behind the Rockcliffe Airforce Base. It was 1961. One night, as I lay in bed in my room on the first floor of one of the row houses in which we lived, I remember feeling I was being watched.

My mother often told me stories about the gremlins who had sabotaged aircraft during the Second World War. She said that the green runway lights, which I could see from my bedroom window, were gremlins. Well, what I saw that night certainly weren't gremlins. I called them spacemen.

They were looking in at me through the window. I remember feeling afraid. The next thing I knew, I was hovering above the housing complex, looking down on a brightly lit area. I could see two or three of them looking into a different window.

That was all I could remember, and I was haunted by this dream-like memory for years. During the hypnotherapy conducted by the doctor, the rest of the "dream" fitted in.

The spacemen, who I thought were wearing large helmets with visors, ended up having large, egg-shaped heads and large, insect-like eyes. They came through the wall of my room, and one of them picked me up. We then floated up to the ceiling, passed through it and through the roof, where I remember looking down at the brightly lit area.

When I looked up, I saw a large, circular craft ringed with two sets of lights. The outer set of lights was white in colour, with intermittently flashing red, yellow, and blue lights. The centre ring was just white.

We rose to the centre area of the craft and a portal opened into a bay area. There were other beings standing there, wearing different apparel, who were slightly taller than my companions, who were only four to five feet in height.

I was taken to what, at first, looked like an elevator. A door opened, and we entered a very dark room. I could still see the "aliens." They moved with the precise, graceful movements of a praying mantis, deftly moving their large heads on delicate necks.

They knew I was observing them and said that their eyes worked much like those of our earthbound insects, except that they were also able to do in-depth analysis with their eyes. Where we see only the surface of things, they can see cellular structures and beyond.

After this telepathic exchange ended, a large oval door opened onto a room with a central walkway. Three or four more beings were waiting for me behind what looked like a hospital gurney, where I was placed.

I was told that they were going to check my eyes. First, they put a dark cloth over them and playfully lifted it off one eye and then the other. Then they took an instrument to retract my lids so they could have a closer look. A large machine, which resembled an x-ray machine, was held over my eyes. There were two long tubes attached to it, and the "aliens" said they were going to try to feed information into my eyes to see how much could be implanted into my brain.

Soon after the procedure began, I got a terrible headache and asked them to stop. They did. I was ushered to a small stool to sit for a while. They soon brought me back to my bedroom the same way I had left it.

I'm sure I've had other encounters in the meantime, but the next major occurrence didn't happen until June 29, 1989. That night I was extremely restless and anxious. I asked my husband to give me some time alone in our bedroom so I could listen to a meditation tape to help me fall asleep.

He was too tired to wait for me to go to sleep, so he decided to sleep that night on the couch in the living room. I finally managed to fall asleep, only to wake up at 3:39 a.m. I noted the precise time on the clock because I had the feeling that something unusual was going to happen.

Feeling pretty jittery, I lay down again and said, "Dear God and guru, please lay the hand of healing on me." Within a second or two, I felt a strange buzzing in my head, and then a paralysis travelled down my body until I was completely immobile. I tried to look behind me, but it felt as if someone was pushing my head into the pillow. I tried to cry out but was unable to.

The next thing I knew, it was five in the morning. I jumped out of bed and flew down the stairs to the living room, where my husband was sleeping. Clinging to him for at least fifteen minutes, I kept repeating over and over again, "You'll never believe what happened to me." Then I resolved to call my poor friend, Betty Stewart, who said I could call her any time of the day or night. I'll tell you, though, it took every ounce of courage I had to pry myself away from my husband's side to walk the few feet into the kitchen to make the call.

The odd thing is, a few nights before, I had been asleep and had felt compelled to open my eyes. In this half-sleep/waking state, I saw three or four seven-foot-tall beings, with extremely thin arms and legs and smallish heads. I remember wondering at the time how difficult it must be for them to support themselves upright. Realizing that something weird was going on (something I didn't want any part of), I went to sleep.

In regression, I found out why they had come. During the June 29th incident, they had taken me up through the roof of my house in Bradford, Ont. They had pointed out a dark boomerang shape in the sky. They said it was a Light Portal and they took me right up to it. We went through it and I was shown an enormous ziggurat-shaped ship, ringed with white running lights on each level. I was told that it was a Light Ship, and that it didn't have to be aerodynamic at all because it travelled inter-dimensionally on light particles (photons, I later learned).

The entities talked about how cumbersome and useless the earth space programs are and how they'll never get us anywhere in space the way we're going. Eventually, they said, physicists would learn how to use photons to propel their ships into the third dimension and alternative dimensions.

Our idea of death is also rather amusing to them. They see us as conservative beings who are stuck in the third dimension.

They have observed that the only time we humans feel we can travel into other dimensions is when we are "dying," because we finally accept that we are headed for some unearthly destination. The "light" at the end of the tunnel is actually a portal to other dimensions. The aliens said that we can pass through the portal without dying, and that we have to shake off our old ideas about space, time, and death.

After this regression, I spoke with a television producer who was considering working on a Home Box Office special about how abductees handle trauma. I told her my story about the long, tall "space-pokes" and what they had said. She recommended that I get in touch with Fred Alan Wolf, the author of the book *Parallel Universes*. She said I talked just like him.

I ordered a copy of the book and found that it was written by a quantum physicist. I wondered how what he had to say could possibly fit into what had been revealed to me. (I knew little, if anything at all, about quantum physics. I hardly understood classical physics.)

Lo and behold, there he was writing about time travel via neutron star clusters and photons. These exist in other universes because they are observed. By whom? Does he mean that they exist in other dimensions? At any rate, it was exciting!

What was even more exciting was a short interview with an engineer on CTV's *Canada A.M.,* which I caught by accident. On December 3rd, 1990, an engineer, who had designed a circular ship with paper-thin sails, said he and five other engineers were planning to "sail" it to Mars in 1992, propelled by the radiation of the sun—by, yes, photons!

Whatever the grand plan is—and nobody is sure about it!—I think we're being given some help. The world is finally coming together and lessons are being learned and walls are coming down.

Abductees are turning up everywhere to finally talk about their experiences. Whenever I mention the subject of UFOs or the possibility of contact with other life forms, there's always someone with a UFO story.

Here is an instance: My son Joseph came to me one morning in October 1989 and said, "Mummy, I had a strange dream last night. I was standing at the window and the moon was big in the sky." There had been a full moon that night. "I saw a rainbow in the sky, and it went swoosh." I asked him to draw the rainbow, and the one he drew was upside-down. This led me to believe that he had seen the lights of a craft leaving the area. In some instances, spacecraft had been known to change their configuration.

Here is another instance: In the summer of 1990, my Uncle Leo came to visit us from Ottawa. He is a very conservative, religious-minded, French-Canadian Roman Catholic.

I had decided to wear a shirt with a UFO design on it and a button that said "I Believe in UFOs" just to tease him a bit. He looked at the button, smiled, and said, "You would."

Later, over a beer, I asked him, "Uncle Leo, have you ever seen a UFO?"

"Yeah," he said.

"You're kidding!" I was aghast. I don't know why; maybe it was because he was the last person on earth I expected to hear a UFO story from. He's the worst tease, and I thought he might be pulling my leg.

I asked him if he was really serious.

"It's not something you kid about or tell just anyone, you know," my uncle said.

I felt ashamed for ridiculing him, so I asked him to tell me his story.

"Well, it was early June in '59. I was on my way to work at about a quarter to five in the morning. I was going down by Empress Street, where they have the big long stairs. I was on my way to the Champlain barn to pick up my streetcar.

"Then there was this bright object in the western sky and it looked like a whole bunch of lights flashing. It just stayed there for two or three minutes, and all of a sudden it took off forward, just as if it had never been there, really fast and toward the west until I couldn't see anything anymore. It just got smaller and smaller, so I knew it was something weird. It was sort of cylindrical in shape. It's kind of hard to describe it because I'd never seen anything like that before.

"Then, of course, I read about strange things that are seen in the sky, so I recalled that's what I saw, so I let it go at that."

Uncle Leo added, "There are always some sightings here and there, and they say there's no explanation for them, and the governments of the United States and Canada and all the rest of them are tight-lipped about them and they won't divulge any information. If they know anything about them, they don't say anything."

Well, they may not be saying anything now, but the egg has cracked. Soon the chick will hatch and it'll probably have large, insect-like, wrap-around eyes, and an egg-shaped head.

# Rendezvous

The late Betty Stewart was among the most articulate and percipient of Canadians who presented themselves as UFO contactees and abductees. A former long-time resident of Toronto, she lived for many years in Bond Head, Ontario, where her "rendezvous" took place.

At my request she prepared this eloquent presentation of her philosophy with an account of her experiences with alien beings. She completed the text on 16 January 1991, and I published it later that year in *UFOs over Canada*, where it attracted a fair amount of favourable attention.

Ms. Stewart's contribution does more than hint at her extended contacts with alien intelligences; it outlines, in some detail, a philosophy of what might be termed, for want of a better word, "alienness." She refers to the Reticulian Greys, a species of extraterrestrials (yet) unknown to science. She offers these insights without fanfare, without apology, as a legacy from "our visiting friends."

◆ ◆ ◆

The experience I am about to relate is, as far as I am able to determine, unique in the annals of UFO research.

Through an act of complete accord and co-operation, a fellow abductee, whose case I wished to examine, was subsequently brought to my home by Extraterrestrials for that purpose and the resultant television and radio exposure my researcher would engender.

I learned about this person through regressionist Ian Currie of Toronto. After I underwent regressive hypnosis at his office on January 9th, 1986, he told me of another client, a woman, who had experienced an implant insertion, as had I. However, where mine was merely a locator placed in the outer cartilage of my ear, her implant was of the more commonly reported type inserted up the nasal passage and often associated with incidences of genetic manipulation. She had sneezed it out twenty years after its injection and had managed to keep the tiny burr-like sphere for some time before it mysteriously vanished from her possession.

I asked Ian for this client's name and telephone number, but he could not remember these details, as her visit had been several years prior to my own. I called his Toronto office regularly, hoping he would come across the information in his files. Then, on July 15th, six months after I had seen him, he called to give me the woman's name and also the telephone number of the Toronto-based Canadian UFO Research Network (CUFORN) which had at one time briefly reviewed the case. They in turn gave me the telephone number of "D."

Here begins the bizarre unfolding of an unprecedented experience in UFO investigation. After a lifetime of personal encounters and abductions, I was in the process of exploring my own experiences and the abduction cases of others. D became, then, one of those under my scrutiny. When I telephoned her on July 15th and introduced myself, there was a gasp of surprise as she recognized my name. She then proceeded to tell of meeting me five days earlier in what she had perceived to be a dream.

With my cautious questioning of where this meeting had taken place, and by D's detailed description, we established beyond doubt that the 2:00 a.m. rendezvous had taken place on my very own property in the large shed attached to my "century home."

I had no recall of the encounter myself, and since the description of my property was astounding, to say the least, I then asked D to describe me as I had appeared at our meeting. This she did with alarming accuracy, right down to the garment I was wearing.

There was no way at that time that D could have known about me through normal channels, and by her own admission she is not clairvoyant. Our only mutual contact was in the person of regressionist Ian Currie, who, to this day, knows nothing about my property and has not spoken to her since he regressed her on that one occasion.

Here was evidence beyond the wildest hope of any researcher—and on my own doorstep. What a significant find! I was ecstatic, but puzzled as to why this had taken place, and in such a manner. Was it my dogged determination in my phone calls to my regressionist seeking D's identity and phone number? My all-out, hell-bent pursuit, which caught the attention of our Extraterrestrial friends? Whatever the impetus, I was grateful for the co-operation shown me by these visitors to our reality.

The reader must bear in mind that I had known of D's existence for more than six months before calling her. She, however, did not know of my existence until she was brought to me five days prior to my calling her on the phone the day Ian gave me her name.

The reason for this extraordinary act of Extraterrestrial assistance eventually made itself clear to me and to all subsequently involved in its telling.

The purpose behind my personal history of lifelong contact, and the many revelations of a technical and philosophical nature attendant upon these contacts, appears to be tied in with my desire to share such information and my lack of concern for any resultant ridicule.

Ian Currie had taped my one-time regression session at his office, and it is well that he did so, for quite apart from my insight into what had taken place during my abductions, I was also given much in the nature of prophetic information.

I was told of the television and radio exposure that my actions would precipitate, and the first of these proved to be CBC Television's *Man Alive* production entitled "The ET Hypothesis," first aired on April 1, 1987; a show which garnered the greatest public response in the program's then twenty-year history. Such a response was certainly indicative of the public's growing interest in the subject.

That regression tape also foretold of the lectures I would be giving and of my book now in progress. For sceptics who may call this a natural sequence of events, or a self-fulfilling prophecy, I will add that many other things have come to pass as well, but space does not permit the telling here.

I will not elaborate the details regarding D's visit to my property other than to say that until we could both separately undergo regressive hypnosis on the meeting in my shed, we refrained from contaminating our testimony by further exchange of information.

CUFORN had arranged for some regressive hypnosis sessions for me with Dr. David Gotlib of Toronto, during which we covered several abduction incidents in my life. These were the first regressions I was to undergo after my initial, one-time session with Ian Currie. Then, following the taping of the program "The ET Hypothesis" with American artist-author Budd Hopkins (*Missing Time* and *Intruders*), and just prior to the show's airing, Budd came to my home with David Cherniak, the program's producer.

Budd is an experienced and disciplined regressionist, a skill he developed through years of dedicated research, and since I had retained no conscious memory of our ET friends' visit to my home with D, the unfolding of that detail under hypnosis was fascinating for all three of us.

D later underwent regressive hypnosis for the same incident, but with Dr. David Gotlib. Until then we had continued to refrain from blurting out detail, even after meeting for the first time on the *Man Alive* show.

During my lifetime I have met several disparate types of Extraterrestrials who have treated me with dignity and respect, and at no time have I been subjected to the often-reported incidents of genetic engineering. I can only assume that these members of an apparently loosely knit cosmic federation have been successful in getting their true intention into action by my reaction. I know that I have their sanction and protection as I happily continue the dissemination of information.

The direction in which our visiting friends have guided me becomes more evident with each new human contact seeking me out and adding to the networking of information both on this continent and abroad.

When I state that I have always been treated with dignity and consideration, that is true. The implantation of the locater in my outer ear, with a subsequent implant in the brain to facilitate exchange of knowledge, in no way contravenes my statement. Since this is the best way to ease my absorption of information, I consider it a privilege and not an invasion. I, in turn, respect the bestowers.

When I refer to abductions, I am not speaking of arbitrary liberties taken against the will of Earthlings, for despite the normal trauma of some abductees, all have in fact agreed to this through their superconscious or they are left untouched.

The abductions are carried out either with the physical body or with the etheric body; the latter action, more common in occurrence and referred to as "bi-location," is conducted with the physical body remaining at rest while the etheric body does the travelling. There is then no risk of molecular damage to the physical body during transfer between realities. Interestingly enough, anything that happens to the etheric body is reflected back upon the physical body. The reverse is also true. If a physical body has lost a member, such as an arm or a leg, the etheric body carries this member and appears as a whole, since this is the pattern or imprint of the individual's existence in time.

(A brief foray into the study of quantum physics will substantiate the plausibility of that which I refer to as the "quasi-state," that of occupying two or more realities at the same instant.)

Our visitors use the intellectual/spiritual development of the subject to convey reality. The stored imagery of the abductee's own memory bank is employed in the assessment and handling during the encounter.

Those hampered by undeveloped capacities will find that our visitors will allow them the continued comfort of their misconceptions, religious or otherwise, for it is not possible to pursue true enlightenment with the unevolved, despite the position and manner in which such lives may function.

There are absolutely no religious overtones in these encounters, except those fostered by the subjects themselves. That there is something of the spiritual essence is obvious to the enlightened but usually misinterpreted by the unready, who turn it back into old patterns they can readily accept.

Man's selfish, organized divisiveness of creed with its corrosive evil is well known to our friends. Warnings of "Earthlings, alter your path" are not threats; they are pleas for spiritual change, and this has nothing to do with the church. It does have to do with the "oneness," the whole of the cosmos, and the supreme essence, or, if you choose to call it that, "God."

When I am sometimes asked, "Where does Jesus fit into all of this?" I am struck with the backwardness of the average citizen, who chooses to deify a master teacher and to "worship" (a word better expunged from the vocabulary of man) as do primitive aborigines upon confronting civilized man for the first time—quite simply put, organized religion, with its misleading dogma, has set man back many millennia in true spiritual development.

That we are to be once again visited by Jesus is all too well documented to be ignored. Referred to as the "second coming," it is in fact further along the line of several such past visitations (although not always in the same physical likeness) in the attempt to help man, for we have been under scrutiny for as long as time has seen fit to usher our development.

We are, ourselves, hybrids, the furtherance of early man through genetic splicing. Our scientific efforts to find the "missing link" have always been a source of amusement to those who know the true reason for the seeming unsubstantiated jump in such findings.

Those who question Jesus' position in the whole scenario come away from my symposiums with a healthier understanding of the Master and how he came to us. The revelation of the in vitro fertilization performed by our visitors with Mary does not shake their belief, as they accept him not as some fundamentalist deity held in awe and worshipped in a manner akin to that of a graven image, but as the man he truly was and is.

These people leave with their faces glowing with renewed faith and understanding, as they gather about at the end of an evening, for all they need is confirmation of their own growing realization. That is why they are in attendance.

I would like to introduce a word here about "guruism." Occasionally, an abductee will prove morally unworthy of the interest vested by our visitors. Whether it is evidenced by selfish intent to impede those of just purpose, or by falling into the trap of overestimating the value of their own role in the experience through egoism and the promotion of cultism, we have a negative situation. When this does occur, the subjects are dropped from further ET contact by a justice both swift and final, for they have negated true purpose. These persons then either accept the condition or, as in instances where considerable publicity has ensued, resort to falsifying continued contact to keep up appearances.

Our visitors may be unable to comprehend the complex emotional makeup of humans, but they do know the steps to take in circumventing the furtherance of destructive behaviour. (We should note that this quiet withdrawal does not interfere with man's free will.)

I have personally witnessed two cases of well-publicized contact where such punitive measures were effected. To this end, one could add "Amen," for are we not all bound by a cosmic cohesion in mutual co-operation?

Those who would explain away the experiences of abductions to fantasy, self-created to supply some nebulous psychological need, do a great disservice to man. Also, that many cases are disturbed or fearful is after the fact, and not the cause of seeming aberration. Such judgements are to be expected of those who enter upon the study at a superficial and biased level.

If critics have not had contact themselves, there is little chance for these surface-skimmers to realize the full force of the matter, since it takes more than reasonable intellect to come to a well-defined conclusion. Unfortunately, we have many articulate but ill-prepared minds producing useless print on the subject. However, the nearest approach to the truth is now being reached by a few good minds going beyond the theories of Albert Einstein, who opened the door but a crack.

The average man on the street does not comprehend, let alone have any desire for, enlightenment regarding the plurality of existence. It is still the stuff of science fiction. Parallel worlds? A few years ago the halls of the academe vibrated with laughter at the mere suggestion. Even as a young person, when I said, "Everything that was, is, or shall be, IS," I was cautioned by those who loved me best not to voice this where I could be ridiculed.

The greatest argument the genuine abductee can have against the groundless attacks of sceptics, most of whom would give their good right arm for a contact of their own, would be, "Have you ever experienced anything like this yourself? And if not, how can you offer any sensible opinion?" Perhaps before too much valuable time is lost, we will have a meeting of minds in place of the now fruitless, windmill jousting. In the meantime, the many cases of abduction are viewed askance. It takes considerable fortitude for these people to come forward and admit to their adventures. They deserve at least a decent hearing from the ill-qualified who would be judge and jury.

There are varying species in contact with Earth, and not all are in complete accord or at the same level of development spiritually and morally. There is, however, adherence to cosmic law, an understanding between species, and though not all share the same interest in Earth and its progress, they work together more or less in harmony despite these differences.

I have had contact with several types of beings—humanoid and also those who assume a very human appearance to cloak that which could be horrifying in aspect, such as the insect-like but highly evolved entities who were a delight to meet in their earthly disguise. A very acceptable and handsome group indeed, totally human in every detail.

I instinctively felt that the appearance was too good to be real, and in 1988 I asked channeller Don Daughtry's "Source" if this was the true appearance or if it was assumed for our acceptance.

My suspicions were well founded, as the description furnished by the "Source" showed an eight-membered, spider-like creature better associated with one's worst imaginings. Two years later, in 1990, to my surprise and satisfaction, I read of the same creature described in identical detail in a quote from Plato's *Symposium*, as told to him by Aristophanes. The more stilted phrasing of the "Source's" archaic English matched point for point with the modern idiomatic translation from Aristophanes's Greek. It is difficult to ignore such strong evidence, and even at my most practical, I cannot.

Do these beings still exist in their time frame, and how long before Plato and Aristophanes? All is relative and wondrous for us to ponder with our limited vision. That these entities care enough about our state to visit and keep an eye on things is a thrilling prospect. Their intrusion into our reality wipes out barriers for those who have witnessed and understand, even to a limited degree, for I am not alone in this particular instance.

A fellow writer from New York, a woman who makes Toronto her second home, has also met these same beings in their altered form. Before I could describe my encounter to her, she furnished me with precise details of the young men and their craft. It was identical to my own in every way. Such corroboration is rare and wonderful, for these cases are fewer than the common reports of the Reticulian Greys.

Since most prominent contacts are with the Greys and the genetic updating involving their species (our ancestors) and Earth Humans, many researchers concentrate their efforts in this direction only and promulgate statements which could lead the unknowing to believe that this is the sum total of contact.

The suggestion that Extraterrestrials are cold and unfeeling, when compared to the emotional morass in which humans wallow, is one of the least understood differences between the species. That many of our visitors have progressed beyond the selfish love of Earthlings is not yet understood. Everything about man and his strivings focuses on self and is therefore selfish. Even man's love, as near as he can express it, focuses on the reflection back to self. We are at one in this with our charming forms of animal life.

Universal love, more correctly defined as an all-encompassing detached concern, since it does not reflect back to self-interest, is a thing of the infinite, radiating ever outward, not inward. It belongs to the "oneness" of the Universe and is not yet part of man.

The ability to travel between realities has much to do with the dropping of useless burdens associated with materiality. Wayward emotion is then also part of the primitive excess left behind as the need lessens for personal expression. Knowing this, we realize we must seem an erratic and volatile breed to those of unified mind and purpose.

The lab-rat syndrome is often felt by abductees under the analysis of otherworldly scientists who pick them up many times during a lifespan for the continued study of life specimens on a planet in ecological and spiritual decline. This same feeling is even more strongly experienced by the victims of genetic engineering. We use the word "victim" only in the sense that the conscious self is not aware of the acceptance by the unconscious self.

Those with a better handle on what is taking place are more inclined to realize that this is a necessary step in man's evolution, and co-operation is therefore of importance over any personal objection.

Abductees are frequently told, "You are our chosen one." The more intelligent realize that this is employed to compensate for the commonly experienced lack of self-worth. There have been instances where the abductees were shown a "book" with strange writing. Since any meaningful communication is achieved through telepathic exchange, this would appear to be a material ploy to elicit co-operation and nothing more significant than that.

One can understand the use of simple subterfuge with a species like our own, for a glimpse of the deviousness within the cerebral cortices of Earthlings would surely give rise to the use of a similar device to attain an end. It hardly smacks then of moral issue in its employment since man has knowingly and willingly set himself up for anything else in a passing parade of intrusions. Man does know right from wrong but refuses to join the righteousness of cosmic law.

And so it continues, the enlightened receive further enlightenment while the ill-equipped cling to specious concepts. Those whose belief systems are shaken will either come away wiser or crawl farther back into the caves of ignorance, each governed by his degree of evolutionary and spiritual progress.

Our dedicated researchers have touched only briefly on the understanding of that which is taking place. But despite the interference and denials of officialdom, progress in that understanding is coming about.

The most dramatic issue of ET contact continues to be that of genetic engineering, and those who do not deny its existence are endeavouring to solve the mystery. Of course, our scientists still direct their radio telescopes out into the blue hoping for responses which won't come about until we are ready to understand the morality and intent behind the visitations.

The real purpose of the genetic manipulation has yet to be established, although erroneous statements have been made to the effect that Earth Man will soon become sterile and therefore the intervention is taking place for this reason—all too simplistic. At our present rate of population increase and moral decay, such a situation would be a blessing in disguise.

My own sources indicate that the hybridization of our species is being carried out to facilitate ease of travel between realities and as a furtherance of the genetic engineering which took place long ago. We are the degenerated remnants of that society which had fluidity of access between realities, until the denser, coarse vibratory level of this earth plane finally took its toll. The finer abilities deteriorated. We lost our longevity, our immunities to disease and the full use of our brain capacities (control over matter and telepathic communication), and all through spiritual decline.

The Reticulian Greys are our ancestors, who have progressed to their present state of evolution in time. They are from our own future and have stepped back in time to continue their work. Since we are they, and they are we, there is no dispute in cosmic law and time manipulation, because the original connecting thread in time still exists.

Do we lose all control over our existence because of this? Certainly not! Free will still prevails. Realize, then, that spiritual development is of paramount importance and that the separateness of Earth Mind, which grants us the right to accept or not as we choose, can also delay or exclude us from ultimate unity with the cosmos.

# PART VI
# CURIOSITIES, CROP
# CIRCLES, CONSPIRACIES

*Yet, across the gulf of space, minds that are to our*
*minds as ours are to those of the beasts that perish,*
*intellects vast and cool and unsympathetic, regarded this*
*earth with envious eyes, and slowly and surely drew their*
*plans against us. And early in the twentieth century*
*came the great disillusionment.*
—H.G. Wells' influential novel
*The War of the Worlds* (1898)

I chose to title this chapter "Curiosities, Crop Circles, Conspiracies"
because it incorporates miscellaneous, hard-to-classify material (like a
*real* Canadian flying saucer), and information on conspiracy theories
(CT), and considerations of crop circles (CC).

Conspiracies are ever-popular, but never more popular than during
the 1980s, when lack of physical evidence of UFO landings (called
Crash / Retrievals) was explained by "coverups" like those popularized
by Stanton T. Friedman and the TV program *The X Files*. Where is the
aileron of a crashed UFO? If it is absent, it is missing; if it is missing,
it is hidden; if it is hidden, it is in someone's possession; if it is in someone's possession, it is in the government's possession; if it is in the
government's possession, the governments of the world are in league to
suppress proof of alien-human encounters and interactions, including
the "reverse engineering" of alien craft!

This chapter includes descriptions and discussions of crop circles.
The connection between alien beings and crop circles—the geometric

and other figures that overnight appear in farmers' fields—is a tenuous one at best. It is easiest to account for their formation by assuming them to be the work of hoaxers with energy, imagination, and ingenuity. Indeed, hoaxers have confessed to preparing a number of them, but not all of them, and the best connection between these forms and aliens is a Canadian case, the Langenburg circles, which is discussed starting on page 254. It predates the enthusiasm for crop circles that was the rage in England in the 1980s.

# Flying Saucers

The cover of the October 1953 issue of *Fate* magazine shows an aerial view of a bright, metallic, saucer-like vehicle. The craft emits a trail of orange-coloured exhaust as it streams far above an airplane hangar. The words on the cover explain it all: CANADA BUILDS FLYING SAUCER.

If that is not explanation enough, here is what it is all about.

◆ ◆ ◆

Did Canada build its own flying saucer in the 1950s? That is what *Fate* maintained in its October 1953 "Special Saucer Issue." A report from a Canadian newspaper stated that a highly secret "flying saucer was indeed under construction designed to take off and land vertically and fly horizontally at around 1,500 mph." The *Fate* article described the craft and why it may or may not have been possible and feasible. Was there any truth to these reports? Perhaps the skies hold the answers to that question...

Do not look to the skies for the answers. What is being described in "a Canadian newspaper" and in the magazine's rewrite is the fact that the A.V. Roe aviation company at Malton, Ontario, under contract to the Canadian and United States defence departments, produced proto-types of the so-called *Avro Aerocar*, which manoeuvred vertically as well as horizontally. Indeed, it is felt that some reports of flying-saucer activity over Toronto's skies in the mid-1950s might well be little more than rumours connected with the tests of the *Aerocar*.

It is interesting that the A.V. Roe company has given rise to two urban legends. The first legend is that it designed and constructed an opera-tional "flying saucer." As with most legends, of the urban or rural kind, there is some truth to this. Movie footage does exist of a heavy-set, saucer-shaped craft rising vertically from the tarmac, wobbling all the while, hovering a few feet above in the air for some seconds, attaining a small amount of horizontal motion, and then flopping back onto the tarmac. The Martians or the Reticulian Greys would not be impressed.

The second legend is somewhat more substantial because it has to do with the *Avro Arrow*, a sleek fighter jet that proved its worth in the skies but had the misfortune to be launched the day the Russians fired their *Sputnik* satellite into space, thereby inaugurating the space race and the apparent need for intercontinental ballistic missiles rather than fighter aircraft of superior design.

# The Langenburg Crop Circles

The farm of Edwin Fuhr lies northeast of the town of Langenburg, Saskatchewan, close to the Manitoba border. Fuhr lived on the farm with his parents. He was a respected member of the farming community and was thirty-six years of age in 1974 when, while harvesting a crop of rape, he made a remarkable UFO sighting and then came upon "physical traces" in the form of crop circles.

The Langenburg Crop Circles sighting occurred about 10:00 a.m. on 1 September 1974. The sighting was investigated by the Royal Canadian Mounted Police. Then, on 21–2 September, the incident was the subject of an investigation by Ted Phillips from the Centre for UFO Studies.

From a distance of about fifty feet, Fuhr reported seeing a metal dome spinning at a high rate of speed above the level of the grassy field near the slough. He approached to within fifteen feet of the spinning dome. Then, after retreating, he saw that there were four more metal domes. The five domes, arranged in a rough semicircle, were silently spinning a foot or two above the ground. Then, all at once, the objects ascended, remaining stationary in the sky for a couple of minutes before disappearing into the low cloud cover. When he approached the landing site, Fuhr found five rings of depressed grass, swirled in a clockwise direction, some of it scorched or burned. On 3 September, the sixth ring was found, and on 15 September, the seventh.

The Langenburg Crop Circles are classic instances of formations that later came to be known as "agriglyphs." The discovery of crop circles on Fuhr's farm in rural Saskatchewan predates by close to a decade the intense interest in crop circles found on all social levels in Britain. It is now known that historical records yield innumerable descriptions of "devil's circles," "fairy circles," etc. The Langenburg Crop Circles are a very early instance of such formations. They are interesting in yet another way. Fuhr's description of the metal domes is one of the very few links between the crop circles and UFO activity.

Here is an interview with Fuhr conducted by Phillips. It appeared in *The Edge of Reality: A Progress Report on Unidentified Flying Objects* (1975) by J. Allen Hynek and Jacques Vallée.

◆ ◆ ◆

*Taped Account of the Event, Recorded 9/21/74*

Fuhr: I had about an acre and a half left on this end. I was coming up very slowly at about ½ mph. I was about 75 feet from that slough and I had to slow down because the rape was laying flat. I was about 50 feet from that object, see, I knew I had to turn around and I looked up and I saw that, I call it a goose blind. I thought, "What the hell is that guy doing in that damn slough?" I got off and walked up to it, not thinking a thing about it. I had jumped off the swather, moved toward it. I walked to about 15 feet of the circle, to about here, and the rape was standing up here yet (4 or 5 feet high), I stopped, this wasn't swathed yet. I was just standing looking at it. I couldn't figure why the grass was wiggling around. The grass was standing up here and it was moving. I couldn't figure what the devil it could be. I stood there about two minutes and thought, "Look, the whole damn thing is turning." I must have stood there at least two minutes and I couldn't figure out what the devil it could be, so I backed up slowly to the swather. I never turned my back on it once, I just backed up slowly to the swather, got around behind it and got up on the left side of it. When I got on, I sat down in the swather and then I saw those four on the left-hand side of me. They were all revolving, all four of them. I sat there like I was froze, I couldn't move nothing. I didn't know what the devil to do. I sat there for, it could have been 15 or 20 minutes, I don't know, it could have been even less than 15 minutes. They all went up, straight up, to, I would say, about 200 feet and they stopped at that distance. If you had winked you would have missed the takeoff from the ground to the point where they stopped (200 feet). When they hit the 200-foot mark, they stopped spinning and a vapour floated out, an exhaust. The exhaust was only about 6 feet long, like a vapour, it was from two ports at the bottom of it.

Phillips: Now, you could see these ports, could you see holes or—

Fuhr: You could see they were about 12-inch diameter ports and they were all like that. They were in a formation like a step, the lower was the last to go up. And after that, I would say only a second, there was a downward wind, a pressure that flattened the rape that was standing, and I thought, "Oh, hell, here goes my crop," and there was just a downward wind, no twirling wind, I had to hold onto my hat. After about two minutes they were gone. It took just seconds to get to that height (20 feet) and then they were just standing and after that, into the clouds and they were gone. I sat two minutes in the swather to be sure they were gone. It was overcast and it was raining and I would say the temperature was about 38°. I got off and went to the swather to see if it was warm; it was cool. If the machine was hot, it should have been steaming with the cool rain falling, but it wasn't. The colour of the machine was like a brushed stainless steel. It was rough and you could see while revolving that it was sort of grooved all around, you could see kind of grooves, they were darker grey. The dome shape and the bottom part had that lip on it and it was a dark grey in colour like it had been hot at one time, like steel that gets hot and cools off. To my knowledge, the whole thing was spinning.

Phillips: Did it appear that the objects were about the same size as the swirled areas here?

Fuhr: They seemed to be, I can't be sure, I was, I guess, kind of in shock. Now that the whole thing's over, sometimes I sit down and just wonder, "They couldn't have been larger?" I just don't know, after a while it makes you wonder, "Well, jeez, you must have seen them." People tell you all these stories and pump you so full of b—s— that you don't know if you are coming or going. So, I don't know. I'm damn sure they were all the same size; I couldn't tell any difference.

Phillips: The one nearest you took off first?

Fuhr: Yes, this one here took off first and then the one there and those two that were close together took off together and then the last one. That's the way they were in the air too, in a step formation. When they got to that height (200 feet) and they were straight back, they looked like they were standing, and I thought, "My God, are they coming back again?" That's when I didn't know what to do. After that vapour, the wind and then into the clouds. The vapour came out as they stopped, you could see it for just a second, then the wind, the downward pressure. The vapour was a dark grey and toward the end (lower end) it was lighter and lighter, just disappearing.

Phillips: How large did the objects appear to be?

Fuhr: The top was about 5 feet and from straight across it was maybe 11 feet with that lip on. When I was sitting on the swather I couldn't see the bottom part, I just noticed that all five of them were sitting there, and I was watching them at an angle, and I could see all of them at the same time. That one looked like there was something out of it, it looked like something was probing around in the grass. It was like, oh, I would say, the size of a fifty-cent piece, a probe it looked like, and the grass was all twisted and you could see marks like something had jumped here and there, all over.

Phillips: While you were looking at the near object on the ground, what did you think it was?

Fuhr: I thought someone was playing a trick on me. I took it for granted. I have a neighbour who will play tricks and when I saw it I thought, "What the devil's he doing now?" I thought it was one of those new metal goose blinds and I thought, "What the devil could it be doing there in that slough? There's no geese or water in there." And I thought, "Well, I'll walk up there and scare him," and it scared me instead. It didn't look like a goose blind then; it was revolving. If it had been on the ground or stationary, I probably would have walked right up to it.

Phillips: Could you tell if it was on the ground?

Fuhr: I couldn't see the bottom, but it was probably 12 or 18 inches above the ground; it wasn't on the ground at all. The grass around it was always moving, it was moving steady.

Phillips: When you were within 15 feet of it, did it start to climb?

Fuhr: No, it was sitting in the same spot, 'cause I backed up to the swather and I seen those over there and they were all sitting at about the same height off the ground, about 12 or 18 inches or so. They all seemed to be revolving at the same speed too, according to the way the grass was turning. They were revolving clockwise. When I backed up, I went slow back, I didn't turn my back on it, no way. When I sat down on the swather, that's when I saw the other four and that's when I couldn't move. I know the swather throttle was wide open, I had never slowed it down. When I got close, my head wanted to go fast back but my feet didn't want to move. When I got to the swather, I didn't know what to do, but when I got to the house, that was worse yet, I didn't know what to do. I wasn't going to tell them, they asked me, "What's the matter with you?" I told them I had seen something out in the slough, they wanted to know, "What did you see?" So I told them. They said, "No, no, you couldn't, you gotta be nuts." And I said, "No, come out and look, the swathe is all down. When I told Dad he never said too much, he never said yes or no, but Mom said, "No, that's impossible." I told Dad to come and look; he wouldn't go by himself so I went with him. He looked, jeez, he couldn't believe his eyes, he went to each one, looked at all of them. Then we found that one spot on the grass where something had been out, and you could see what looked like probes, where something had probed around. The grass was all tangled up. He was crawling around on his hands and knees all Sunday afternoon in that one spot there.

Phillips: From the very first observation until they disappeared into the clouds, how long did you see them?

Fuhr: The most it could have been was 15 to 20 minutes, it could have lasted more or less, I can't be sure.

Phillips: You have dogs. Did they bark during the observation?

Fuhr: Well, he barked, when was it?... *Saturday night*, they barked [the night before the reported event]. The neighbour's dogs barked too. They all barked at the same time, Saturday night, about midnight. Then they barked about *three in the morning*. Jack, our neighbour, had a babysitter who was frightened because the dogs were barking, and when Jack came home, he said the dogs were still barking. On Monday night about 10:30 the dogs were barking. My dog had been out in the field area, and he backed up to the house. The television was acting up about then too. *The dog wouldn't go into the field.* He usually follows me, but he wouldn't go out there. But the dogs were barking on Monday night, and on Tuesday morning I found that mark there. When I heard the dogs barking Monday night, I thought, "It couldn't be out there again. Even if it is, no way am I going out there!"

Phillips: I understand that your neighbour's cattle were disturbed...

Fuhr: Yes, the cattle were making a lot of noise that Sunday morning. The fence was broken in four places.

Phillips: When they reached the 200-foot level, did they line up right away?

Fuhr: Yes, they all seemed to be just like man-controlled; well, the way they took off they looked as if they were man-controlled, to take off in a formation like that... They were in a step formation, the lowest one was at the far end, and when they were up there they looked like they were straight across when they were at that level. I don't think they were radio-controlled; they landed just so many feet from the rape crop, all the way around the field, each one. Now those two over there were real close together; they looked like they were only six inches apart.

Phillips: When did you find [the seventh] site?

Fuhr: The Saturday night after [September 14], the dogs were barking again, and we found that one.

Phillips: When you went to the sites after the objects had ascended, how did the grass appear?

Fuhr: Well, I checked for burns but I couldn't find any. *The grass wasn't broken off, it was flat, pressed down.* It didn't seem different from the other grass except it was flattened, it wasn't dead or burnt or anything. Some sprouts are coming up there now—it's not dead.

Phillips: After the objects left, you waited two minutes, then what did you do?

Fuhr: After I looked at the marks, I continued to swathe for quite a while because I didn't know how to go home and tell those guys at home, that was my problem. When I got home, they asked me, "What's the matter?" I was all pale in the face, I didn't say nothing. I washed and tried to eat and I was trying to think how I could tell them about this thing. I went in for lunch at about 12:30.

Phillips: When the objects ascended, did you feel any kind of sensation?

Fuhr: None. I had to put my head back to watch them, no sensation, just that gust of wind, that downward gust of wind. I couldn't hear any sound because of the swather motor.

Phillips: What do your friends think about your sighting?

Fuhr: Well, I've had lots of calls from the news people; most of them seem to be really interested. Most of the younger people in Langenburg believe it. Some of the older ones don't, but they don't believe the United States has landed on the moon. People say, Why don't you carry a camera? How the hell could you carry a camera on a swather?

Phillips: What did the RCMP people think of the event?

Fuhr: Constable Morier was really interested, but the Corporal said not to repeat the story, he said, "Keep it under your hat for a while and don't report nothing."

Phillips: Before you saw these things, did you believe in flying saucers?

Fuhr: No, I thought it was a bunch of bull, I had never seen one, so why should I believe in them? God knows I do now.

*Taped Interview with Edwin Fuhr's Mother*

Mrs. Fuhr: I was just here from the church when Edwin came in...he acted altogether different. He was sorta, you know, sorta worked up. He was so worked up that he couldn't hardly eat dinner. We only had lunch for dinner, so I said, "Why don't you eat the rest?" He said, "I don't want nothing. I'm not really hungry." I said, "Why?" And he said, "I saw something this morning." And his dad was sitting there and said, "What do you mean you saw something?" And Edwin said, "Oh, I can't even describe it to you." And I had a little bowl sitting on the table, a little stainless steel bowl, and he described it on that bowl. He said, "That's what it looked like, that stainless steel bowl."

Phillips: So you were gone to church?

Mrs. Fuhr: Yes, we were gone to church and when we come home, his dad was home listening to the news on the radio. So I and Edwin's wife went to church that morning. Edwin was just getting ready to go out when we went to church, that was a little after ten. I didn't want to believe it, but he said, "Are you silly? I'm not going to tell you any stories, it is true." His dad went out with him to look at the marks, and Edwin came back pale as a ghost and said, "What next is going to happen?" I wouldn't go out there for five days, it was on a Friday; oh, they were fresh. I even dreamed about them.

*Taped Interview with Constable Ron Morier, RCMP: 9/21/74*

Phillips: How did you first learn of the Langenburg report?

Morier: Well, first of all, the fellow's [Fuhr's] brother-in-law lives next door here, and he is a good friend of the Corporal. I was on duty Sunday night and he phoned. He stalled a bit, and I could see that something was on his mind. He asked me, first of all, if we had had any reports of any mysterious sightings or anything like that. I said that we hadn't. He stalled then and wasn't going to tell me. Finally he did tell me that Mr. Fuhr had seen something; at that time he hadn't seen the rings as it was dark when he heard about it. He was at the farm visiting and he was told by his brother-in-law what had gone on—that he had seen the saucers—and he was sceptical as hell, but he thought that he would check with us. So I said, "No, but it sounds awful interesting. If he says there are circles out there, let's go out and have a look at them in the morning." I was off duty at the time. I figured it would be interesting.

I got up about 8 o'clock and went out there and met Edwin, and I could see that he was still, it appeared to me, quite shaken, you know, about this whole thing. He was jumpy, and you could see by just looking at the guy that he had been scared. But he took us out there and sure as hell there they were, five circles. I was sceptical too, but I was curious. There they were. I had never seen anything like them before, and listening to his story and everything... so I got on the phone and called the Corporal and told him what I had seen and told him that I thought that someone should get some pictures. So they did, they came out shortly and they took pictures. *These pictures were taken after only about four people had actually seen the rings*, Edwin, his father, myself and _____. So, that's how I came about the report.

Phillips: When you were there, they did appear to be quite fresh?

Morier: Yes, they were. The thing that really stood out was that the grass was all flattened out in a clockwise fashion. I got down on my knees and put my face near the grass, trying to smell some kind of exhaust or afterburn or something like that. There was no odour to it at all. But it was really swished tight, you know, *I mean it was really flattened and matted together.* I noticed, going out again, as the days went by, that the sun had dried the grass and it wasn't as prominent as before.

Phillips: So the pictures were taken 22 hours after... that would have been September 2nd?

Morier: Yes, the second of September.

Phillips: You know, in talking with people around town, and the CBC did street interviews with local people, you get the impression that the local people feel that Fuhr is reliable and sincere. In your opinion, based on your discussions with him, do you believe him to be an honest man?

Morier: Yes, I do.

Phillips: Do you believe he is sincere about the event?

Morier: Yes, I believe that he saw something, and I don't see why he would exaggerate what he saw. There is no way that this is a hoax. Just talking to people who know him, of course, I wondered as to his credibility too, but I have spoken to different people too, including relatives of his, in-laws, etc., and they all believe that he did see something out there. They've all seen the circles. They are convinced that something was there, and I am too. *I think that there is no way that anything was wheeled in and out of that field,* because there had to be some trace, and you saw yourself in those slides that when the swather was wheeled in there and the pictures were taken that you could see the tracks clearly.

Phillips: And there was no evidence of that in any of the areas?

Morier: No, sir, it was in the slough grounds, the grass was green and it was long and it was undisturbed except for the circles, and whatever was in there, it came out of the air and departed the same way, as far as I could tell.

Phillips: So, to your knowledge, Fuhr did not report the sighting to the news media himself?

Morier: No sir, it got out through other people.

# A Round of Circles

"During 1986 and 1987," wrote Pat Delgado, "I was asked by the Canadian Broadcasting Corporation to talk about circles and rings on a program called *Quirks and Quarks*, which was transmitted throughout Canada. The following are extracts from letters I received as a result of the programs."

Pat Delgado, the British investigator of crop circles, is referring to the so-called circles and rings he discussed on CBC Radio's popular science program. These strange formations in fields of wheat, oats, and barley are also known as "agriglyphs."

Delgado and Colin Andrews are the authors of *Circular Evidence: A Detailed Investigation of the Flattened Swirled Crops Phenomenon* (1989). Here are the relevant parts of letters Delgado received from listeners across Canada.

◆ ◆ ◆

*Correspondent, Sidney, British Columbia*

My experience happened about six years ago, in a meadow being grown for hay, I think about ten acres. It was in the middle of May, as the grass was nearly two feet high, as far as I can remember. We hay here earlier than in England. I was walking along the headland with my dog. Everything was silent about me, blue sky and sun, when this almighty bang came and my dog jumped, wondering what on earth was happening. It was a much louder bang than a gun. I have belonged to shooting clubs for years, so I know what they sound like. The grass was going around in a clockwise direction, banging and cracking, and the grass was wild as could be. I thought it would be torn out by the roots. We stood there and watched. Only eight metres from where we were, with a blink of an eye shall we say, there was dead silence, all as quiet as before, no sign of wind or any movement of trees. I walked over to the circle and stood looking at it, the grass was limp and partly flattened, not torn a bit, it just looked tired. The circle was as far as I can remember about three metres around, with upstanding grass all round like the rest of the meadow, just that one circle that was now different from the rest of the meadow. I did not notice any spiral pattern in the centre, it all looked the same. After studying it for a while, I shook my head and made some comment to my dog about finishing our walk around the meadow. No sign of disturbance in the rest of my walk or anywhere else in the meadow.

*Correspondent, Sarnia, Ontario*

I have examined three circular impressions, two in a pasture/woodland environment in the Pontiac County area of Quebec and one near Grand Bend, Ontario. The Grand Bend effect was located in a corn field. The Pontiac impressions are located about 9.5 and 20 kilometres from Shawville, Quebec. This is just across the Ottawa River from Renfrew County, Ontario. Let me begin by describing one Pontiac impression, which is nearly identical to the second Pontiac impression. Examination of the site revealed a donut-shaped impression of dead grass on a green, living background. The outer ring was about nine metres in diameter, while the inner hole of the donut was seven metres across. Within this one-metre-wide ring, the dead grass was swept in a clockwise bend. It appeared that the grass died from severe induction heating of the soil. The stems were not damaged, but the root structure of the grass was destroyed. Grass within the hole of the donut was green and healthy. The ring-like impression was located on a 5° slope, below a large ironwood tree. Whatever produced the ring also burnt the branches of the tree. It appeared as if a "vehicle" of some sort descended from above, forcing down the branches of the tree, burning them and trapping them between the vehicle and the ground. The soil and grass were not as severely damaged in the area below the trapped branches. Soil sampled from inside and outside the ring was normal. At the inner edge of the ring (bordering the donut hole), two granite rocks showed temperature discoloration, as if scorched by induction heating. Two young ironwood trees (about eighty centimetres in height) located inside the outside edge of the ring, were bent and deformed and contained severe burn marks, but they were living and growing. The farmer explained that two or three similar-sized poplar seedlings had died. Poplars have shallower root structures than ironwoods and apparently suffered the same fate as the grass. This impression was at least two years old when I first saw it, and the effect is still visible about ten years later! The individual who first discovered the donut impression said that it appeared overnight. He knew this because he had crossed this section of pasture as a shortcut to reach his car pool each morning and had returned late each afternoon by the same route. I am sure that no one reaped financial gain from this oddity, so a financially perpetuated hoax is out. The farmer reported that "government men" took samples at the site but no conclusions were published. The above incident takes on an eerie twist because UFOs were reported in this area at the time when the impressions appeared. Quite a number of local residents reported visible sightings, and certain sightings were witnessed by more than one observer at the same time.

The second donut was found near Ladysmith, Quebec. Ladysmith is twenty kilometres from Shawville and about sixteen kilometres from the first site. This impression is also on a 5° slope next to a large ironwood tree and in a secluded location. The dimensions of the donut are the same as the first one, or possibly a bit smaller. Apparently, this incident occurred in late December, in the early evening, with snow on the ground. A villager about one kilometre away phoned the farmer who owned the property where this second impression was found, informing him that there was a fire in his bush. Apparently, snow, steam, and reflected, refracted and scattered light simulated the effects of fire. According to the report, the barn blocked the farmer's line of vision and he observed no flames or smoke, so he pursued the matter no further. About half an hour later, neighbours reported a brightly lit stationary aerial object over nearby Gray's Lake. After five minutes or so, the object accelerated away at high speed into the southeast sky.

*Correspondent, Lac du Bonnet, Manitoba*

In my last parish in Langenburg, Saskatchewan, we had quite an experience with these rings. One of my parishioners was harvesting canola [rape seed oil] on a September morning, when, in his own words, he came across about five UFOs in his field, rotating, and then they took off and disappeared. Needless to say this event sparked a great deal of media hype, and he underwent a great deal of personal ridicule and abuse.

However, the rings were solid evidence and were exactly as described on your show. As well, I believe they also appeared on a neighbouring farm.

I disagree that these were caused by turbulence, however, as no such weather conditions were in evidence. What I do believe might be a cause of these rings is piezoelectric forces that could have affected my parishioner, causing him to hallucinate these UFOs. The swirling nature of the phenomenon his brain registered suggests that some sort of vortex force was involved, which generated an image quite like what he imagined a UFO would be. At any rate the fact that several cattle and dogs were also greatly disturbed during this "flap" suggests that some force was acting on them that perhaps is similar to what animals sense prior to earthquakes.

I am not a physicist, but I did want to share this letter with you. The date of this was in the late 1970s. Newspaper accounts and photos are available from local newspapers, and the local television station also took film of the circles.

## *Correspondent, Calgary, Alberta*

I was driving down a gravel road near Arrowwood, Alberta, when suddenly about 100 feet in front me and off to the right in a fallow field a great explosion of dust took place. The soil went into the air at about 30 feet and fell back to earth with slight drifting in the direction of the wind. I stopped the car and went back to examine the area. My first thought was that a seismic crew was working, but that did not prove to be the case. It was not a whirlwind or dust devil since the dust fell gently back down to the ground. Upon close examination of the area where this took place, I could find no markings whatsoever on the surface of the field. My perception was that this dust explosion was no more than one metre in diameter. After examining the area and finding no markings, I truly began to feel that I had been seeing things.

## *Correspondent, Labrador City, Newfoundland*

Our permanent home is now at New Ross, Nova Scotia, a country place, but without any wheatlands—the crop is Christmas trees. However, there is much meadowland and behind our house a large meadow where I believe there was once a stone circle. On that meadow strange lights have been seen at night—not marsh gas, as it is a flattened hilltop and very dry. Some of the lights seemed to take the form of what are called UFOs. They seemed to be attached to circular objects that rose from or landed on the ground. Some of them would rise and stay in one place in the sky all night, or would move about in various directions including from west to east, or would appear to be playing leapfrog with each other. I examined the ground where one had appeared to land, but the grass was too short for me to be certain that any mark or depression had been left. However, another man, a farmer, who lives about 100 miles from us, did find a circular mark on grass on his property. So UFOs are one possible explanation.

With regard to UFOs, these are not always visible, especially in day-light. I am pretty certain of this because when one passed over during the night, it would often affect the time on our clock—in fact we were all "turned back" in time, even in our conversation or the radio, TV or stereo. This sometimes also happened in the daytime, but although we looked we could see nothing in the sky even on a clear day. The UFOs we experienced and sometimes saw were elliptical in shape, and it occurred to me that they might have been made of the thought-energy I had also been seeing, though I can't say for certain that I actually saw one forming. The nearest I came to that was when one suddenly appeared on the meadow, initially it was a ring of light.

*Correspondent, Pembroke, Ontario*

My observations of some mysterious rings were made in 1967, in Grattan, County Renfrew, Ontario. On a flat area, adjacent to the shore of Garvin Lake, I had noticed these conspicuous rings, which were almost perfectly circular (almost too precise to be caused by nature). The site, an old abandoned farm property, was grown over by species of wild grasses, within which two very distinct rings were visible, side by side.

These two rings were approximately four metres in diameter and perhaps one metre wide. The grass that had grown within the ring area appeared to be totally dried up and sort of stunted or tramped down. There was evidence that the site had been used by deer hunters, who had erected makeshift tents. My thoughts were that these rings were caused by hunting dogs that had been tied to a picket in the ground and then ran around in a circle, tramping all the remaining grass.

Several months later, a farmer near Chapeau, Quebec, discovered similar rings of about eight metres diameter in his pasture. The grass there appeared to be burnt, according to his report to the *Pembroke Observer*. I never visited the site. However, the incident led me to look more closely at the rings I had discovered, but I could not find evidence of either burn marks nor any indication that dogs were ever tied up there. As I often returned to that site for hunting and fishing purposes, I could notice that the grass appeared stunted for another two years. In the third year these things could no longer be distinguished.

# Major Crop Formation

The following report, an exceptionally detailed one of a major crop formation in British Columbia, comes from the Internet's *CNI News*, Volume 4, Number 14, Part 1, 16 September 1998, where it was headed "Global News on Contact with Non-human Intelligence."

*CNI News* is a twice-monthly electronic news journal addressing UFO phenomena, claims of human-alien contact, space exploration and related issues, including the cultural and political impacts of contact with other intelligent life. *CNI News* is edited by Michael Lindemann and distributed by the 2020 Group.

◆ ◆ ◆

*Major Crop Formation in British Columbia, Canada*

As reported in the September 1, 1998, edition of *CNI News*, Canada has witnessed a number of interesting crop circle formations in recent weeks. Undoubtedly the most impressive to date was reported in the small farm community of Vanderhoof, about 50 miles west of Prince George, British Columbia. The formation, consisting of three clusters of perfect circles totalling eleven circles in all, appeared in a field of oats during the night of August 27–28. As seen and photographed from the air, the formation is immediately intriguing for one simple reason: unlike in English crop fields, there are no tractor or tram tracks through which a would-be hoaxer might enter this field. Yet there is not the slightest hint of disturbance of the oat crop between the field edge and the circles, which start about 175 feet inside the field, and which are also separated from each other by as much as 500 feet of pristine, undisturbed crop. If a hoaxer made this formation, one might suppose he or she had a talent for levitation.

*The following report was produced on the scene by Chad Deetken, one of Canada's leading crop circle researchers, and is reproduced (slightly edited for length) with permission.* CNI News *thanks Chad for sharing this report, and also thanks researchers Michael Strainic of MUFON Canada and Paul Anderson of Circles Phenomenon Research Canada for first bringing this case to our attention.*

British Columbia's first verified crop formation, consisting of 11 circles ranging in size from 18'6" to 99 feet in diameter, was located in a field of oats next to runway No. 250 at the small Vanderhoof airport.

One of the first people to see them was pilot Eric Stier. He was returning from aerial fire patrol on Friday, August 28, and was just approaching the runway at 4:15 p.m. when he spotted the distinct pattern. He had flown over the same field the day before and says there was nothing in it then.

Soon after landing, he and friends Neil Weibe, John McQueen and Bryan Wallace went back into the air for a second look. They took numerous photos and scrutinised the field very carefully but said they could see no tracks or points of entry. They had no idea what to make of these strange circles.

The next morning, Saturday, they walked into the field. Still suspecting a possible prank, they looked very carefully for paths and other signs of human involvement but found nothing. At this point, they told the owner of Vanderhoof Flying Services, Brent Miskuski, of their find, and he in turn notified farmers Frank and Margaret Smith, who lease the land.

Up to this point, only a handful of people knew about the formation and so it was relatively undisturbed. However, by Monday, the press found out, and from that moment on interest and visits to the site began. [A newspaper account of the circles appeared in the *Prince George Citizen* on Tuesday, September 1.]

My wife, Gwen, and I first learned about the formation on Tuesday morning, and within an hour and a half were on our way for the 9-½ hour drive from Vancouver. We arrived after dark at about 9:00 p.m. We entered the formation at 10:00 a.m. on Wednesday.

Since numerous people had already visited the site, it was difficult to detect certain features which would indicate whether or not it was genuine. However, there were still numerous areas that had not been walked on. In these areas, I found no obvious signs of damage to the stalks or compaction of the soil. Also, the lay looked quite good and dowsing the circles indicated a strong energy.

During the three days we were at the site, we spoke to many people who had experiences which may be related to the arrival of the formations:

Many people told us their dogs barked incessantly or acted strangely the night the formation appeared. One woman, Rosie Martins, told us her dog was so out of control that the family cat took fright and jumped into her son's bed to hide, scratching him badly. Another woman, Mae Frankel, said her son's dogs were in a barking frenzy all that night. Also, Margaret Smith's mother visited the circles and when she returned home, her dogs and cats refused to come near her. And a couple who were visiting the formation with their small dog said the dog was desperate to get out of the large circle.

A woman told us that at 2:00 a.m. on Friday, the night the formations appeared, she saw an eerie glow in the forest a few miles from her house. She thought it might be a fire and so woke her husband, but after an hour it simply blinked out. She said it was a fiery orange light which lit up a large area, and that there was no smoke.

That same Friday, during the day, two men in a neighbouring town said they saw two silver objects rising from the lake they were fishing on. At first it seemed they might be looking at reflections in the water about a half mile away, but then whatever it was rose and took off rapidly. These men say they are not believers in the paranormal and seemed embarrassed by their sighting. Neither could explain what they had seen, and they did not know of the existence of the crop circles.

We collected 53 sets of stalk samples from circles and 101 control samples. Each sampling contains about 20 stalks. In addition, we took an equal number of soil samples. These will be sent to the Burke/Levengood/Talbot team for analysis.

Size and lay of the circles:

1) In a cluster of 5
   —one was 51' diameter and clockwise
   —one was 23'10" diameter and counterclockwise
   —one was 50'2" diameter and clockwise
   —one was 41'8" diameter and counterclockwise
   —one was 46'6" diameter and clockwise

2) In a cluster of 3
   —one was 19'8" diameter and counterclockwise
   —one was 19'6" diameter and clockwise
   —one was 18'6" diameter and counterclockwise

3) In the other cluster of 3
   —one was 99' diameter and counterclockwise
   —one was 21' 8" diameter and clockwise
   —one was 22' and clockwise

The distances that separated the circles in each cluster ranged from 1 foot to 2'8". The distance between the two circles farthest from each other was 535 feet. The closest distance to the edge of the field was 175 feet. The distance from the runway to the closest circle is 600 feet.

It is noteworthy to mention that after we had completed our sampling, hundreds of people from the surrounding area began visiting the field. We talked to a great many of them, always asking if they knew of any pranksters who might be capable of this or if they had heard of the slightest rumour suggesting a hoax. Every single person, regardless of their personal belief as to the circle's origins, said they had heard nothing.

# Odd Happenings

I am frequently asked if anything strange or mysterious has ever happened to me. I suspect that people who ask me this question really want me to answer yes. Then they will tell me about their encounter with a ghost or a UFO. When I collected Canadian quotations, nobody ever asked me if I "believed in" Canadian quotations. But now that I collect ghosts and spirits, or at least reports of them, people always ask me if I "believe in" them.

I have had some odd experiences in my day, but nothing as alarming as meeting a denizen of the spirit world, though I did spend a couple of hours walking around the streets in the vicinity of the intersection of Yonge Street and St. Clair Avenue in uptown Toronto with a woman companion who claimed to be in continuous contact with alien entities. She would point out a man in a raincoat who was standing at the intersection or a woman who was crossing the street with a child and assert that they were aliens who were keeping her—and me—under surveillance. I would look at the harmless man or the middle-aged woman, and the feeling would come over me that my woman companion was right: They *were* keeping their eyes peeled on us. My companion was strikingly attractive and stylishly dressed, so maybe her appearance was attracting attention, or maybe there was something else going on...

Two MUFON representatives organized a series of talks on UFOs to be held at the OISE auditorium in Toronto. (MUFON stands for Mutual UFO Network, an organization for members of the general public who are interested in unexplained aerial phenomena, and OISE stands for the Ontario Institute for Studies in Education.) The series was held during the hot summer of 1992, as I recall, and I was one of the invited speakers. About forty people were present, and they paid fifteen dollars apiece to attend.

I have a fairly standard presentation and an affable patter. For about fifty minutes I discussed the pros and cons of flying saucers and unidentified flying objects. The audience seemed attentive. I presented the arguments by drawing on the work of investigators like J. Allen Hynek and sceptics like Philip Klass. I discussed the implications of ETH (the Extraterrestrial Hypothesis, which holds that UFOs come from outer space) as well as the FFF interpretation (Fraud, Foolishness, and Fantasy). But I did conclude that the study of the phenomenon (what people report, why they report it) sheds light on human nature if not on alien psychology and that this was eminently worthwhile.

While I was speaking I was aware that there was a middle-aged man, rather poorly dressed, sitting close to the front row, but off to one side of the auditorium, who was paying rapt attention. I instinctively felt that he was essentially biding his time, waiting for an opportunity to speak, whether to object to what I was saying or to agree with it, I did not know.

When the session was turned over to members of the audience for questions or comments, this man was among the first to stand and speak. I am not exaggerating when I say that his question took me by surprise. This is what he had to say.

"Who designed the cover of your book?"

He had in mind my first book on UFOlogy, which was then in print, to which I had made reference in the talk. Its title is *UFOs over Canada,* and it had been published in a trade paperback edition about two years earlier.

"You are asking me the name of the designer of *UFOs over Canada?*" I believe in repeating questions so everyone in the auditorium can hear them.

"Yes. Who designed it?"

"Gerry Williams," I answered, naming the freelance designer who did a lot of work for the publisher, Hounslow Press. "Why?"

"Did he see UFOs over the CN Tower?"

I held up a copy of the book with the cover facing the audience. It shows two UFOs cavorting over the Toronto skyline, and the skyline is dominated by the CN Tower.

"Gerry is a friend of mine. He has designed a number of my books and many more for Hounslow. No, he did not see two flying saucers over Toronto. To my knowledge he has never seen a UFO. About the only thing odd about him is that he is a vegetarian."

"I saw them. I saw them in the same position that he drew them. Are you sure he did not photograph them in the sky next to the CN Tower?"

"I am certain he did not, or he would have mentioned it. The illustration on the cover is Gerry's artwork, an original design and not a photograph."

"Well," he continued, "I saw them in the same place in the sky as he painted them, with the CN Tower between them. It was about three years ago."

"This is curious," I added, feeling we were getting nowhere. "It's must be a case of art imitating reality." Then I added, "I would like to chat with you later. Could you stick around after the talk?"

He nodded yes and sat down. There were other questions about my talk and about recent UFO flaps and crop circles but nothing to match in interest the man's question.

When the session was over, I mingled with the crowd, signed a couple of books, greeted a few familiar faces, and looked around for the man who had seen the UFOs in the sky alongside the CN Tower.

He was nowhere to be found.

The next day I phoned Gerry and asked him about the source of inspiration for the cover design.

"I made it up," he said. "I copied some basic UFO designs from a book, changed them, positioned them in the sky, and added a sketch of the CN Tower."

"You never saw a UFO yourself?" I asked.

"No, never," he said. "But I guess, from what you told me, I must have drawn two real ones!"

The only detail to add is a coincidental one. Gerry Williams is the name of my designer, who lives in Toronto. It is also the name of a New York–based designer. That Gerry Williams drew the picture of the gaunt alien being that appears on the jacket of Whitley Strieber's *Communion: A True Story* (1989). It is the prototypical image of the alien being.

Coincidences!

# The Carp Crash-Retrieval Report

Carp is a species of fish, but it is also a small community located on the outskirts of Ottawa, not far from Kanata, the community that houses the country's defence-related computer industry, its Silicon Valley. Carp is recalled, when recalled at all, as the site of the original "Diefenbunker," the inglorious name of the Central Emergency Government Headquarters erected during the coldest years of the Cold War. It was here that Prime Minister John G. Diefenbaker authorized the construction of the gigantic "bomb shelter" to be used as a refuge, redoubt, or refugium for 535 key officials—government officials, public servants, military experts, and staff members—in the event of an atomic attack on Parliament Hill, Ottawa. Completed at tremendous cost in 1958, the four-level underground bunker has never been used, yet it has been maintained to the present day. If it serves a purpose in the 2000s, that purpose is not a matter of public record.

Carp happens to be the location of a curious crash-retrieval report. I have reproduced the report verbatim from the pages of *Notes from the Hangar*, Volume 1, Number 2, Third Quarter 1991. This publication is subtitled "The Quarterly Journal of the National UFO Museum." The National UFO Museum is a private collection of UFO-related materials located in Sun Valley, not far from Las Vegas, Nevada.

The editors of the journal did not know what to make of the report, but they decided to publish it anyway, hoping that their readers might be able to make something of it. By turns the report is knowledgeable and nonsensical. Paranoia seems part of it. Do its claims have any basis at all in fact? Is it true to type? Here is how the editors introduced the report:

"Hardly a week goes by without at least one anonymous letter, article or package arriving here at NUFOM. Things have been slipped under our door, mailed without return address, slipped to us by passing strangers, and even wilder! Apparently we are not alone. This article was received anonymously at the UFO Contact Newsline of Los Angeles in an envelope postmarked "Ontario, Canada." Is it true? A hoax? Wild ravings, or a courageous person coming forward with a truly terrifying truth? Frankly, we haven't a clue, but we found it of sufficient interest that we thought it prudent to share it with you. Can anyone shed any light on this startling tale? Admittedly this sounds too contrived to be much more than a transparent piece of disinformation— one or two bits of truth, and a lot of wild fingerpointing; and yet... We have reprinted it here just as we received it, weird grammar, punctuation and all. Please send us your comments and information!"

The reader might well question the wisdom of reprinting a tract of unknown authorship and provenance that perpetuates a probable hoax, thereby enhancing the unknown originator's sense of alienation. Yet the report is of specific Canadian interest. Given the limited number of outlets for material of this sort, and given the equally limited readership reached by these publications, it seems that the sole outlet in this country for marginal material that has a curious and even controversial nature is publication in a book-length collection like this one. (After all, it was Vachel Lindsay who once said, "The place to hide something is in a book.")

At the same time, the report is exemplary in at least one respect. It is a fine instance of the type of communication that turns up in UFO circles every few years. The report implies a conspiracy or "cover-up" on the part of the media, the military, and the top levels of government. What is being suppressed, apparently with limited success, is all knowledge of crash-retrievals of unidentified flying objects. Conspiracy theories constitute the most vivid of all contributions to present-day UFOlore. They are the most dramatic of all the aspects of contemporary UFOlogy—in this instance, at once global and Canadian.

The editors of *From the Hangar* were not alone in receiving the report reproduced starting on page 282. A copy of it was also sent to CUFORN (Canadian UFO Network), a well-established research group based in Toronto. Lawrence J. Fenwick, editor of the *CUFORN Bulletin*, discussed the communication in the January–February 1990 issue under the title "Something 'Fishy' in Carp." Fenwick's article is reproduced here; the informants' names are disguised.

◆ ◆ ◆

In early March 1990, your editor received an anonymous two-page typewritten story and two photographs supposedly recounting a crash-retrieval of a UFO in a swamp in Carp, Ontario, just outside Ottawa, Canada's capital.

The outlandish scenario painted by the author might have been scrapped by some UFOlogists as a piece of disinformation. CUFORN decided to check into the details of the story. So far we have had corroboration by several eyewitnesses to something strange seen on the date in question, November 4, 1989. Investigators Bob Graham, Arthur Bray and Clive Nadin were assigned to the case. Graham sent us a copy of his five-page story, which he first sent to Bray. Co-Director Harry Tokarz co-ordinated the investigation.

Graham is a field representative for a farmer's organization, so he used the cover story when interviewing people that he was probing a story of cattle being disturbed in the area.

The event occurred just east of the intersection of Corkery Road and Old Almonte Road, according to the aerial map sent anonymously to us. Graham's witnesses confirmed the location. D.L. said there had been helicopter activity over the swamp on that weekend. J.C. recalled as many as six 'copters flying over the swamp on November 4. Mrs. L. said that, about dusk, 5:00 to 5:30 p.m., Sat., Nov. 4, several 'copters of different kinds had hovered over the trees in the swamp, moving up and down, using their searchlights. They left about 8:00 p.m. Shortly after, she saw a blinding light, "brighter than lightning," that lit up the interior of her house. It was steady and lasted two minutes. B.F. said local farmer A.H.'s cattle stampeded and bawled all that night. Ian and J.C. remembered seeing the light. Three people recalled their dogs being disturbed that night.

It is noteworthy that 8:00 p.m. was the exact time mentioned in the mysterious article when Canadian military radar picked up the UFO's landing. The investigation is continuing.

◆ ◆ ◆

The investigation continues, the mystery deepens... a second communication appeared. CUFORN was sent the following item in a plain envelope, postmarked Ottawa. It arrived in mid-October 1991, and was presumably released by the same source that released the original report:

All information on ALIEN contact is being systematically released by the BROTHERHOOD. A group responsible for the founding of the New World, NORTH AMERICA. It is also known as the HOLY GRAIL. The GRAIL exists. From the ancient Middle East, to Europe, to Canada. This group protects the Blood of God. It has members in every level of modern Society. Its beliefs centre around the secret knowledge of the creation of man, & the ongoing relations between the forces of heaven. The release of ALIEN information is in an effort to stop RED CHINA. China is preparing an all out nuclear, biochemical attack on the Soviet Union, Europe & North America. The attack will have millions dead in minutes, billions in months. If successful all major Judeo-Christian systems of belief would be wiped out within a year by COMMUNISM. Classified information in photo, videotape, autopsy reports, films is going to be leaked to the press over the next three yrs. Most of this information is on the CARP Ontario landings, Monuments-bases on the darkside of the moon, and phobos mars installations & the final origin of the ALIENS.

The above statement, made "by the BROTHERHOOD," has been reproduced as it was received, complete with errors and peculiarities of spelling and punctuation, etc. These considerations add a charm (if not a harm) of their own. The statement by "the BROTHERHOOD" seems oddly dated; after all, in recent years "COMMUNISM" has not been perceived to be the menace that it once was or may have been, and "Red" China's commissars are a menace to their own people, not to the population of what used to be the Soviet Union. At the same time, in another way, the statement is fairly current, indeed fashionable, for it makes reference to "the HOLY GRAIL" in Canada. It is likely that the author or authors of the communication, and presumably of the report reproduced below, are familiar with Michael Bradley's book *Holy Grail across the Atlantic* (1987), which argued that the *sangreal* (the blood-line and specifically the descendants of Jesus Christ, not a chalice or goblet associated with the last days of Jesus) found their refugium in a Templar's Castle, the ruins of which are discernible at "The Cross" (New Ross, Nova Scotia). So this statement is an odd linking of the legend of the Grail from the Middle Ages and a contemporary UFO sighting.

◆ ◆ ◆

Canadian and American Security Agencies are engaged in a conspiracy of silence. To withhold from the world the alien vessel seized in the swamps of Corkery Road, Carp, in 1989.

UFO sightings in the Ontario region had intensified in the 1980s, specifically around nuclear power generating stations. On November 4, 1989 at 20:00 Hrs Canadian Defense Department radars picked up a globe shaped object travelling at a phenomenal speed over Carp, Ontario. The UFO abruptly stopped, and dropped like a stone.

Canadian and American Security agencies were immediately notified of the landing. Monitoring satellites traced the movements of the aliens to a triangular area, (See Aerial Map) [Sorry, no map enclosure in the package we received.] off Old Almonte and Corkery Roads.

The ship had landed in deep swamp near Corkery Road. Two AH-64 Apaches and a UH-60 Blackhawk headed for the area the following night. The helicopters carried full weapon loads. They were part of a covert American unit that specialized in the recovery of alien craft.

Flying low over Ontario pine trees the Apache attack choppers soon spotted a glowing, blue, 20 metre in diameter sphere. As targeting lasers looked-on, both gunships unleashed their full weapon loads of eight missiles each. All sixteen were exploded in proximity bursts ten metres downwind form the ship.

The missiles were carrying VEXXON,—a deadly neuroactive gas which kills on contact. Exposed to air the gas breaks down quickly into inert components. Immediately after having completed their mission the gunships turned around, and headed back across the border.

Now the Blackhawk landed, as men exploded form its open doors. In seconds the six man striketeam had entered the UFO through a seven metre hatchless, oval, portal. No resistance was encountered. At the controls, three dead crewmen were found.

With the ship captured, the United States Airforce, Pentagon, and Office of Naval Intelligence were notified. Through the night a special team of technicians had shut-down and disassembled the sphere. Early the next morning November 6, 1989, construction equipment and trucks were brought into the swamp. The UFO parts were transported to a secret facility in Kanata, Ontario.

As a cover story the local were informed that a road was being built through the swamp. No smokescreen was needed for the military activity as Canadian forces regularly train in the Carp region. Officially nothing unusual was reported in the area. Although someone anonymous turned in a 35mm roll of film. It was received by the National Research Council of Canada, in Ottawa. The film contained several clear shots of an entity holding a light. (See Photograph) [Sorry, no photo enclosed either.] At this time the photographer is still unidentified.

The humanoids were packed in ice and sent to an isolation chamber at the University of Ottawa. CIA physiologists performed the autopsies. The three reptilian, fetus-shaped beings, were listed as CLASS 1 NTEE's (Non Terrestrial Entities). Like others recovered in previous operations, they were muscular, grey-white skinned,—humanoids.

The ship was partially reassembled at the underground facility in Kanata. Unlike previous recoveries this one is pure military. Built as a "Starfighter" it is heavily armed and armoured. In design no rivets, bolts, or welds were used in fastening, yet when reconstructed there are no seams. The UFO itself is made up of a matrixed dielectric magnesium alloy.

It is driven by pulsed electromagnetic fields generated by a cold fusion reactor. All offensive capabilities utilize independently targeting electronic beam weapons. In the cargo hold were found ordnance racks containing fifty Soviet nuclear warheads. Their purpose was revealed by advanced tactical/combat computers located in the flight deck.

Threatened by recent East-West relations, and the revolutionary movements within itself. Red China is preparing for the final ideological war. The aliens have agreed to defend China from the free world's combined military and nuclear forces.

At this time China is arming the Middle East with their own nuclear arsenals. In order that they can successfully take on Israel. Unifying the Arabs under one Chinese command was simple. Especially with Israel's recent "Iron Fist" attitude towards the occupied Arab territories.

The Soviet warheads found in the UFO were destined for Syria. CIA operatives in the Middle East have noticed huge movements of Chinese "technicians" and "advisors." China is also supplying the Arabs with bacteriological agents, Migs, Hind gunships, tanks, and missile launchers.

The use of "Soviet" instead of "Chinese" nukes is part of a disinformation campaign. To break up East-West relations after the annihilation of Israel. The warheads were hijacked from Soviet submarines in the Dragon's Triangle. A section of alien controlled Pacific once frequented by Russian subs. After losing some—900—high yield warheads and thirteen vessels, the Commanders were ordered to steer clear of the area.

The most important alien-technology find were the two millimetre, spheroid, brain implants. Surgically inserted through the nasal orifice the individual can be fully monitored and controlled. The CIA and Canadian Government have actively supported mind-slave experiments for years. Currently the University of Ottawa is involved in extremely Low frequency (ELF) wave mind control programs. A continuation of the CIA psychological warfare project known as MKULTRA, started at the Allen Memorial Institute in Montreal.

Using ELF signals transmitted at the same wavelength the human brain uses, the researchers could subliminally control the test subject.

The alien implants utilize the same principles except that the whole unit is subminiaturized and contained in the brain. Fortunately the implants can be detected by magnetic resolution scanning technology. All individuals implanted by the aliens are classified as ZOMBIES.

The ZOMBIES have been programmed to help overthrow Mankind in the near future. When China finishes with Israel it will invade Europe. At the same time Chinese space-based bacteriological weapons will be launched at the Arctic. The winds will carry the disease into Russia and North America. In days hundreds of millions will be dead,—the survivors will have to deal with the Chinese, the aliens, and the ZOMBIES.

The aliens want all out war so that human resistance would be minimal, when they invade. They tried this same tactic once before with Nazi Germany. Most of the scientific advances we have today came from German science which was based on alien technology. Had Hitler won the war, the earth would have become a concentration camp. In order to depopulate the continents for the aliens.

Data aboard the sphere explained why the aliens are so comfortable in our world. They preceded man on the evolutionary scale by millions of years; created with the dinosaurs. Some 65 million years ago an inter-dimensional war destroyed most of their civilization, and forced them to leave the earth. Now they have chosen to reclaim what was once theirs...

# Acknowledgements

Some expressions of appreciation are in order. I am grateful to researcher Alice Neal and librarian Philip Singer for their assistance with past publications as well as their continuing commitment to present ones. Three researchers with special insight into anomalous phenomena who have made significant contributions are Dwight Whalen, Chris Rutkowski, and W. Ritchie Benedict. Contributions were also made by Ed Butts, David A. Gotlib, and Cyril Greenland. Anna Porter, publisher of Key Porter Books, commissioned the work, and editor Janie Yoon made signal contributions along the way. My wife, Ruth, remains a beacon of inspiration.

I am ever on the watch for accounts of events and experiences of an extraordinary nature that have occurred to Canadians. I hope readers who wish to share their episodes will feel free to contact me. They may do so in one of three ways: care of the editorial department of the publishers; through my email address: *jrc@ca.inter.net*; or by means of my website: *www.colombo.ca*.

Keep watching the skies!

# True
# Canadian UFO
# Stories

## Some Other Books by John Robert Colombo